PRESS PASS

PRESS PASS

*A Woman Reporter's
Story*

BY KATHLEEN ANN SMALLZRIED

New York · 1940

E. P. DUTTON & COMPANY, INC.

DEDICATED TO THE

A.B.S.E.N.T.

ACKNOWLEDGMENT

DAN MAHONEY AND NED BUSH *were Sunday editors of the* SOUTH BEND NEWS-TIMES *at different times during my career there as reporter. They had in common their opinion of my work. In print it goes something like this: "How anybody that writes as well as you do can also write as badly as you do is a mystery to me. Look at this sentence. Just* look *at* it!"

My trouble was in being like a mother with children. I loved the good and the bad alike. In fact they all looked good to me. But my experience indicated that if I wanted to write I had better learn something about it.

So I took the first draft of this manuscript to my friend, Dorothy James Roberts, and told her what was on my mind.

ACKNOWLEDGMENT

She called me a foreign word that sounds something like "dumbcup," threw the pages in the air and on the floor and made me start all over again—and again—and again.

I guess it was worth while, though, because I sold the book and I want her to know that I deeply appreciate her assistance to me in the preparation of the manuscript.

Contents

9

CONTENTS

PRESS PASS

CHAPTER I

On Your Mark—Get Set!

I WENT INTO A DEPARTMENT STORE to buy a pair of gloves. It was after I had been a reporter on the *South Bend News-Times* for several years and had had a number of signed articles printed, which I read, and forced upon my family. I hardly dared hope that anyone else, except Frank Ahearn, my city editor, who made me rewrite each one ten times before he'd accept it, read them. On this day I said, "Charge the gloves to K. A. Smallzried." When you have a name like Smallzried (pronounced Small-zzzz-reed) you don't bother much with first and middle names. The girl paused, looked up at me, and said, "Are you K. A. Smallzried, the writer?" I told Ahearn about it when I gave him a knockout feature on the last wooden Indian in South Bend, and he said, "Nevertheless, you are going to rewrite this story. And put some life into it. It's the Indian that's supposed to be wooden." (That's what you get for trying to be somebody, instead of nobody.)

Another time I was at a meeting of a woman's club and a member came up to me and said: "Do you know, my daughter came in the other day, her hat on the back of her head, her coat flying open, carrying her gloves, her galoshes unfastened. I said to her, 'Mercy, child, you'll catch your death of pneumonia,' and she said, 'I'm trying to be like Kay Smallzried.'"

I told my grandmother about that and she said, "Huh! You go hacking around town, staying up 'til all hours 'til your eyes look like two burnt holes in a blanket, half-killing yourself for that newspaper. Haven't they got any other reporters? There's no sense in the way you tear around at all."

Maybe there wasn't any sense in it, but you can't tell that to a city editor. In a way, Ahearn was a very flattering person. He thought I was made of iron and didn't need to sleep or eat. I fancied I couldn't bear him, and that I was going to have a nervous breakdown the next minute. Actually I wouldn't have traded my experience for a trip to Havana with Robert Taylor thrown in and all the drinks on the house at Sloppy Joe's.

But before we get too deeply into the business of being a reporter, let's catch up on my early life.

I was born on March 21, 1909, in Wabash, Indiana. It is a small town on the banks of the Wabash River, and although it was the first electrically lighted city in the world, all anybody ever thinks about when you say "Wabash" is the river (a filthy, muddy stream) which was immortalized in a song. I've about given down on trying to clear up the distinction between the town and the river and simply let it go that I was born on a shanty boat. (But really, of course, I wasn't.)

I weighed eight pounds and had lots of hair and my parents were proud of me. I was their first-born. I shall always love them for not having me photographed in the nude back-side up. They are individualists and felt then, as they do now, that having my picture taken as God made me is my own affair. So far I have resisted.

I decided when I was four that I wanted to be rich and famous, an idea which has only fifty per cent deserted me. I still want to be rich. But now I like the anonymity of being nobody. However, if being nobody interfered with my being rich, I think it only fair to say that I'd sell my birthright of non-identity for a mess of negotiable pottage any day.

A turning point in my life almost came when I was five years old. My mother and my grandmother were reading the papers. I felt at a loss for something to do. It wasn't bedtime, and it was clear to me that thumb twiddling was no occupation for an ambitious young lady. I walked up and slapped the newspapers out of my elders' hands.

"Here, here," mother remonstrated, "what's the matter?"

I clenched my fists. "I don't like it here," I said, "and I'm going to run away."

To my surprise and consternation, my mother calmly agreed to my decision. She got out my red coat and red hat, my best outfit which I was only allowed to wear for momentous occasions. But this time I did not feel the joyful pride in them I was used to experiencing. I cast a glance in the direction of my grandmother, who on one or two occasions had saved me from a spanking and had shown an interest in my problems. She had the engaged impersonality of a movie audience. Mother opened the door and I walked out into the still, cold night. I was furious and trembling. Before proceeding I must have a plan. I sat down on a step of the side porch and considered. It was so unjust. To go back was unthinkable, but where could I go at this late hour? It was all of seven-thirty. After ten, cold, lonesome, miserable minutes, I reached my decision. I should stay out in the cold while they were in by the stove! I knocked on the door, ignored my mother and grandmother, who said with exaggerated surprise, "Well, are you really back?" and went straight to bed with never another word.

Like everybody else, I entered school when I was six. I liked it, too. Learning, I thought, was my dish, and I went after high grades for all I was worth. I finished high school with seventh scholastic position in a class of eighty. Mother decided that college was outside our financial possibilities, and scholarships (I had knocked down one to the State university) didn't provide enough. So much for learning.

I was elected cheer leader my junior year in high school, the first girl the school ever had in that office. I was awarded an athletic sweater for the job, and I had a short-lived pride in the fact that I was the first girl ever to get one. It was a large, orange coat-sweater with black stripes on the sleeve. But what I really wanted was a slip-over. I felt as if the hand that had been feeding me had bit me! School spirit, eh? They could have it.

The war, which has been well-nigh the entire content of many recent biographies, rates but a few paragraphs in mine. I was nine years old when it ended. I had been shrouded in robes, sweltering through pageants, blistering my heels in uncomfortable white shoes while I paraded for the cause, and snipping flannel at the Red Cross weekly for almost two years, when the Armistice was signed. Never let it be said of my father that he didn't do his share, too. He was a drum major in the liberty guards, and he sang at entertainments to help raise money to carry on the war. At two o'clock of that historic November morning my father came into my bedroom and woke me up. "The war's over," he said. "Come on, Tossy, let's celebrate." The relief from the arduous war discipline which he and I had been subjected to was indeed reason for celebration.

I climbed sleepily into my clothes, took him by the hand, and started out. I don't remember exactly how it happened, but almost immediately we were walking at the head of a parade, I still clinging to my father's hand and both of us shouting, "Hip, hip, hurray!" We waved to our friends on the sidewalk, from whose number one would occasionally dash and offer Father a drink. The parade was composed of happily inebriated patriots who had also served by standing and waiting, waiting for the war to be over, I guess. An improvised band was blaring, "Hail, hail, the gang's all here," and the musicians paused only long enough to warm up with drinks. I remember my mother laughing with neighbors, and for years after, over the boys in the band.

The more they drank and the longer the parade lasted, the shorter their uneasy steps became, until they were hopping in their agonized impatience to get to the Elks' Club, where the celebration was to reach its unconfined top.

At the Club everybody was drinking and drinking. Father didn't think I ought to drink, so he bought me candy and pop and sandwiches. Some of the men, enough older than I was to give me a thrill, asked me to dance, and I did my brave best. I noticed that my father was getting awfully warm, but I didn't think much about it. Later he wanted to go home, and I saw that he was very pale. What I didn't realize was that he was really ill. He was not a drinking man, and the celebration had got the best of him. My only thought was that he was unjust, and I felt badly treated to think he wouldn't stay when the party was obviously going to last for hours yet. Father almost died for his country that night, for I kept him there until six in the morning. Nevertheless, I was glad to get home, because I was sick from eating so much, and felt better when I had coughed up the surplus. However, when I woke up and Mother asked me if I had had a good time, all I could remember was that I had been brought home before I was ready to come. So I said, "No, and it's all Dad's fault." My father was dismayed when mother told him, and he asked me if he hadn't treated me well. I can appreciate now what reflections on the ingratitude of children must have gone through his mind. Even then something in his face, as pale as his pillow, moved my selfish little heart, and in five minutes I was declaring I had never been better treated in my life.

Movies and reading provided my major recreations. For a long time, between my ninth and twelfth years, Gloria Swanson was my favorite, and then Nita Naldi, and next Greta Garbo. La Garbo still rates high in my cinemaffections (I picked that up from *Time*) but I like Myrna Loy, too. This is no time, however, to tell all about the movies and me. I only mean I still enjoy a good movie as much as anything else I can think of. It's probably the escapist in me. Anyway, when I see Ginger Rogers and Fred Astaire, Ginger simply fades away and lo, and behold, there I am dancing with Fred. If I had my life to live over, I should be a professional dancer, preferably in a dance team. If—

As for reading: first there were the magazines: *Vogue, Harper's Bazaar, Country Life, House and Garden, Good Housekeeping, Woman's Home Companion,* movie magazines, and occasionally a *Red Book* or *International Studio.* For books I took out a library card as soon as I could read, and when I had done with the Bobbsey Twins and Camp Fire Girls series I read *The Three Musketeers, Hugh Wynn, Richard Carvel, The Virginian, Jane Eyre, Lorna Doone, Oliver Twist* and *Vanity Fair.* I read *The Three Musketeers* six times. When I was twelve I wanted to read Shakespeare. I had read about him in other books and heard about him at school. If he was the best there was, I reasoned, why should I wait? I read *Macbeth, Antony and Cleopatra* (Cleo was one of my *very* favorite historical characters),

As You Like It, Twelfth Night, The Taming of the Shrew, and *The Merchant of Venice.* I wrote a character analysis of Marc Antony for a book review when I was in the seventh grade. I read it before the class and the teacher, a Miss Plummer, took it very calmly and corrected me on only one thing. I said that Cleopatra vamped Marc Antony. The teacher suggested that I say she fascinated him. From Shakespeare I took an uncritical leap to the best sellers. I would as soon have been caught without my dress in public as without a glib judgment of Messers and Mesdames: Cabell, Arlen, Cather, Fitzgerald, Glasgow, Millay, Kaye-Smith, Ertz, Hutchins, et al.

I started early thinking about my career, but before I settled on acting or dancing definitely two things happened to turn my ambition in another direction. The first thing was my father's getting a job as manager of a hotel. There was a very distinguished guest at the hotel, a man about fifty, who looked as though he might be a lawyer. Father liked him because he had nice manners and talked interestingly and unobtrusively about various places he had traveled. He talked always about his journeys of five or six years back, never about the places where he had spent his immediate past. My father suspected he was associated with an ex-governor of Illinois who contributed to the political scandals of that state for a number of years. However, our guest was nice to my father, who as a result adopted a *laissez-faire* policy, successful in the hotel as in other businesses. This man, whom I shall call Mr. J., was a guest at our house for dinner one evening, sat with me for a while and talked about books. He told me I ought to read *Blennerhasset,* and that Aaron Burr was a very interesting man. He spoke a good bit about writing and what a worthy occupation it was. He said a young person could do no better than to study history and people and write about them. He talked to me as he would to an adult, at least I thought so, and I was flattered and inspired. I decided I would be an author. I talked to him several times afterwards and finally told him of my decision. He shook hands with me and wished me every success and said how nice it was that I knew so young what I wanted to do so I could prepare myself for it. He told me not to be afraid of what I learned.

When I read in an issue of the *Chicago Tribune* about a year later that he had been arrested for embezzlement of thirty thousand dollars of the State of Illinois public funds I wasn't disconcerted. That was his affair. I was still young enough to hold his personality of more value than his morality. I think it is significant that during the time he was hiding out in Wabash he was registered under his right name. There was never a whisper about him. Believe me, when you live in a small town for six months without a whisper against you, that's something.

At the same time Mr. J. was living in the hotel a nephew of his was a guest there, too, and was courting the proprietor's daughter, a very pretty girl. The proprietor was only lukewarm about the idea and told the girl to wait awhile. It's a good thing she did, or else it isn't, depending on the way you look at it. Anyway, the nephew went down to Martinsville, Indiana, one week end and blew a safe in a bank. Being a novice and not as resourceful as the late Mr. Dillinger, he was caught. Ten years! Though I didn't blame the uncle for his misstep, I did blame the nephew. He had curly hair and nice eyes. He had betrayed us!

The second thing which strengthened my resolution to be a writer happened when I was in the seventh grade. I took second place in a city-wide music-memory contest sponsored by a local newspaper. When I went to the office to get my prize, a reporter, Katherine Ramsey, who still writes for the *Wabash Plain Dealer*, asked me about my taste in music. I told her I wasn't really interested in music, that I had just happened to have a pretty good memory. I further told her I wanted to be a writer, an ambition in which she encouraged me. So I went home to begin my career. My first result was a little nature poem which my school friends and I liked very much. At their instigation and accompanied by a group of them, I stopped at the paper office one afternoon and asked how much it cost to have something published. We were told that the price was a cent a word. We put all our funds together and counted the words in the poem. We didn't have enough money. The girl at the desk didn't ask me what I wanted to have published and I didn't tell her. I looked around the office and listened to the pounding of the press in the basement. I decided that, after all, my failure to get my poetry into print didn't greatly matter. What I really wanted to be, and this time I was certain, was not a poet but a reporter.

From that time on I didn't change. When I was a senior in high school I told my principal, Mr. M. C.

Darnell, what was pressing my mind. So he got me a job reporting high school news for the *Wabash Citizen*, a morning paper. That was in March. The paper was just starting to publish. My boss was Foster Riddick, a gentle-mannered redhead, who looked over my copy and told me how to improve it, what constituted a lead and so on. I was simply enchanted with my job. My popularity with my classmates, which had been fairish, was at once tripled. I began to get my first inkling of the fact that I was losing my identity with them. I wasn't really Kay Smallzried any more, but a reporter, someone who could put their names in the paper.

The city editor will say, "We'll send our Miss Smallzried to cover the sideshow." This makes you feel very good, as if you were somebody. But by-and-by you overhear a club chairman say, "We want some publicity on this. Be sure and ask that reporter. You know, what's-her-name!" And then you realize you're nobody. Just a useful piece of sturdy ectoplasm! Almost I called this book *Nobody's Autobiography*, but I refrained because a book with such a title might be written by a janitor or a house-mother of a sorority, and I have never been either, although there were times—!

So at eighteen I was a full-fledged newspaper woman. One of the things I liked best about my new life was meeting and working with unconventional people. There was a city editor who was always trying to kiss me and who swore every time he spoke. There was a circulation manager who had blue eyes and long curly eyelashes. He always wanted to kiss me, too. His wife didn't understand him, he said. I told him I was sorry, but I couldn't help him. He told me I could if I wanted to. I gave up the logical approach and just stuck to saying no.

There were three other girls on the paper, a society editor, a reporter, and a bookkeeper. The bookkeeper could swear as fluently as the city editor. She wore magnificent clothes and the society editor told me she didn't buy them with her salary. I didn't care. She had a better sense of humor than the society editor. The reporter was quite a gal, too. She let the city editor kiss her as often as he wanted. I would watch them unabashed and when his hands got to wandering she would say, "Don't. It's bad for the youngster." It is the only time, as far as I can remember, that anyone tried to protect me from the naughty facts.

In addition to getting an insight into human nature at the *Citizen*, I managed, by dint of will and intention, to learn something about newspaper work. Mr. Riddick kept me on the staff after my graduation to do some reporting and also to sell advertising—and, what is different, to collect for it. It was while I was engaged in this work that I learned what profiting by one's mistakes means.

So that you may better understand my lesson I should explain to you that the paper was backed by Ku Klux Klan capital, not so much for purposes of propaganda, as to provide an outlet for advertising by merchants who were members of the organization. The opposition paper was anti-Klan. While the fact of the *Citizen's* Klan association was not printed on the masthead, it was generally known around town, and if I'd had a lick of sense I would have known better than to ask a Catholic baker for an ad. But I didn't have a lick of sense, so I asked him. His reply was, quote: "Get the hell outa here." Unquote.

I walked back to the office in a fine fit of pouts. Heretofore I had been opposed to the Klan and the intolerance it stood for. But the attitude of the baker was certainly not calculated to win my friendship or influence me. I began thinking perhaps the Klan was right after all.

But no sooner had I sat down at my desk to cool off than the telephone rang, and it was the baker calling: "I been thinkin' it over," he said. "Sorry I was so brusque. Now here. You can run this. I'm introducing a new type bread tomorrow. Corn-top."

Well, it was rather noisy in the office and I was new to the business anyway, and I didn't quite understand him. "Corncob bread," I said, writing it down.

"Yeah, corn-top bread," he said.

So I asked him how big an ad he wanted and I think it was something like a quarter-page. I fixed it up and sent it to the composing room, meantime reflecting that Catholics weren't so bad after all and the Klan certainly had the wrong attitude.

But whoopy-doo! You should have heard that man when he called me up next day. "What the hell you tryin' to do?" he roared. "Make a monkey outa me? Corncob bread! Corncob bread!" His voice cracked on this but he continued. "Jesus! Who ever heard of corncob bread!"

"What *did* you say then?" I asked.

25

"Corn-top. T-o-p, top," he screamed. "I'll never pay for this ad. Never!" And *bang* went the receiver.

With this I was again ready to join the Klan, and went around all day burning fiery crosses in my mind. But that afternoon he called me up once more and said, "Say, I want you to drop around. I've got something for you."

It wasn't hard for me to imagine any number of things he might have for me, but I went anyway, wondering if you could taste cyanide on sticky buns and if it was a very painful death.

"I—I've come to see what you've got for me," I said, standing just inside the door. "I'm sorry—"

"Oh, think nothing of it." He was all smiles. "We've had thousands of orders today for that bread. Everybody wants to know what'n hell corncob bread is. Here." He handed me a three-pound box of candy. "Thought you might like this. Best business we've had in years."

Now that's what I call profiting by a mistake! I've tried and tried to make similar mistakes which might net me more candy or even an original Mainbocher, but to no avail.

On the fourth day of July that year I had more experience in getting out a paper than I had all the rest of the time put together. It was in the evening and Dad was touching off Roman candles and other fireworks, presumably to amuse me and my younger sisters, Elinor and Mary, when the phone rang. It was the printer and he asked if I could come to the plant. I said I could. When I got there I found he wanted me to help him make up the pages, for the incredible reason that no one else had shown up. The managing editor had gone away for the holiday, which was all right, but the others should have been there—all except me, that is. Not being important, I had been told to take the day off. It was clear that each thought someone else would turn up. It's a good thing we didn't have two printers or I should probably have had to set the type, as well. The material was all in, but it needed to be placed in order in the pages, proof had to be read, heads written, and so on. I fell to, told the printer what to do, and left him to see that the paper was printed and ready for delivery next morning. I thought what I'd been doing was easy, for after all, hadn't I been assistant art editor on the high school annual? Compared to the demands of art editing, I decided, getting out a newspaper was a task for Simple Simon.

The day after I put the paper to press I told the city editor what I'd done, and what do you think! He thanked me for it.

On some occasions, in my capacity as assistant in advertising, I would lay out a page whose advertisers I arbitrarily picked among the town merchants. Then I would call on my victims and sell them the space I had allotted them. I remember once laying out a page boost for the football team and returning with seventy-five subscribers, all pulled out of one afternoon's tramping. Among them was a hardware merchant who had never spent a cent for advertising since he began doing business. The city editor looked at his name and said, "My

God, Kay. We'll strike a chromo for you." For this work I was paid two dollars a day. I seldom worked a full week.

One of my jobs was stopping at a local bank to pick up its weekly ad. The secretary there watched me come and go and finally she figured the institution needed a bright young girl like me. No, I'm not being conceited. She said I was bright, and little did she know about it. I left the *Citizen* in October to work in the bank for thirty-five dollars a month.

MALADJUSTMENT

Everybody makes at least one mistake during his life and I'm glad I made mine early. I never spent a more unhappy time than the period during which I worked in a bank. I don't like being regimented! Filing checks all morning, working a posting machine all afternoon— ugh! Two of the women there made life unbearable. Gripe, gripe and sniping remarks!

It turned out that I was a genius at making mistakes. The bank employees were supposed to be free at three o'clock in the afternoon. But if a mistake showed up in the balance made by the head bookkeeper at about ten minutes past three everybody had to stay until the error was located. And day after wearying day the crime would be found in my province. That wasn't all. So clever was I in burying my mistake that often it was five, six or even eight o'clock before the bookkeeper could find in just what transaction I had hid my misstep for the day. As a result I was only popular with most of the men, who didn't care about brains anyway, and one married woman who had patience and a sense of humor.

I may not have worked hard, but I did work vigorously. One day I pulled a drawer out of a cabinet so hard I fell over backwards, and one of the boys who was a woman-hater had to pick me up and tell me to pull my skirt down. And another day, sitting on a chair with rollers, I pushed myself away from the posting machine, went over backwards again, and had to have two cracked ribs taped.

My father began working in South Bend while I was at the bank and after a couple of trips to see him the family decided to move there. This was in July of 1929. I went straight to the *News-Times* to ask for a job. A shoemaker should stick to his last and I knew what my first, last and always was. McCready Huston, author of short stories and novels, was managing editor. He gave me a job proofreading on Saturdays, and in September hired me steady to write obituaries, and whatever else the city editor might assign me to.

I loved it then, and I still do. I like the anonymity of it. You are nobody and yet you have thirty thousand readers every night. You are the one thing the rich woman, the woman in the tar-paper shack, the man at the front desk, and the man on the assembly line have in common. A friend who went around with me on a day's assignments said, "But what does it all mean? Cardinal Pacelli, the twenty-three-ounce baby, the WCTU protest, the medical convention? Why aren't you confused, distracted, writing at top speed and with forty calls a morning?"

"Listen," I said, "what does everybody do? They eat,

drink, fornicate, and read a newspaper. Those four pleasures they have in common. And the purveyors of those things are the least common denominator. That's what it means. Maybe I do get confused, but what of it? You remember what Cowper said: 'He comes, the herald of a noisy world—' "

I'm warming up to my subject.

CHAPTER II

Obit Reporter

"WITUCKI UNDERTAKERS."

"*News-Times* calling."

"Nuttin' doing."

"O. K."

I dial the next number. There are fifteen undertakers and I call them all every morning. I've done it off and on for seven years. The next one is the second Polish undertaker. I'm halfway down my list now.

"*News-Times* calling."

"O.K. I've got one for you. Casimir Przybysz."

The last name is pronounced Psheebeesh, with the "p" sound barely perceptible. I never can remember how to spell it so I ask the undertaker to spell it out for me. Then I spell it back to him: P as in Paul, R as in Robert, Z the last letter in the alphabet, and so on. I repeat after him, "2516 Pilsudski Street." All this is important. South Bend has a large west side populated with

Poles and Hungarians. Several thousand of our thirty-five-thousand circulation goes to the west side. An error can mean anywhere from five to twenty-five circulation stops, depending on the size of the family and the number of friends. And a man has more friends in death than in life. At least some men do.

Carefully I note that he died at three-forty-seven in the morning, and wonder if they had a stop watch going to record so precisely the moment death occurred. He had been ill four days of pneumonia. So much for the facts of his death. Next I take up with the undertaker the facts of his birth and life. He was born February twenty-third, 1886, in Poland, and he came to this country as a child with his parents. He had lived in South Bend for thirty years. His marriage took place June fifteenth, 1909, in South Bend, to Angella Chelminiak, who survives. I spell out Angella to determine whether it has one or two l's, and also Chelminiak, just in case it has a different spelling from the usual.

Next the survivors are listed: three daughters and five sons. Two of the daughters are married and their names have to be spelled out. The third daughter is in a convent. Her name is Sister Severina. Then the five sons. Their names are easy: Stanley, Michael, Ladislaw, Peter, and Ted. I explain that we don't use nicknames in the paper and ask for Ted's correct name. Grudgingly (it's a class pride with undertakers to make an issue when they are questioned) he admits that it is Theodore. Then the brothers and sisters are listed. Four sisters and five brothers. There is one grandchild.

The deceased's occupation is confided next. He had

been employed at the Studebaker factory since his marriage—not counting the time he was laid off during the depression.

At last come the funeral arrangements. The body may be viewed at the residence until the hour of service, which will be at nine Tuesday morning in the St. Stanislaus Roman Catholic Church. The Rev. B. J. Sztuczko, C.S.C., will officiate. Interment will be in St. Joseph's cemetery.

"Anything else?"

"He was a member of the Holy Name Society of the church and of the Polish Post of the American Legion, Number 357."

"Then he was a war veteran?"

"Yes."

"You didn't tell me that."

"Well!" Questioned again, he is good and sore. There is a pause. "It wasn't down here." He is referring to his obituary blank.

"O. K.," I say. "Thanks."

It has taken me about seven minutes to write down this information. I push it to one side on my desk and continue my calls. This may be my only "obit" for the day. On the other hand, I may have a dozen more. One time in January when there was a lot of sickness I had nineteen, and they took nearly two columns. (The conversation above, by the way, is intended as an example of gathering obituary information and the names are not intended to be those of people living or dead.)

There is no charge for obituaries in the average-sized city newspaper in the Middle West. I don't know what the customs are in other sections of the country. Once when the paper was sold to an advertising man who had big ideas about improving it, this policy of no charge was changed for about twenty-four hours. The chief (it was his idea that the staff call him that) told the undertakers to add the price of the obituary onto their bills, remit to him, and nobody would ever know the difference. The first person who was to have the dubious opportunity of having an obituary in the *News-Times* paid for happened to live, or rather die, in Mishawaka, a sort of twin city to South Bend, four miles away. A young undertaker went out and gathered the information, made the arrangements, and presented the bill. A bereaved daughter of forty years or more looked at the items and noticed a dollar and a half unexplained.

"What's this for?" she asked.

"That's for the obituary in the *News-Times,*" said the honest undertaker.

The body wasn't back from the mortuary yet when the subscription of that family was canceled. That was the last of the paid obituaries.

For some reason the writing of obituaries is given to the cub reporter. I mean, my first day of reporting for the *News-Times* I sat down and called all the undertakers. There was one obit. The name was something like Broadripple and I misunderstood it and it came out in the paper Broadrittle. My city editor informed me there was "no God damn excuse for it." Ever since that day I have spelled every name out: B as in bastard, R as in Rat, and so on. I even spell Smith, because the family might spell it Smythe.

34

I have in common with the late Ring Lardner the curiosity to know why this job is assigned the cub reporter. Mr. Lardner,* by the way, also served his apprenticeship in newspaper work on the *South Bend News-Times* and wrote obits. So did Walter O'Keefe, Charles Butterworth, and J. P. McEvoy. Just why obituary reporting should have served as a prelude to the successful careers of these gentlemen in the fields of humor and comedy, I don't know. Perhaps their chance to observe how people behave when death visits their midst may have something to do with it.

I never thought much about obit reporting beyond griping now and then because, once I was past the cub stage, I wasn't relieved of it. But one evening last August when I was having dinner with a friend who knows very little about newspaper work I had cause to think of it. We hadn't known each other very long, and she was interested in what I did, and I started by telling her that for nearly seven years I had written obituaries.

"Obituaries!" she exclaimed. "What's it done to you?"

"Done to me?" I said.

"Yes. You couldn't have been associated with that sort of thing all these years without having something change in your attitude."

It was a new idea to me. I hadn't considered it beyond doing it as carefully as I could, as I might put on silk hose each morning, being watchful not to snag them. She asked me why papers were interested in people's

* To be fussy about it, I guess Mr. Lardner and Mr. McEvoy worked on either the *News* or the *Times*, before these two paper were consolidated.

deaths. (She was one of those rare birds who are publicity-shy, and it was no pose, either.) Now I confronted myself with questions about it. Why was death news, everybody's death, that is? When people ought to want privacy, why did they want publicity, instead? What is grief? This last question puzzled me for quite a while. I had observed what the newspaper calls "bereaved" people rather closely. Not all, but most of them seemed to welcome the hysteria of tears to cover up a loss they felt but knew not how to express. And that passed as grief.

Once in one of those "now, my child" moods, Pi Warren, my news editor, who had a habit of mumbling civil words as though he were ashamed of the fact that he wasn't swearing, said to me, "We figure that a guy has a right to have his name in the paper three times in his life, when he's born, when he's married, and when he dies. And it should be spelled correctly."

So by all means, "Mr. and Mrs. America" should have their obits in the paper. Many, many persons read the obituary column before they read anything else, snugly glad to be alive when their neighbors are dead. For one thing, the notice serves to inform friends of the death and the funeral arrangements. The family like to see it, too. They read it and burst into a fresh paroxysm of grief. And above all, the family like to have pictures of the deceased in the paper. They bring me snapshots taken ten years before, dim, hopeless prints, and are highly indignant because the city editor refuses them. It's no good explaining that the pictures won't reproduce. They simply reiterate, "If it was a Studebaker you could get it in." It would be no use to tell them that the Studebakers would have ten-dollar Bachrach prints available.

Another practice fairly common is the writing of the obituary by some member of the family. The home-written obit is a sad affair with explicit details about the many friends who mourn the loss. These little boasts are omitted when the paragraph gets into print. If a prominent individual dies suddenly the paper will say that the death was a shock to the many acquaintances of the deceased. Notice the word acquaintances. The paper will not even assume that the man has friends. If the occasion justifies it the reporter may refer to a man as prominent or widely known, but never well known. "For all you know," the city editor once said to me, "the business men around this town may think he's a son of a bitch. That's how well known he may be."

When a member of a family comes in to give information the reporter has to assume all the impersonal sorrow of an undertaker and be kindly, solicitous, interested. The written account may have been painstakingly scrawled on letter paper from Woolworth's. The first paragraph will be almost usable, since some member of the family may have taken a look at printed obits and discovered how the details of place, time, and occasion are handled. But the next paragraph! There's where the belly laugh will be. The family pride comes to the forefront, that one fact about themselves which they hold to be unique. Once I had such an obit written by the brother of John Doe, seventy-three, who had died suddenly at his farm. The second paragraph read: "He is survived by his widow and five brothers and their wives, Charles, seventy-five, Joseph, seventy, Richard, sixty-eight, Andrew, sixty-seven, and Paul, sixty-five, none of whom have ever been sick a day in their lives until John took sick Friday, and none of whom have ever had a divorce." There it is—John is kindly admonished by the survivors for having up and died among so many healthy people. An interesting sociological note blooms in the boast "no divorces." It's illegal for the reporter to wonder if the brothers' good health was responsible for their success as husbands. I questioned John's brother and discovered that the deceased had several children, a fact which hadn't seemed important to the obit writer.

The learning of any business brings its series of errors and tribulations to the neophyte, and the newspaper business is no exception. The horrible part about making an error on the newspaper is the extraordinary number of persons with whom you share it. You make a mistake Tuesday morning, and Tuesday evening thirty-five thousand people know it. If the same could be said about bankers the bank holiday might have been avoided.

When I had been on the paper about three days I was sent out to a home to get a picture of a man who had died. He was not very prominent but he had been active in the Knights of Pythias or Odd Fellows or something like that and the city editor decided he was worth a one-column cut. I took a cab and told the driver to wait for me. The undertaker cautiously opened the door and to my horror I saw that I had arrived while the funeral service was going on. I was standing in a little cubicle of a hall and could look into the parlor where a quartet was standing over the deceased singing "The End of a Perfect Day."

I whispered to the undertaker, "I'd like his picture."

"Don't you know better than to come here at a time like this?"

"But I didn't know the service was going on."

"That doesn't make any difference." The undertaker forgot himself and began bawling me out in resounding tones that threw the soprano off key. "This is the most heartless demonstration I have ever seen from the press in all my life, in all my years of—"

I opened the door and walked out. I felt humiliated and ashamed. I told my editor about it and he laughed. "So our little Nell got her feelings hurt." I know now that, people being what they are, the family would probably have been glad to stop the service while they found a picture for me.

My next embarrassment came when two World War veterans died the same morning. The police reporter came in and told me the chief of the detective bureau, who was a member of the American Legion, had told him the American Legion was going to hold a military funeral for a war veteran. For some reason, probably inexperience, I didn't check on it, but arbitrarily added the flourish to the account I had already written for one of my veterans. There was no reason for choosing him more than the other—I just shut my eyes and pointed. That evening the opposition paper held that the other hero was to have the military funeral. So the next day I wrote the funeral again and put the military rites with the correct service. The girl over at the other paper, however, had evidently been on the mat for having it wrong. At any rate, the next evening she had reversed her story, too. The opposition, it seemed, chose to be just as impartial in awarding military honors as I had been. If anyone is interested, she was right in the first place.

One day when I was not at my starry-eyed best (the evening before, I had been), I didn't remember what day it was. I thought it might be Thursday, though as a matter of fact it was Wednesday. I wrote eight obituaries in which I said that the subjects died on Thursday. The error was not caught by the man on the desk, the linotype operator, nor the proofreader. It came out in the paper and the press had to be stopped until the page could be made over and the error corrected. I got a desk calendar given to me after that.

Undertakers are a rather good sort, I learned. My list included one fashionable undertaker, Protestant, one fashionable, Catholic, two Hungarian, two Polish, three Negro, and six serving the solid citizenry in various neighborhoods and suburbs. A good story is told of Art Russell, the fashionable undertaker, Protestant. He lived in a home in one of the older and more elaborate residential sections. One evening the late Rome Stephenson, one-time president of the American Bankers' Association, called him up and said, "I say, Art, my wife's out of town, and I'm getting dressed for a dinner and can't tie my tie. She always does it for me. I wonder if you can come over and help me." Art went over and did his level best with the recalcitrant ribbon, but couldn't get it to assume the neatness he desired. Finally he said,

"Well, Rome, I can't tie it either. But if you lie down, then I can do it." *

Once when I was covering a Kiwanis luncheon an undertaker at my table and a doctor at the next table were arguing. I didn't pay much attention until I heard the undertaker say with some finality, "Well, we get 'em when you're through with 'em. Poor old Mrs. Ballardson." Mrs. Ballardson's name reminded me of a funny thing which had happened in connection with her obituary, one I had written. She was eighty-two at her death, had been survived by eight children and twenty-three grandchildren. For some reason the number of her grandchildren appeared in the paper as ninety-two. I hadn't thought twenty-three was so bad, myself, but the linotype operator evidently was out for a record, and the proofreader took his word against mine.

It isn't unusual for the family to call the paper and ask that the reporter be at the undertaker's at the same time they plan to be there. The main objection to this procedure from the reporter's standpoint is that obits are only part of the day's work, and time spent in gathering facts on one story with the help (or the hindrance) of the family will take from twenty minutes to an hour, when five minutes would do if the reporter had a free hand. I recall one time when the undertaker called the papers at the family's request and asked for a reporter. The girl on the other paper and I answered and sat respectfully to one side while the family made all the arrangements for the funeral. The undertaker was hold-

* Cruel friends tell me this is a standard undertaker's joke, but it was told to me for the gospel truth and I repeat it as I heard it.

ing out for having the coffin closed during the service. The widow wanted it opened. It was no good our suggesting that we had a deadline to make. We must sit there for forty-five minutes while the undertaker said, "But I think it's just a little more private, just a little more delicate to have the coffin closed."

The widow would muffle a sob and contend, "I wanted those last few minutes, that last little while—"

The undertaker won. Fifteen stories I had for that day didn't get in until the last edition, a street-sale paper, was rolling. I had fifteen calls next morning wanting to know why the items weren't in the paper delivered to subscribers. How could I tell my "reliable sources" that an argument over a coffin lid was the reason?

Death may be solemnity or sordidness. Seldom, to the obit reporter at least, does it seem tragic. An instance of death as a solemnity was to serve as my measuring stick in finding tragedy. It was a solemn occasion for all South Bend society when the wife of a prominent industrialist died. The publisher of our sheet was named as honorary pallbearer, so the city editor decided I had better cover the funeral, though this sort of coverage was not customary. The family of this woman had all the loyalty and cohesion of a Jewish family. They lived in a large brick and stone house which had a huge hall and a two-way marble staircase at one end, like the hotel lobbies of the Nineties. I sat in the hall during the service. The house had been built at the insistence of the wife so that her children, six, I think, and grandchildren might live under one roof. Flowers banked every available space that was not occupied by industrialists, bankers, and business leaders who looked on the ceremony with an assurance that this woman who had occupied such a comfortable and well-respected berth here would surely have an equally good berth in heaven. The undertaker asked me if I wanted to view the body. I felt a little guilty because I hadn't known her very well. It seemed an intrusion to look at her. But thinking about cats and kings, and realizing that to refuse would be a serious social error, I went in. The undertaker stood by, proud and solemn. I almost said, "Very nice, indeed," a compliment he would have taken, I am sure, in the spirit in which it was given.

Three church dignitaries officiated: a Methodist bishop, a former pastor of the church which her father had built, and its present pastor. The bishop and the former pastor confined their participation to prayer and a brief eulogy. The incumbent pastor, however, had other plans. It was his big opportunity. The woman had been his wealthiest patron. So he took off on a description of her reunion in heaven with those members of her family who had gone before, her father and mother, her daughter, a son, perhaps a grandchild. With each one he mentioned, the family burst afresh into tears. He went on happily sweating over the job for an hour. For his pains in trying to hold up his end of the service he was not asked back as pastor of the church.

The sense of tragedy I spoke of was associated with the death of a young CCC worker. On a Sunday afternoon's recreation he dove off a springboard and broke his neck. I went to his home to get a picture.

A young girl opened the door and I told her what I

wanted. She was a sister to the dead boy. I stepped from the porch into the living room, a shabby, but clean, little chamber, from whose open doors I could see every other room in the house. Without asking me to sit down she went to look for a photograph of the boy. I glanced into her bedroom and saw hanging on the wall two large pictures, one of the Virgin Mary and one of the Sacred Heart of Jesus. On her dresser stood a framed picture of Clark Gable.

I could see the mother seated in the dining room. She was rocking her body back and forth, uttering prayers and ejaculations between sobs. "Oh, Jesus, Mary and Joseph,"—"Oh, my son, my boy." Two friends, silent and miserable as punished dogs, sat beside her. My heart flooded open with pity. Poor mother, helpless wretched woman, married in her teens, bearing children every other year of her married life, husband gone, and children gone—no one left except the daughter who had let me in, a child really, who worked as a maid for four dollars a week.

Sing the Mass, priests, and commend a Christian soul to God. Jesus, Mary and Joseph, comfort this woman. The days of her life are overlong. What will she and the matriarch of the marble stairs have to say to each other, I wonder?

The girl returns and gives me a picture. I thank her and go away.

Naturally many of the obits I write are of deaths from auto accidents, sometimes among my friends. I would have seen a boy I knew with his date at a bar or night club on Saturday night before they decided to drive somewhere else, to a near-by lake, perhaps. Monday morning I would write, "—only son of—" "—only daughter of—" "killed in crash—" "the funeral to be—" "—the body will not be viewed—" It has made me careful of my driving.

The funeral I remember most vividly was one I did not write. It was that of Knute Rockne, famed Notre Dame football coach. It was in April of 1931 on the Saturday afternoon preceding Easter. It is unusual for a funeral to be held in a Catholic church on Saturday afternoon, and this service is not to be confused with the funeral mass. The Rev. Charles O'Donnell, C.S.C., who was soon to follow Rockne, gave the oration. It was broadcast. The whole city of South Bend was draped in mourning. Merchants had put pictures of the coach and his championship teams in their windows and draped them with black and purple. The sense of loss and grief was very genuine. Rockne had not only brought Notre Dame to the foreground. He had attracted much business to the city. And people liked him. When he looked at you all his vitality, imagination, and perception shone in his blue eyes, bright, keen, alert, the focus of the phenomenal strength of his personality that knew no rest. Everybody remembered him that way. His friends agreed that the airplane crash was the only way for him to die.

My Saturday beat was early, and I was off at three. I didn't have to go to the funeral, but I went anyway. I drove with friends to a lot near the campus and waited until the service was over. Several thousands of autos were parked for blocks around, filled with people who

wanted to see the cortege pass. Our car was parked
facing the university administration building atop which
is the gold dome and the statue of Our Lady of Per-
petual Help.* All the buildings on the campus were
draped in purple and black. To the right several rods
away was the new football stadium which had been
used for the first time the autumn before, when Notre
Dame for the second consecutive year had completed
its schedule with no defeats and captured the national
championship. Its yellow brick shone in the afternoon
sunlight. Straight ahead was the spire of the church from
which the bell tolled solemnly and slowly, one sound
from its great throat for each year of Rockne's life. At
last the service was over and the long motor caravan
began its measured procession to the cemetery. Thousands climbed out of their cars and stood by the roadside and wept. People who had no personal cause for
tears caught the mood and openly cried. The murmur
of their grief, the low tone of automobile engines held
in first gear, and the grit of tires and feet on the graveled
road were the only sounds. The hearse, Rockne's family, priests, bishops in red and purple robes, college presidents, football coaches from other colleges, business
men who had once played on his teams or perhaps played
with him, all looked sorrowfully ahead. The fragile
spring foliage of the trees lining the campus avenue
trembled in the warm spring breeze.

* Notre Dame friends began an argument as to the correct name of
the statue atop the gold dome. I wrote Tom Barry, publicity director
at the university, when I had completed this work, and he wrote back
first that I was right, and later that I was wrong. It is simply known
as Our Lady.

After it was over we drove back to town and I dropped off at the *News-Times*. There I found a newspaper office more quiet than any I had ever seen. I went into the society coop and picked up an old copy of the *New Yorker*. Pretty soon I laughed aloud and everybody gave me dirty looks, from the city editor down to the assistant high school sports reporter. I couldn't help it. I had just read about a Negro woman who had died in Washington. It seems that there are a number of Negro insurance and mutual benefit societies which for a couple of cents a week guarantee the policy holder burial in a cemetery and an obituary notice in the paper. This woman belonged to thirteen such companies and received thirteen notices. Commented the *New Yorker:* "It was a rather impressive passing, even for Washington."

A couple of summers ago I had the first indication of what the trailer era is going to mean to cemetery family lots—and to obit reporters. An undertaker called with an obit on a woman seventy-five years old who had been taken sick at a trailer camp, hastily moved to a hospital in South Bend, and died. She was en route with her son and his family from Detroit to California. She had no relatives in South Bend. She had never lived there. My curiosity was aroused. I asked why she was being buried there.

"Oh," said the undertaker, "she said she wanted to be buried just wherever she died."

I suppose writing obituaries has done something for my attitudes. It has enabled me to distinguish between the man who belongs to an organization because he believes in it and is interested and thinks he may be able to do some good there, and the man who joins churches and clubs and lodges and associations because he wants a good, substantial obituary notice to follow after him. It has also led me to believe that the writers of the old melodramas were right: there is a fate worse than death, but not for the survivors.

CHAPTER III

Meet Me Friends

IT HAS JUST OCCURRED TO ME that maybe you would like to know something about the people I worked with. If I keep on just talking about myself you will get the idea that I was pretty near the whole *News-Times* staff. And, as a matter of fact, I never did actually get out the paper single-handed.

When I went to the *News-Times* everybody around the office was congenial and made wisecracks and I very quickly felt at home. Although I was a little timid, I tried not to show it, and soon I wasn't afraid of my bosses, and they weren't afraid of me.

I say "bosses," because in a newspaper office you have to please practically everybody from the office boy up and down. But I must say for Mr. J. M. Stephenson, the publisher of the paper, that he placed his faith pretty much in the people he hired, and therefore, if you pleased your city editor and your managing editor, you were almost sure to please Mr. Stephenson. For this reason I didn't have much contact with Mr. Stephenson during my early years on the paper, although I did later on.

The door of his office was always open but I had no reason to darken it until I had been there quite some time. One day McCready Huston, who was then managing editor, told me Senator Robert M. LaFollette was in Mr. Stephenson's office and that if I could find some pretext to go in I might be introduced to him.

It might seem on the surface of things that this was a sort of practical joke. But it wasn't. Mr. Huston realized, I think, that I looked with longing at the assignments given other reporters to interview the great and the famous, and judged, rightly, that I would get a kick out of being eye to eye with a real live senator.

So I overs to Mr. Stephenson's office and goes in to see his secretary, Peggy Douglas. Peggy was a swell gal and we double-dated lots. I told Peggy what I had come over for in a stage whisper that could probably have been heard beyond the footlights of the Shubert Theater in New York, and just as if he had read my mind Mr. Stephenson asked me in and introduced Senator La-Follette. I said, "How do you do," and then just stood looking at him. He chatted amiably a few minutes and I searched my mind for an intelligent question and finally ended up by asking him if the government in Washington still carried on, or something to that effect. I walked out of the office in a state of adolescent confusion feeling as though my hands were swinging about my knees like an ape's.

The senator was in South Bend as a guest of Stephenson and although Tom Coman or John Ches our two crack reporters, interviewed him, there was no mention of his host in the story. It was a policy of Mr. Stephenson's not to use his paper to exploit himself or his family. When his children were born we carried stories on that because it was news the other paper would have, and there was no use our being scooped. He was friendly to his employees but not familiar with them. Once or twice he gave swimming parties for them at his private pool. As for his policies, there were two that I could see. One was that the paper should be wet and the other that it should be Democratic. He was at that time, and may still be for all I know, president of the Conservative Life Insurance Company, as well as publisher of the paper.

In command of the business interests of the paper was the late Mortimer P. Reed, secretary-treasurer. Mr. Reed was a widower with two grown daughters and a young son. I liked Mr. Reed, and if he were not dead I might say something here that would please and amuse him and introduce him to the reader. But he has gone beyond the hearing of my admiration. For that I am sorry. The first time I went into his office I did so to get the money to take the spelling bee champion to Washington, D. C., to the national contest. He gave me $300 and I brought back $65 of it and accounted for every penny I spent. He said I was the most economical reporter he had ever sent on such a trip. The last time I went into his office was to get $75 to take the Soap Box Derby champion to Akron, to the national finals. It was just for a week end, mind you, and I had only $4.45 left over and couldn't tell how any of it was spent. That shows you what experience will do for you. He didn't say anything about how economical I was on that last trip, but he didn't say anything else, either, from which I conclude that he was plenty o.k. (We're going to come to a chapter on those champions in just a minute. So hold on.)

The first time I ever went into Mr. Huston's office was, of course, when I applied for my job. As I have already said, he wrote short stories and novels on the side and he always encouraged any of his staff who felt like doing the same thing. As a result, two of the ace reporters were hard at it on the Great American Novel. The city editor didn't know about it (he wouldn't have believed it) and so he was sometimes hard put trying to find these two. He would have the office boy call all the speakeasies and other places in town where they might be, and when they weren't there he would swear horrid oaths. Mr. Huston would listen awhile and then say, "Have you tried their homes? I think they're working on their novels."

One of the reasons I am writing this book, besides the hope of money, I mean, is that I want to prove newspaper work is not exactly what the movies say it is. Nor is it all the business of being foreign correspondents (as other writing journalists, Stanley Walker excepted, might lead you to believe). But in Pi Warren we did have something of the movie-type city editor. Pi hailed from Muncie, Indiana, and received his nickname because, as a high school mathematics student, no matter what the question was, he began his answer, "Well, you take pi—and well, pi—"

As deadline drew near he would bawl out across the room, "Come on, slaves. More copy." Then he would scoop up a great handful of it and take it out to the composing room (the office boy having gone to lunch) and as he reached the door he would turn around, look over the room at his busy staff pounding 25 typewriters furiously, and say, "Jesus Christ, nothing but Boy Scouts and Camp Fire Girls, and they expect me to get out a paper!"

I remember one evening when I was ready to leave, I walked to the head of the stairs that led down to the street, turned around, and said, "Well, good night, everybody." Pi, sitting over at the city desk, looked up and said, "Oh, were you here today?"

That made me laugh but just the same I spent part of the night trying to think up a funny answer, and the next morning when I went in I said, "Gee, I wish you were more like my mother," and Pi said, "Why?" and quick as a wink I replied, "Because she's always glad to see me." (Ain't I the one, though!)

Pi left the paper to go to the *Chicago Herald and Examiner* and Frank Ahearn moved up into the slot. (That's newspaper terminology. The city desk in some offices is a round table with a slot in one side for the top man.) I am grateful to Mr. Huston for the opportunities he gave me, a stranger in South Bend, to meet people who would be helpful contacts in my work. But it is to Frank Ahearn that I am grateful for the training to write, in whatever degree I do, pictorially, dramatically, and occasionally with humor. (If he doesn't like this book, and the chances are he won't, he'll kill me for that. But for years I've been wanting to leave him holding the bag on something, and blaming this book on him is too good a chance to miss.)

Frank came from Northampton, Mass. He entered Notre Dame and from there went to the *News-Times*. Part of the time I was there he wrote a Sunday column, and it was about himself, and Loretta, his wife, or his baby, Jim, or his little dog, Panic, or maybe about something he had thought.

I remember one column he wrote about life's little annoyances. It seems he had been meaning to buy himself some shoestrings and forgetting to do it. He wrote that his shoes "looked as though they were laced up with marbles." Another time he was discussing the qualities of prohibition liquor and referred to some that would "melt the teeth on a rake." That was Frank for you. Time after time I've seen him take a drab story and rewrite it into a wow, proving that it wasn't the story that was drab, alas, but the writer. I've often thought that the only thing in this world that strikes him as being dull is a conversation between two women. He was certainly skeptical of women as reporters, and I must say that no woman working for him will ever get into mischief from idle hands. The only things about me that are slender are my hands and my feet, my hands from always typing the stories that Frank Ahearn thought up for me, and my feet from running after them.

As an example of how Mr. Ahearn taught me to write, let's take a story through its revampings. At one time the board of directors of the Community Fund informed the executive committee they would no longer back them in their plans. I opened my story about it something like this: "Members of the board of directors Tuesday night informed the executive committee of the Community Fund that they would no longer back them in their plans. Blah, blah, blah, etc.—"

With a smug little smile I walked over and turned the story in. In a moment Ahearn comes forth with, "Holy Mackerel! Miss Smallzried." It was times like this that taught me resignation. I walked over to the desk again, my smugness one with the ages. "Did the executive committee know this action was coming?" he asked.

"No."

"It was a surprise to them?"

"Yes."

"A bombshell?"

"Yes."

"Say so."

I rewrote the lead: "The board of directors of the South Bend Community Fund Tuesday night surprised its executive committee by announcing that it would no longer back the executive group in its plans."

Again I took the story over. Again Mr. Ahearn called me back. It seems I might as well have said that the board of directors had stuck its head from behind a door and said "Boo." Didn't I know a bombshell when I sat on one?

Third and final time: "Members of the South Bend

Community Fund board of directors tossed a bombshell in Tuesday night's quarterly meeting by walking out on the executive committee."

You see, a bombshell had not actually been thrown, and I was too literal-minded to translate explosive facts into explosive terms. The executive committee proved as unimaginative as I, and it was some time before I heard the last echoes of the bombshell from them. Which was exactly what Frank had wanted—a vivid, pictorial report that people would talk about.

Frank could be as pictorial in his speech as he was in his writing. One time when I had made the same mistake in a lead four times, using different words to do it, he picked up the copy, waved it in the air as he rushed over to my desk, and cried, "Jesus Christ, Miss Smallzried, if you make this mistake again I'll cut and mangle your body and strew it from here to the corner."

That's what I liked about newspaper work. You were never in doubt about what people thought. Frank left the *News-Times* to go to the Associated Press in Detroit and later went to Hartford, Connecticut, as assistant city editor on a paper there.

Hard as he was to write for, there was one other, Jerry Holland, Sunday editor, who was worse yet. When I first went to the paper I had said I would like to do book criticisms. At the age of fourteen I had read a copy of the *American Mercury* and I thought if you hated a thing bad enough and said so, you were good. Well, time wears down all things, even stone. If this weren't so I think I would still be at the *News-Times* rewriting my first book review. It seems that not only was my writing bad, my punctuation was atrocious. When I turned my criticism in to Mr. Holland for the sixth time (it was one page on a sloppy Russian novel), I said, "I'll have you know when I was a freshman in high school I took first honors in a college freshman English exam."

"It's too bad you didn't stick to that system," Holland replied. "This system you've invented is terrible."

Holland wasn't just an ogre at that. I found out somehow that he liked poetry and it wasn't long before I was lingering in front of his little glass cage with trifles of my own. I remember one of them that he liked a little bit:

> Tonight I shall sit alone
> Drinking this bitter wine:
> Eyes that held their secret from me,
> Lips that were never mine.

(Never mind. I was only twenty.) Jerry had a real talent for poetry and I have lamented time and again his lack of ambition in doing anything about it. It is with his permission and with humility on my part that I quote in this crazy book the following lovely quatrain he wrote for a friend of his who died:

> Dressed in her moon-made shroud
> And slippered by the mist,
> Death, as a lonely lady,
> Came to me to be kissed. *

* When I wrote Jerry to ask his permission to print this he wrote me: "My dear young lady: I would not dream of spoiling your fun by giving my permission, when you will do as you please anyway."

Jerry, a Notre Dame man, was and is a bachelor. He was a terribly handy person to have around because he remembered everything he had ever read and if he was in a good mood and I was in doubt all I had to do was to ask him. But if he was in a mood of thinking I ought to do my own work, then I had to look it up myself, in the dictionary or city directory.

Jerry's always being so smart about everything began to make me a little sore, because I had never looked upon myself as a blue ribbon dumbbell. So I began nursing a secret desire to be right when he was wrong. If I could score my victory in the realm of information about the Catholic Church, the fruits would be sweet indeed, because Jerry was the kind of Catholic who knew its history backwards and forwards.

One Saturday the pastor of St. Joseph's Church called up to say the Most Rev. John Francis Noll, D.D., etc., Bishop of Fort Wayne diocese, was going to baptize a number of Negroes at the early service next morning. That night, when I had gone up to the office to finish my day's work, Jerry was just getting around to writing a head on the story and he said I couldn't possibly be right. "A bishop," said Jerry, "never baptizes." We began a loud and fierce argument only to be shouted down by the city editor. Finally I got a vicious inspiration. "Change it," said I. "I'm probably wrong."

Monday morning first thing, I called the pastor, who said that I was right and wondered why I had not written the story as he had given it to me. So I rushed over to Jerry's office and began dancing back and forth saying in a singsong voice, "I was right and you were wrong and you can write the correction."

You will be thinking by now that if I wasn't the only person on the staff I was at least the only girl. But that, also, is not so. There was, among others, Dorothy J. Konold. She was tops, professionally and personally. Mrs. Konold was book review editor and feature writer. I hadn't been there half an hour before I was looking in her direction and thinking, "Oh, to be Do (pronounced Doe) Konold." She came in at 10 A.M. I came in at eight. Nary a hair on her head was ever out of place. Mine always looked as though it had just been "done" which was bad, or needed to be "done" which was worse. Do was always perfectly made up. My nose was always shiny. Do wore her clothes with *Vogue*-like smartness. Mine were worn as though they had followed me out of the house and jumped on me.

And this was not all. Do never had to rewrite ANY of her copy. I had to rewrite practically everything but the obits. She wrote the lead book review. Heaven only knew what spot on the page I might hit. Her Sunday features were on the first page of the society section. At this stage of the game I hadn't even been trusted to write a Sunday feature. This viewing-at-a-distance business continued until the middle of the winter when the *News-Times* editorial staff went on a sleigh-ride party. Do brought her husband, Ed, and we went riding and singing every place. Somebody had provided a little liquor in case of snake-bite and things went along at a gala pace. We all sang:

Caviar comes from virgin sturgeon,
Virgin sturgeon, very fine fish;
Virgin sturgeon need no urgin'
That's why caviar's such a rare dish.

Then we went back to the *News-Times* and had beer
and coffee and sandwiches. We turned on the radio and
danced and sang some more and told jokes. That was
the first time I was ever out with the Konolds, but not
the last time. It's characteristic of newspaper people to
have a lot of their social life with each other. But the
Konolds had many friends outside the paper, too, and
I've been to parties at their house, both with and without "me friends." But whichever way it was, there
wasn't anywhere more fun to be had.

Do has been asked by two different publishing houses
to write a novel. But she has two pretty daughters, the
genial and good-looking Ed, and a nice home. So she
has never bothered with the novels.

Well, let's go back to talking about the boys again.
It's easy to do that, especially when the boys are Dick
Jackson and Jim Doran. Dick was a Hoosier born and
bred. So was Jim, for that matter, but he had once
worked on the *Boston Transcript*. Dick was very
clothes-minded and wore spats and a mustache, and
Holland called him "the sartorial Jackson." He had
very long eyelashes. It's hard, in a way, to describe
Dick, because he was so deft, and had so many unex-
pected talents. Once when he was at my house we fell
to playing with my sister Mary's yo-yo. Dick just gave

it a flick at the bottom and it rolled right up into his hand. He was like that—whether it was yo-yos or cutting a fish dead center and extracting the bones with one operation. He could do tricks no one else could. He mixed marvelous drinks and told good stories. He also wrote a night-club column, which was once very nearly my undoing. It happened while I was doing publicity for St. Mary's College. Dick and some of me other friends had been having a cocktail or two at my house and settling the business of life, love and literature once and for all. Dick wrote about it in his column. It had been his honest intention to refer to "Kay's salon" but the linotype operator, who, perhaps, dwelt more with beer and skittles than with pink-ladies and theories designed to make life more abundant, felt that Dick might have been a little eentsie-weentsie bit in his cups when he wrote the column. So it came out in the paper "Kay's Saloon," and I had some tall and fancy explaining to do to everybody.

One noon Frank Ahearn, Wally Mansell and one or two others and I were having lunch in a Greek quick and dirty down the street from the *News-Times*. It was more or less our custom to choose among the items that passed as food at this *culinaire* by shutting our eyes and pointing. On this day Frank (he was from Massachusetts, remember, and still felt the touch of the divine madness of Back Bay) had drawn some grayish-looking strings and brown rubbery tubes, identified on the menu as sauerkraut and wieners. He had his fork lifted when Dick came in and looked in fascinated wonder at the stuff Frank was holding. He picked a thread of it

61

off Frank's fork and held it aloft. "What's that?" he whispered. "New England boiled dinner?"

"Oh, dear God," said Frank, dropping his fork to his plate and closing his eyes in disgust.

The thing you were likely to notice first about Jim Doran, outside the fact that he was handsome as Robert Taylor, was a sort of devil-may-care attitude combined with an eager restlessness. He was one of the few newspaper men who could "double in brass," that is to say, work on the desk or as a reporter with equal facility. For this reason he never found it very hard to get jobs elsewhere. He was always going off, but he always came back. There would be something in the new setup he didn't like and since he was good, he knew he could always have his old job again. Once he went off to take Youngstown, Ohio, by storm, and he was gone about ten days. When we knew he was coming back Frank Ahearn spread the word around that we were to greet him with deadpan expressions and just say "Hi, Jim," as if he had been there every day, and besides that, we loathed him. We carried out the order to cruel perfection, and Jim's face got kind of long, and Frank looked up after what was to Jim a considerably long and embarrassing silence, and said, "Well, I see the homing-pigeon of the *News-Times* is back again."

"Youngstown," said Jim, "is the dung-hole of the world."

The last time Jim left the paper it was to go to Albany, N. Y., and Dick Jackson left with him, and I guess they are still there.

One afternoon when I was sitting back in the society

section writing a feature or something, a tall, good-looking blonde came in and sat down at the typewriter on the desk beside mine. She took off her gloves and left her hat on, with professional air, and began to type. I stopped doing whatever time-killing chore I was engaged in and looked over her shoulder to see what it was all about. She inserted her paper and typed "WEST SIDE NEWS" and underneath it, "by Helen Minczewski."

"My name is Kay Smallzried," I said.

"Mine is Helen Min-ches-ski."

And thus began a long and honorable friendship. Helen had a couple of years at St. Mary's College, figured she was destined for bigger and better things, and came down and got herself a job covering the West Side News. There are 40,000 Poles, 10,000 Hungarians, and a large population of Germans, Swedes and Belgians in South Bend and its environs, and it was the news of these foreign peoples that she was to cover. She had a natural flair for the work, found news where there wasn't any and wrote it into headline stuff. She met the Polish consul from Chicago, and did a crackerjack job of interviewing him. As a result of her good work and her personableness she was chosen one of the outstanding young people of Polish descent in America and sent to the old homeland for a visit.

We not only had fun in contributing our share to what Pi Warren scored as "horseplay" in the office, but also double-dated to some extent and took in the night clubs and entertainments. The night the moon was in total eclipse we drove around and looked through people's telescopes and watched the young people in the park who were watching the eclipse (what they could see of it). I remember we drove downtown and saw two men at a street corner with a mounted telescope, so we stopped, got out, paid our dimes and took a look. Helen asked them how long they had been doing this kind of work.

"About six months, ma'am," one of them replied. "We were brick masons, but we got out of work and took what little money we had to buy a telescope. We go around from town to town and charge people a dime to see through it. We make a real good livin' at it, too, an honest livin'."

One afternoon when Helen and I were trying to get up enough energy to ask each other where to go and what to do, Barbara Green (that isn't her real name), who worked on the society desk, allowed as how she had a quart of absinthe and didn't know how to mix it.

"Just you go along home," I said, "and we'll be out pretty soon."

For years I had been reading *Vanity Fair*, hoping to be sophisticated or the life of the party or something. And here was my chance, because a recent issue had an absinthe cocktail recipe in it and I remembered it. We met Mary Doran Bolt, who worked in the business office, as we were leaving, and invited her to go too. We went to the soda fountain across the street and got some simple syrup and took our way to Barbara's.

The recipe called for a jigger of absinthe, the white of an egg, and simple syrup. Shake well with crushed ice. That's all.

64

It was a hellishly hot day and we sat in the Green library languidly sipping our cocktails. I think it was Barbara who spoke first and said, "It's awfully good and cool and all, but I don't feel it a bit, do you?"

And we didn't. It was just like having mint ice cream. Soooo, we had another one. This kept on for a while, and by-and-by Barbara's father came home, and he had one, and said we were very foolish to waste our time on such things. He made us Scotch highballs. That kept on for a while, too.

Then some people came to take Helen to a party, and Mary and I got up to go. We accompanied Helen as far as a little flight of three steps, which led from Barbara's lawn to the sidewalk. I shall always remember Helen as she was poised and silhouetted against the setting sun. She had forgotten that there were three steps. She did not anticipate even one step. She literally floated out into space. Mary and I watched with a fascinated horror. But Helen was not disturbed. Unaware that her progress had been in jeopardy she landed on both feet, turned and bade us a cheerful good evening, and with dignity entered the car.

We all reported for work the next morning, Mary swearing she was going home that night and tie herself to a bedpost. It was four o'clock in the afternoon before any of us achieved that mental coherence which gives our lives an undercurrent of security.

Helen married a Notre Dame grad named Charles Spangenberg and lives in Chicago; Mary married a chap named Scoops Weatherby and lives in Elkhart; Barbara quit to take another job, and I—I hung a picture of

Picasso's "The Absinthe Drinker" over my bookcase and said to myself, "There now, let that be a lesson to you."

You will get the idea that the turnover in a newspaper office is pretty high, and it is high during a depression, and also when depression salaries continue in to good times. But even so, I'm not mentioning everyone who worked at the *News-Times* while I was there —only the ones who made day-to-day life more stimulating and amusing.

Take the sports department for instance. Costin to Hoenig to Danch. Jim Costin was the sports editor and wrote as chatty a column from the doghouse as a person could wish to read. Jim lived more or less permanently in the doghouse because he invented the Costin system of playing bridge. The little woman, according to his column confessions, felt that, while the Culbertson system might fail to satisfy Jim's creative genius, it did pay better dividends. All this about Jim's bridge game is, I realize, purely personal, but his column was a lot like that too. He told all about sports and himself and as a result was so entertaining that my grandmother wouldn't think of skipping a day without reading him.

Jim is still with the *News-Times*. He has a break that lots of sports reporters would give their gold bridgework for. I mean with Notre Dame right in the back yard of South Bend, he is never at a loss. He travels around with the team and can tell you all the best eating places from coast to coast. I guess nobody needs to be reminded of the Ohio State-Notre Dame game of 1935, when the Irish staged a fourth-quarter rally that beat the Buckeyes 20-18. Whenever things get a little dull he just writes in his column "Remember the time—" and South Bend dies for Notre Dame all over again.

His assistant, Bobby Hoenig, was the best dancer the sports department ever had. Just the same Bobby could write boxing to a fare-you-well, and he handled the Golden Gloves contests each year, and in addition planned the make-up of the pages, wrote the headlines, edited the telegraph copy, and was in general a sports editor's dream of a handy man. The first year I was on the paper he entered the Golden Gloves matches and was the champion in his weight. I asked him recently if his dancing in the ring had anything to do with his polishing off the Big Apple when he hits the dance floor but he just laughed me away.

The lad who supervised the high school sports reporters and handled stories on the myriad other local sports, wrestling, industrial teams of all kinds, bowling, and what not, was Elmer Danch. Never will I forget the first day Elmer came to work for the *News-Times*. He was the reporter for James Whitcomb Riley High School sports. The boys ganged up on him.

It's a common fault of young reporters to write five paragraphs of material into about two columns of type. Danch, like myself, had this fault, and his first day's copy looked like a mile out of the Dixie highway. The composing-room foreman, Walter "It-can't-be-done" Worth, called Danch out and told him he would have to go over to the *Tribune* composing room and get a column stretcher.

Now there ain't no such thing! Type is set automat-

ically into just the wid h you read it in your newspaper.
And long lead rules are set between the columns. But
nobody bothers to tell a young reporter this, and it
seems reasonable that the lead rules can be made to give
enough to get your brain children before the public the
way you have written them. At any rate, Danch
thought so, and set off for the *Tribune*. Meantime the
Tribune composing room was advised by telephone of
the crisis which threatened to send the *News-Times* to
bed way past press time. So the *Trib* boys obligingly
wrapped up some lead and gave it to Elmer. We all
rushed to the window to watch him bring it back. The
opposition was located one block down and across the
street. When Elmer got back he was told that it wasn't
big enough, and he was sent back for more. The boys,
enchanted with their success, repeated the gag two or
three times. Finally, wilting under a hot September sun
as he threaded his faltering way through traffic, Elmer
brought some 60 or 70 pounds of lead "column
stretcher," and said if that wouldn't do they could cut
the story.

Jay Walz was our music critic and one of our better
writers. He had a swell sense of humor and in his column "Half-Notes," often included those program in-
cidents which are "unrehearsed." One had to do with a
performance of the *Lenore* "Overture." To the chagrin
of the conductor the off-stage horn did not come in
when supposed to. At the conclusion of the piece the
conductor rushed back stage to find the unhappy soloist
arguing with a stage-hand. "You can't play that thing
back here," the s.h. said, "there's an orchestra playing

out front." Jay married a very brilliant girl, Audrey Boyers, who did her sincere best to turn me into a presentable poet. She objected to my nights-in-Singapore attempts and said I would be better off if I wrote about what I knew and felt. Once we both were on a poetry program together, Audrey with first prize and I with honorable mention.

Practically every daily paper in the United States has to have correspondents in adjacent suburbs and country villages. Even the *New York Times* has an East Orange, N. J., correspondent. So you can readily understand that there is no reason for the *South Bend News-Times* to flout this laudable example. My Alma Mater has approximately thirty such zealous newshawks in northern Indiana and southern Michigan, for the city is only six miles from the state line. These correspondents take full advantage of the "freedom of the press." There's nothing they don't tell and it's all right with their readers. I remember that once a man in Plymouth, Indiana, wrote to cancel his subscription because, although the Plymouth correspondent had correctly reported that his wife had a "major" operation, the paper printed it "minor" operation.

During my tenure we had two state editors who sorted this welter of correspondence. The second was Tom Philipson, for whom I have a soft spot in my heart because he always says to me, "Do you love me as much as you always did?" And I say, "Just as much, Tommy," and sigh.

The first one was George Scheuer (pronounced Shoyer) who is Tommy's cousin. George is one of those people to whom the world presents few mysteries. He has an amateur radio operator's license. He has a pilot's license. He can cut wood blocks, and always designs his own Christmas cards. He can write a good story (he's going to do a guest chapter for me later on). And last but not least, he has gone from the state job to the Associated Press, so you can see that straightening out the news of thirty urban centers can be a stepping-stone to bigger and better things.

There was only one person ever connected with the *News-Times* who presented a more spectacular array of talent than George, and that was Harry Elmore, a photographer. We all called him "the Great Elmore," and not without reason. He was about five feet five inches tall and deceptively slight. He had one of the softest speaking voices I ever heard—but no matter how soft he spoke, a woman could still overhear him saying, "She's the sweetest subject for a picture I've ever had." He certainly did know how to get his women subjects to be their best in front of the camera. Now if he had men subjects it might be a different story.

For instance. One time he was sent to Mishawaka to get a picture of some Belgian pigeon racers. He was gone hours and hours, and when he came back he had a dim and useless picture of a lot of men who looked as if they would make squab meat out of any piegon they met. The city editor wanted to know what the hell, and Elmore just laughed and jingled a pocket full of change. He'd been playing darts with the Belgians (who are the best dart-throwers there are) and he'd beaten them all and cleaned them out.

70

Another instance. There might be a group of local boxers standing around the sports desk chatting and Harry would drop by and, hearing the conversation, remark, "I was champion boxer in my weight when I was in the Navy. I knocked out twenty-seven men in one night." Of course everybody would say, "Aw, you did not." And he would say, "Want to bet?" and of course they did. Then he would go over to his studio and come back presently with the press clippings to prove it.

That isn't all. The amateur senior golfers held a championship tournament one year in South Bend and Harry allowed as how he'd enter. The office felt, "Well, this'll show him." You know the answer. He won. Another year his wife will win the women's championship if she hasn't already taken it.

Then there's the matter of tennis. I know you don't believe it, but I can prove it. In his youth he was state champion of Nebraska. You stood more chance winning money playing an eight-horse parlay than you did when you bet against Elmore. I've seen him wrap a hankie around his fist and drive a nail through a two by four.

He took all the publicity and program pictures for Notre Dame and St. Mary's. When he was in a kidding mood he would say, "I've been head man at St. Mary's for twenty years." And, my friends, he didn't eat meat. Only fruits and vegetables.

All photographers have a flavory individualism. There was Johnny Woodruff, who was always on the scene when good news pictures were to be had. More of Johnny later. There was a boy named Jack, who never—no matter what the time of day—went for a picture without having a drink first. He finally bawled out the bosses and got himself fired. And there was Dutch Hennings.

Dutch had curly hair and dimples, and was kind of chunky and wore glasses. He talked like Bob Burns and had nearly as many good stories to tell. At the time of the last election Dutch and the rest of the staff did night duty on the returns. We had a big blackboard up at one end of the office where the results were posted as they came in, so that the telephone girls in various parts of the room could see them and answer inquiries. Dutch stood up by the board and yelled out, "At the turn it's Roosevelt"—"in the stretch it's Roosevelt—"—"the winnah—Roosevelt. It's a photo finish between Landon and Thomas for second." Since every man-jack there played the horses, Dutch started a game which quickly got out of hand. Phil "Sunflower" Nicar, the Republican political reporter on the staff, was all ready to do battle, and Ross Nelson, the city editor, who was trying to get out an extra, tried vainly to restore order. But by that time it seemed to be Dutch in the stretch and to hell with the extra.

In 1931 the paper was sold to Fred Millis, an advertising man from Indianapolis who thought up "Say it with flowers" and sundry other slogans which in the Fabulous Twenties paid him very well indeed. At the first staff meeting he assured us that we hadn't been sold down the river, that ever since he had carried papers as a little shaver he had wanted to own a paper, and that he took a fatherly interest in us all.

My depression promotions all occurred under the Millis regime. My salary, which had been cut once from $27.50 to $23 a week before he came, was cut to $13.60 in the one and a half years he was there. My work was tripled. I stood it because I was a kid, because I was still burning with the joy of being a real reporter. This (apologies to Mrs. Roosevelt) is a fairly accurate calendar of "My Day": To work at 8 A.M.; work on society until 11 A.M.; then called the undertakers and wrote obits, church news (there were eighty churches some of which had meetings or such each day), poor relief, the social welfare agencies and the Parent-Teacher association news until 2 P.M., the deadline for the last edition; had half hour for lunch; came back and either worked on Sunday features or went out to cover afternoon meetings of various organizations; got home for dinner whenever I could; and about four or five nights a week covered meetings and then went back to the office to write up all I had collected in the afternoon and night for the next day, because we had compositors working at night who could set it and get it out of the way; to bed anywhere from midnight to 1:30 A.M. I also went out with the photographer and supervised the taking of all pictures for the society pages. What happened to me happened to everybody who didn't get fired. One time during this melee I got a job with the township trustee. I resigned from the *News-Times* and when Mr. Millis heard it, he called in the gentleman who had hired me and suggested that if he wanted favorable publicity in his political ambitions, he had better hold up my job. At least I didn't have to worry about losing my job. I was the only girl left except Winifred Whitmore, society editor, who wrote only society news, clipped the paper for future meetings and made the society layout for Sunday.

Mr. Millis believed in sensational journalism and did his best to blow up little stories into big headline stuff. The paper began a dizzy tail spin, and in a little better than a year and a half lost 7,000 of its 30,000 circulation. Advertising dropped, too, and the paper went into receivership to Mr. Reed, with Mr. Stephenson returning as publisher. Mr. Millis went to the Orient. It was Byron J. "Speed" Lewis, who, as managing editor, put the sheet together again and once more made it a newspaper. "Speed" Lewis was and is a real newspaper man.

But before Mr. Millis retired to the land of the Rising Sun he spent about a quarter of a million dollars in improving the property. He put in a new press, covered the outside of the building with structural glass, and put up blue neon signs. He painted the walls of the editorial room green with a black stripe to separate them from the cream ceiling. He got some new desks and painted them dark green and had them all face the same way (at the suggestion of his wife) like a schoolroom. He even gave Bill Moyer, news editor at the time, a copy of a freshman journalism textbook and suggested that the staff read it. Oh yes, and then he put up a panel fence in the editorial room to separate the society and sports departments from each other and from the news department. And, oh, last but not least, he put rugs on the floor. He had Oriental rugs in his own office.

When he was going through the office one day shortly after the completion of the improvements, he put his hand on the editorial room fence and said proudly, "Well, boys, what do you think of it?" And Wally Mansell, the telegraph editor, said, "Well, we can't eat it."

It really remained for the late Carl Cooper to put the correct comment on this affair. Carl was a true gentleman of the old school. He was tall and in appearance much like Lionel Barrymore. He wore a banker's gray suit, and a navy blue overcoat with black velvet collar, and a derby hat, and spats, and carried a cane. He wore pince-nez glasses with a chain and loop over one ear. When he had a particularly good story on his typewriter you could hear him softly singing:

> Oh, my name is Sam
> And I don't give a damn
> And I'd rather be a nigger
> Than a newspaper man.

He believed that woman's place was in the home, and chided us career girls for not marrying. He had been on a number of papers and had traveled extensively. He looked like a judge of the Supreme Court, and Elizabeth Anderson, now society editor, said once that if she had a million dollars she would give a good bit of it to "Coop" without letting him know where it came from and let him live up to his magnificent appearance and salty personality. Coop had been in Gary politics in the city's young days and was familiar with the way both halves of the world lived. He seldom passed judgment, but always knew the facts.

He had been ill during the several days that Mr. Millis's improvement of the plant had been going on. And when he came back and saw the new fence, the green walls and the cream ceiling, there's no telling the extent of past observations it all recalled to his mind. At any rate he stood at the head of the stairs which made entrance to the room, crossed his hands on his cane, and, looking around, said, "Oh, girls, there's a gentleman in the parlor."

CHAPTER IV

Hail the Champeen!

OF BEES

IT'S ALMOST AS MUCH as a person can do, sometimes, to pick up a paper and find the news. I mean, what with contests and premiums, it would seem that the business of newspapers is to supplement the income or replace the household furnishings of Mr. and Mrs. America. The news is hardly more than the cement which holds the prize announcements together.

The reason for contests and premiums is no secret to the subscriber. With one paper having the rights to "Pop-Eye," and the other paper having the rights to "Dan Dunn," the competition to hold your readers is something terrific. So if you can get them interested in contests or premiums your chances of keeping the circulation up are materially improved.

There are some contests, however, mostly those directed towards children, which are designed less to gain subscribers than to give the paper a certain prestige. That is, the paper offers a contest with the kind of prizes which give children opportunities they otherwise would miss, trips, college educations and the like. And any child may enter, whether or not parents subscribe. But, of course, no paper is above hinting that if they do subscribe, the children will be kept in touch with the contest news.

Maybe you think handling one of these contests is so much molasses in your hair. But, believe me, if you've never done it before, that assignment is like getting a blank check on the mint. My first job of this kind was promoting the *News-Times* Spelling Bee in the spring of 1931. My elation when I was told to do it can hardly be described. The high feelings came partly from the fact that I would chaperon the winner on a trip to Washington, D. C., for the finals, and partly from something else which I will keep as a surprise to you.

This spelling bee is sponsored nationally by the *Louisville Courier-Journal* in co-operation with other newspapers throughout the United States. My first step as local promoter was to go into the morgue (file room to you) and look up the papers from the year before to see how my predecessor handled the event. (It was Dorothy J. Konold, incidentally, who had taken care of it. So I was one step nearer being as good as she was. Or so I hoped.)

The method was to have a splash story on a Sunday in February, page one, section two, giving the details of the contest, which was carried on in the public schools of the city and county and in parochial schools.

The superintendents and principals and priests were quoted as saying what a laudable thing they thought the contest was and how nice of the *News-Times* to do it.

After the first story the teachers in all the schools began to hold special oral spelling lessons each day in grades from third through eighth. At first I wrote two stories a week and then increased these to a daily story, visiting as many of the schools entered as I could and running pictures of possible winners, of teachers and of principals. This went on for about five weeks. Then the room eliminations were held, and next the school eliminations to select the winners for the county-wide contest. I had more than thirty winners in all, so many that we had to have a junior spell-down in the afternoon whose survivor took his place with the older contestants at night.

I know you can't picture a spelling bee as exciting. But there's something about seeing those youngsters sitting in a semicircle, repeating the word slowly and then embarking on the long course from its first letter to its last, that starts a thrill playing on the spinal column. A little girl comes to the middle of the word, falters, reddens, her eyes grow large, and then—she finishes "excellent"—a-n-t. And the reader says, "No," glances at the next contestant and says, "excellent." Meantime the little girl drops her head and closes her eyes, trying not to cry. It's no time to be soft-hearted, though. You must save your feelings for the winner.

The auditorium of the senior high school is jammed with the largest crowd ever to attend the final eliminations. People are standing in the back. Over at one side a row of Dominican nuns (out at night for the first time in their history in South Bend, and this by special permission from their superior) bow their heads to pray for their contestant. And she's good, too.

Finally only two children remain, the little girl favored by prayers, and a small crippled boy, who carries a crutch. The girl is very dramatic. She closes her eyes when she spells. The crowd leans forward staring at her, catching its breath. She speaks the letters slowly, allowing several seconds to elapse between each one. "R-a-r-"—here there is an unusually long silence, and the nuns move their lips—"Mary, Mother"— The audience is a single, silent block, their only thought for the next letter. She speaks again, "e-f-y. Rarefy." The nuns smile. The boy spells "embarrass" slowly but with confidence. "Comparable," says the reader, turning to the girl. Again the tension. But this time she says "i" when she should have said "a". The crowd gasps. The boy tries. "C-o-m-p-a-r-a-b-l-e."

The winnah!— Ladies and gentlemen! For the first time in the history of the contest a boy has won; first time a public school child has won; first time a student of a school outside South Bend has won. Stand up, Roland! I give you Roland Light, of Mishawaka Beiger Public School. I interview him on the spot, and urge him to make a little speech, which he does with charming self-possession.

I hurry back to the office. It is after eleven o'clock Saturday night. I begin to write my story in a state of excitement equal to that of a cheer leader whose team has won in the last few minutes of play. The Saturday night editor looks over my shoulder as I write, but not even that dismays me. He takes the copy page by page as it comes from my typewriter and sends it to the city desk to have the headlines written. In half an hour it is all over.

And oh, glorious, glorious—on Sunday morning a great big black banner on THE FRONT PAGE tells all about the contest. I knew, when I was given the assignment, that I'd wind up here, but I never could really believe it. I read the story three times, loving every word of it. I've made it at last. Oh, boy, there it is. I am in such a state that my family threatens to keep me from going to Washington if I don't calm down.

A whole week of unspeakably long days elapsed before we entrained for the nation's capital. My family, Mr. Mortimer P. Reed, the photographer, Roland's teacher and family all drove with us to LaPaz, Indiana, where we boarded the B. and O.'s crack Capitol Limited. It was my first trip away from home.

Once we were settled in our Pullman compartment Roland and I opened boxes of candy which had been given us, and tried to keep the gooey cherry syrup from running onto our best clothes.

Having finished with the candy we decided to go to the dining car and order dinner. I thought he ordered a lot, but as I look back on it I realize I wasn't very far behind him. We had both eaten before and would do so again, but you would never have guessed it from the meal we had that evening.

When we were back in the Pullman again Roland

and a boy across the way, in Western boots and high hat, made friends and chatted until bedtime. I asked for a table and typed my first release back to the office from the train. I told what Roland ate, what he thought, what he wore, what he wanted to be when he grew up (a trap drummer). I described his preparations to retire to his berth and his concern over what to do with his money. (His concern was not far behind my own. Three hundred dollars is a lot of cash, especially if it belongs to someone else.)

The next morning we were up early to look at Harper's Ferry. There are some feelings and experiences incapable of description, and the reaction of the two of us as we looked out on that historic place is one of them. We kept our noses to the glass all the way to Washington. Flat-landers by birth, we had never seen hill country before, and it is a wonder the force of our combined gaze didn't start a landslide. Those big, soft purple ridges did something to me. I can't tell you what, but I wish you'd spend twenty years on the prairie sometime, and then jump, over night, into the foothills. It's a journey that just twelve hours of time passing can't account for.

On our arrival we found our way to a cab, gave the name of the hotel (I forget what it was but I remember that it was at 14th and K streets), and then abandoned ourselves to staring at everything we could see. The dome of the capitol building took our breaths for a moment, with its white massiveness against a blue sky; the innumerable monuments and plazas we found magical.

At the hotel we registered at spelling-bee headquarters. We were told to report for trips next day and a dinner the following evening. We met some of the contestants and talked awhile, and then I asked Roland what he wanted to do, and he said to find a miniature golf course.

So we set out, after having received directions for locating one from a desk clerk trained not to show surprise. We stopped to look at everything, and turned corners and rounded circles until we were good and lost. We were enjoying ourselves, however, and didn't much mind. I saw a white building across the street and said, "Let's go over and look at that."

There was an expansive driveway in front of it and I said to Roland, "We'll just round that drive and get a better look." And we would have too, if one of the White House guards hadn't stopped us. My word! Was I ever embarrassed! Not knowing the White House when I met it head on!

After that we stuck to the business of finding the golf course and had a brisk little game. The course had all the intricacies of a Walt Disney castle.

That gave us an appetite, and I asked Roland where he wanted to eat, and he said someplace where there was music. We went to a rather mild little Chinese dine and dance place. We spelled words a bit that evening, and he went to bed, and I wrote my story and dispatched it by Western Union.

The next few days were beyond our wildest expectations. There were trips to the Bureau of Engraving, where we saw the money and the stamps being printed; to the zoo; to the aquarium; to the Smithsonian Insti-

tute, where Lindbergh's trim little *Spirit of St. Louis*
and the dresses of former presidents' wives are displayed
in anachronistic neighborliness; to the Lincoln Memorial which I fell in love with on the spot—(my name is
in the cornerstone, too, because I took pennies to help
build it when I was in grade school); up the Washington Monument, where some of the more adventurous
contestants delayed the party by walking down the five
hundred steps; past the awful State Department Building, which looks as though it had been built out of ar-
chitectural scraps to save waste, tried government practice notwithstanding; to the senate building, where we
had a ride in the subterranean railroad because Roland's
teacher had told him about it (I don't remember how I
wangled that); down to Alexandria and Mt. Vernon
where I could have lived forever and just daydreamed
about being a movie picture actress or something; to
old Christ Episcopal Church where Washington and
Lee worshiped; to the old Presbyterian church and its
cemetery (here one of the boys, who was chaperoned
by two nuns, startled the party with the comment, "My
grandfather proposed to my grandmother in a cemetery." The embarrassed nuns giggled and said, "Oh,
George!" And George insisted, "Well, he did."), out
to the great Episcopal Cathedral, where George and
I got lost from our respective companions and had to
go back to the hotel in a taxicab, the nuns when we
arrived being in a state near collapse from worrying
over George, but Roland worrying nary a bit about
me.

If the days were exciting, the nights (after Roland

had gone to bed) were twice as much so. One evening
I went to the press room (after we had been to the
Library of Congress) to file the account of the day's
activities. Roland had been especially thrilled at seeing
the Declaration of Independence in the Library, and I
felt that was a fact his public deserved to know. Another reporter was there, a boy from the West, and a
red-headed gal who acted as secretary. After I had sent
a messenger off with my story, the reporter inquired
if I would like a drink, and I said, "Yes." So he called
somebody (this was during prohibition) and said three
typewriters needed to be fixed in the press room, and
presently three quarts of Golden Wedding Whiskey
arrived. Well, I just sipped mine, because (this will be
hard for you to believe) I really did have my duty as
chaperon pretty much on my mind. The redhead and
the reporter, however, fell to with gusto. Then he
wanted to know if I'd like something to eat, and I said,
"Yes." So he called again and had what he referred to
as "Horrors doover" sent up. If he'd just waved a wand
the effect couldn't have been more astonishing, because
six waiters appeared with tray loads. For once I had all
the caviar I wanted. Meantime the redhead was getting meditative. Right out of a clear sky she asked me
about my love life, and I took a drink of ice water and
said the first thing which came into my head, which
was, "I'm divorced." You know how it is. You're away
from home for the first time in your life, and you're
all stuffed with caviar, and somebody asks you something, and all at once you feel giddy and lovely, and
you make up a crazy answer. But saying I was divorced

was the wrong thing, for she really had been. She launched into a set of confessions such as I had never heard before and never expect to hear again. I certainly learned at one fell swoop what every young girl should know.

All the time I was listening goggle-eyed to this revelation, however, I also kept an eye on the reporter, who was becoming decidedly tight. My duties as a chaperon began to assume sizable proportions. While I was wondering what my next move should be (don't ask me why I didn't get up and go; I don't know) the reporter said, "What do you think I should do?" and I said, "Oh, why don't you take a ride? The night air is so exhilarating." And he got up and went out. Half my problem was solved.

The secretary, who had an apartment and was not staying at the hotel, had gone cultural on me and was talking about her books. So I said, "Why don't we go over to your apartment and look at them?" She readily agreed. Up to this point she had been against going home. So we got a cab and went, and I told her to get out first, and once she was out I closed the door and ordered the cabby back to the hotel. I felt pretty diplomatic. I went into the press room and picked up the liquor and took it to my room, rather than have it discovered by somebody who might have made trouble.

The next morning the reporter told me he had taken a fifty-dollar cab ride and had no idea where he had been, and the secretary was as friendly and confidential as ever.

During the day the prize money, which amounted

to nearly $2,000, was converted into cash, and I was asked to take care of it. I know it seems incredible, but the young man who had charge of the contest didn't want to carry it around with him. I don't know why he picked on me unless he figured God protects the young and innocent. That night a number of us were going to a night club, so when I left the press room I took the money with me and put it in the medicine chest in the bathroom. I looked in on Roland and he was all right, sound asleep.

Well, it was one of those evenings. After we had dined and danced we drove along the Potomac River, and every so often one of the boys would get out and pick peony blooms for us, and we laughed and told funny stories and made wisecracks. We got back around three-thirty A.M. I was going to an early Communion service at the Episcopal Cathedral later, so there wasn't much sleep in store for me. When I got to my room I found I had locked myself out. I knocked on Roland's door but I couldn't arouse him. I turned this over in my mind and finally decided to go down and stay with a little reporter from Tennessee. She was a honey. She gave me a pair of her pajamas and since she was about four feet eleven and I am five-five, you can imagine how I looked. She talked to me a lot.

"If mah husbund knew how Ah'm ca'ryin' on, would he be mad!" she giggled. "He's jus' so ju-ellous."

Then she began to laugh about the aunt of her contestant who was also on the trip. "She's goin' to take some senatah's trunk home," my companion said, "and she's jus' been goin' 'round tellin' ev'ybody about it."

I knew precisely what she was talking about, for the charming lady had waylaid me earlier to explain the honorable and sacred duty which had been accorded her. I had listened respectfully, because I thought she was probably somebody important, and had some reason for telling me about the senator's trunk. But now I know she was one of the one hundred or so oddities that turn up at conventions and contests—people without a past or future, whose only function seems to be to add a crazy note to your own none too steady present.

Next morning I leaped gazelle-like out of bed and went upstairs to see if I could waken Roland. I didn't want to go to church in my evening clothes, and also with dawn came my memory of the two thousand dollars safely reposing, I hoped, behind my tooth glass. It was. At Communion I took occasion to thank God for that fact.

This was the day of the big contest, in case you had forgotten what the purpose of the trip was. It was scheduled for the afternoon and I had been invited to have lunch with the *News-Times* Washington correspondent, Frederick William Wile. I asked one of the other reporters to keep an eye on Roland for me until I joined the group later. Mr. Wile called for me promptly at twelve-fifteen and took me to the Columbia Club. We talked about the depression, about Coolidge, about Hoover, and I ate chicken a la king and thought how truly marvelous life could be. The waiter handed me a menu and stood ready to write down my choice of dessert. I ordered rhubarb pie a la mode with chocolate ice cream. The waiter just stood and stared

88

at me, and even Mr. Wile looked startled. "You want rhubarb pie a la mode with—ah—chocolate ice cream?" he asked gently. "Yes." The waiter moved off muttering. "A person could tell you're from Indiana," Mr. Wile said. But when the pie came he had collected himself and without flinching he watched me eat it.

From the club I went to the Museum of Natural History where the contest, for some reason into which it is not the business of a reporter to inquire, was to take place. Following the event we were to have a trip through the building. Since old bones had meant to me only what was left over from Sunday dinner, I was looking forward to both the contest and the visit.

My young charge decided he had time to improve in natural history before the bee, however, and when it came time for the contestants to line up, Roland and one or two others were missing. I went in search of them, looking first forwards and then backwards, until in the latter position I bumped into something, said, "I'm sorry," and when it didn't move, turned around to find myself confronted with a mess of dinosaur bones. I was so surprised I began to sneeze, and when an attendant asked me what I wanted all I could say was, "I—I pzzzzz—I—pzzz—pzz—I—" It was the first I knew that I was allergic to dinosaurs. At last I got hold of Roland in the Indian Room and took him down to the auditorium.

He did pretty well. I think he was tenth or eleventh when he was given the word "indicative." Roland, poor boy, had never heard the word pronounced before and in his reading had always called it "indi-kay-tive." He really did know how to spell it, but not soon enough. So he was spelled down. The winner was a very handsome boy from West Virginia. He had lots of poise and could, I am sure, have won a movie contest with the same ease with which he won his spelling-bee championship.

The next big thing on the program was having our pictures taken with President Herbert Hoover. We went through the White House first and then to the grounds for the picture. Now, Mr. Ahearn, in a spirit of wanting to give me something easy to do, had told me to get a picture of Mr. Hoover shaking hands with Roland Light. When it turned out that Roland wasn't a winner, the assignment became something of a problem. However, the way to do a thing, I had been told, was to do it. So I took a photographer to one side and pointed Roland out. "I'm going to ask Mr. Hoover to shake hands with him," I said, "and you take the picture." I've told you about photographers. They're good at everything but taking pictures.

Anyway I maneuvered Roland into position beside the winner who was standing next to Mr. Hoover. When the president had finished congratulating him, I said, "Mr. President, will you shake hands with my contestant, please?" and he graciously complied. But the photographer (bless him) signaled me that he hadn't got the picture. So I had to say, "Mr. President, I'm sorry the photographer muffed that one. Will you do it again, please?" And he did. I don't think I have ever seen a man look more tired and weary than Mr. Hoover. When he had finished posing, he turned to one of his men and said, "Now, where do we go?" It made me sad, because I had learned that Washington could be a lot of fun, if you went at it in the right spirit.

—AND BOXES

In the early spring of 1935 I went to St. Mary's College as publicity director, but in the summer I again returned to the *News-Times* to work during vacation, filling in on the beats of those who were away. My first assignment was on the desk, editing copy and writing heads. I don't know how long I had been doing this when Pi Warren, who had returned to the paper, asked me to come into Mr. Stephenson's office. The publisher explained to me, "We've had a man doing Soap Box Derby promotion for several weeks and yesterday he sprained his back. We thought the thing was going along all right, but when we checked up after his accident, we learned from the dealers that there hasn't been a thing done.

"Now this Derby is only two weeks away and we can't have a failure. We want you to take it over and go to town with it. Let us know whatever co-operation you need."

My first step, again, was to look at the stories printed previously and see what it was all about. The event was called the *News-Times*-Chevrolet Soap Box Derby and was being promoted in co-operation with two Chevrolet dealers in South Bend and one in Mishawaka. The national sponsor was the Chevrolet Motor Car Company.

The first point was to have the boys with their parents go to the Chevrolet dealers to register. Then the entrants were to build soap-box racers to fit certain specifications as laid down by a rules committee. No boy could spend more than ten dollars. There were two age groups: Class A for boys of high school age, and Class B for junior high and grade school age. When the racers were finished, they were to be inspected, weighed in, and approved. The day for the races was chosen. That was all. It sounds simple, doesn't it?

I set out the morning I got my assignment to visit the dealers and see how many registrations we had. There were exactly six! And registration was to close at the week's end, and the races were to be held in two weeks! My initial story, which was written in juvenile style directed to the boys, informed them that, in order to give everyone an opportunity to enter the event we had been persuaded to keep the registrations open for another ten days. But they would have to hurry if they wanted to build a winning racer in time for the first day's eliminations. I harped on this theme every night, meantime getting some pictures of boys registering, and also pictures of boys building racers.

The American Legion was co-operating by sponsoring entrants from the Children's Home as well as in preparing the racing course. I yanked a couple of members out to the Home and took pictures of boys holding some old wood and wheels, with the Legionnaires benignly looking on.

In a few days the high-pressure stories and pictures began to bear fruit. Boys appeared in the office by tens and twenties. They wanted to enter but they didn't have the money to build a racer. So I began to call the town's business men and civic-minded leaders, and asked them if they would contribute ten dollars to help a boy build a racer. They could run an ad on the side of the car, I told them. I also assured them that thousands of people would be there to see the race. Actually I wondered if anyone except my loyal family and the *News-Times* staff and officials would show up.

At week's end I had one hundred registrations, and by the time the ten days were up there were one hundred sixty. It began to look as though I would have a reasonable crowd of relatives out for the event, if I had no one else. To drum up further enthusiasm I arranged a parade, a sorry affair; wheels came off, the band played out of tune; oh, my! But people came downtown to look at it, and the Soap Box Derby began to have an air of success.

As the day of the race neared, my duties narrowed down to providing a first-aid tent with physician; buying prizes; arranging for officials; having a starting ramp built. I worked on these things during the day and wrote my copy at night.

When the day of inspection dawned my troubles really began. I should explain to you at this point that a good set of wheels, with pneumatic tires, costs around eight dollars. That meant a boy could spend only two dollars for all the rest of his auto. Well, you should have seen how far some of those boys stretched two bucks. I wish I could do as well. As we weighed the cars in at the top of the racing hill, numbered them, and parked them alongside, one parent after another would come to me and say, "Are you going to let this car race?"—"You can't tell me that car cost only ten bucks." —"That car doesn't really weigh two hundred twenty-five pounds. It's loaded."—"Let's get up a petition not to race if that car is allowed."

Oh, sweet diplomacy! Now, the Chevrolet Soap Box Derby is a good-will affair, and while part of its value lies in its practical applications of the rules of sportsmanship and honest competition, part of it unquestionably lies in the mellow mood into which it should induce the contestants' elders. So iron-handed stuff was out. While the happy little sportsmen milled around me, I had to keep their seniors from sabotaging the affair. A soft answer, Moses or Shakespeare said, turneth away wrath. If the wrath I turned away that day could have been harnessed to something useful, I could have made Edison look like a beginner.

First, I explained to angry papa John Doe that the appearance of Richard Roe's car would not help it get down the hill. Its speed was the only thing that counted. Then I temporarily disqualified all cars overweight. If a boy could bring the weight of his car down by one-half hour before race time, he could qualify. I asked some of the boys entering ritzy models how much the tin had cost that covered them. "Oh, that's just an old piece of tin that was given me at the junk shop. I 'spose it's worth twenty cents." Next, the paint cost. "Oh, that's just some old paint we had around the house." I felt that the situation had been handled fairly well when this popped up. "That boy didn't build his car himself.

He had help." Well, there's so much of this in every contest. The boys got along fine. But the parents! There ought to be a law!

The races were exciting. Some of the little models whizzed down the hill at a speed of nearly forty miles an hour. To my pop-eyed amazement better than 10,000 spectators turned out both days, cheering, betting and swearing.

The second day's events took four hours, but nobody seemed to be exhausted but me. The winner was Way Ferdinand, son of a Legionnaire. Way's share of the prizes included a bicycle, a silver trophy, a prize for winning his first heat, and a trip to Akron, Ohio, to participate in the national finals. Way's father drove him to Akron and I went by train.

Those Akron finals are something! I arrived on a Friday night, looked up Way at the hotel and interviewed him, dispatched the story and went to bed thoroughly worn out from weeks of day and night, night and day. The next day Chevrolet officials had arranged to take the boys in a group to see the Akron city races, which were being run as a sort of preliminary to the national event. I decided to save my strength for an emergency and not do anything. But I did go down to the lobby to see the spectacle. There were about 100 young boys in white emblemed sweaters, and little caps with their name and city on them, the gift of Chevrolet. When a champion arrived by train he was met and escorted to the hotel with screaming police motorcycles leading the way. On his arrival a band in front of the hotel set off a blare of welcome. The fanfare for a king is small stuff compared to the reception of a Soap Box Derby champion.

And Chevrolet does right by the press, too. The finals were run off on Sunday. So on Saturday night the boys are taken to a movie to relieve the chaperons of their duty, and a banquet is given for the press. One room is set aside as a private cocktail lounge where drinks are on the house. I wandered in by myself and was quickly taken under the wing of two representatives from St. Louis, Mo. I sat with them, and four other men at dinner. There is something about these contests that attracts the Old South, for (sample of conversation):

Attractive gentleman to my right: "Have you evah been in love with a Vuhginian?"

South Bend reporter in interested voice: "No-ooo."

A. G. to my right: "Well, when a Vuhginian makes love to you, you like it, whethah you like the Vuhginian or not."

I hadn't then, and haven't yet, been made love to by a Virginian, but I must say his voice carried a pleasant note of conviction.

Way almost, but not quite, made the semi-finals the next day. The ceremonies at the track were impressive. A band played the Star-Spangled Banner, and some fifty flags lining the course were raised in unison. Then the parade of champions began marching up the hill.

The trophies were awarded at a Champion's dinner on Sunday night. The winner, a White Plains, N. Y., boy was given a four-year college scholarship at any State university or college of his choosing, and I don't know how many silver trophies. All the boys were given wrist watches.

The second year I handled the Derby was, for the most part, a repetition of the first, with one exception. A party of my friends and I decided we wanted to know what it was like to ride a Soap Box car. So I called several of the boys who had completed sturdy little entries and asked them to bring the racers out to the hill early in the evening, while it was still light enough to take pictures.

Now, on the day of the races this hill is blocked off by city police, and traffic is re-routed. But on the evening we were to have our fun, this provision, of course, was not made. I gaily climbed into a little red racer, had one of the boys give me a push, and started off.

I'll never forget guiding that racer over the brick hill as long as I live. I bounced so hard I thought every bone in my body was breaking, and in the face of my personal agonies, I had to try to avoid an auto that was coming up the hill. Really the auto avoided me. The course was about 1,000 feet and I managed to keep the little speed wagon (which made around thirty-five miles an hour, it seemed like 100) on the street and brought it to a stop about two hundred feet beyond the finish line.

My picture was snapped and when I got out I took the camera and promised to get a picture of Glen Barry, one of the girls from the business office, as she came down. When she hit the bottom, the cable of the steering wheel broke, she lost control, was thrown half out, and dragged into a grassy side line. We were all terrified and rushed to her aid, only to find that, although she was skinned and bruised, she was laughing at the idea of having been thrown from a Soap Box car. The picture, of course, was never printed.

The winner of the second year, Don Troutman, was a very clever young man and had a beautiful little car, but he was outclassed at Akron and didn't make the finals.

So I found out that, for me, the cost of making the front page entailed a lot of anguish, and that anyway if it hadn't been a newspaper promotion, I wouldn't have made it. I simply had to be given a story that would make the front page on its news merit. I wanted to cover a murder. But as the old saying runs, "What you want and what you get are frequently two different things."

CHAPTER V

Be Bloody, Bold and Resolute

AHEARN SAYS, "CHRIST!" and Pi Warren says, "Jesus!" and Cooper says, "My God!" and Mr. Huston just reads the copy in silence.

I don't look up because I know what it's about. I'm writing the funeral notice that will be tacked onto the end of the story. It's the autumn of 1930 and I've been doing obits for a year and am hardened to it. But this one gets me.

The evening before when school dismissed, a man about forty years old approached a little girl, aged nine, and asked her to go with him. She did and he took her to an old barn, threw her down, stifled her childish screams of fear and pain, raped her, and strangled her with a piece of picture wire.

Police, of course, are without clews; the mother is hysterical; the little girl's playmates tell conflicting stories, and no clear description of the man can be

99

gained. The story runs more than a column, but stripped of its details, there it is. The office boy hurries to the composing room with it, comes back for the headlines, carries pictures of the sobbing mother and the scene of the crime to the engraving department. We set about to get our paper on the street before the *Tribune*.

The deadlines of other days are humdrum routine compared with this. Ahearn's shirt-tail is about out, but he doesn't notice it. Pi lights a pipe and a cigarette and puffs first one and then the other. Coop does *not* sing "My name is Sam—" The superior indolence of the society editors has a melancholy air, and the sports writers drop their favorite pastime of bawling at each other, "Remember when—"

Phones ring. A hundred wild and unconfirmed rumors are volunteered by persons who wish to have their names in the paper in connection with the crime: "a suspicious-looking character—"; "a man dressed so and so—"; "driving such and such a car—"; "running down the street away from the direction of the barn—" After a half-dozen of these, I say, "Gee, a ghoul is a nice person compared to these tripes." My wisecrack gets no response.

For days the front pages are filled with the activities of the police as they try to track down the murderer. It is believed (whose beliefs are involved in that mysterious news report that always begins: "It is believed —"?) that the man was no stranger to the little girl. The mother says she knows nothing. Tension hangs over the city like unbroken rain. What child is safe as long as this man is free?

The *News-Times* begins to berate the police department for its failure to capture the criminal. One day Coop comes in, his face flushed, his lips moving as he talks to himself. He marches straight into Huston's office, and Ahearn and Warren are called in. The rest of us look at each other and speculate on the meaning of this conference. I feel confident that Coop will tell me later, since he often flatters me by confiding inside stuff. But this time he lets me down. Says he'll tell me some other time. The only result of the conference that I can see is a further and more furious lambasting of the police department. It is all to no avail, however, and so far as the public is concerned we have had a perfect crime.

The tension dissipates and, like convalescents, we shake off our fears and return to the comfort of the autumn: brisk air—crimson patches of woods over the prairies—the dull grunts of punted footballs heard wherever boys are playing—the even duller grunts of politicians making campaign speeches.

The dahlias bloom and so does the office. Men are at work and Tom Coman writes about business; club women go to tea and Hope Halpin reports the programs; new books are published and Do Konold contributes her deft, intelligent criticisms; the school board fires the superintendent and Jay Walz has a good series of news stories. Ahearn looks forward to a second undefeated season for Notre Dame and the off-year elections as the probably best news breaks.

Not many people die during the fall, so I have a little time to indulge in theory, and I tell Carl I think all sex criminals should be permanently locked up or else rendered incapable of perpetrating such crimes. But he tells me to be a reporter or else get married and not bother with the more profound side of life. I ask him what that private conference was about when the little girl was murdered and he is about to tell me, when Ahearn orders me to return to my desk and stop bothering the help.

Then—one Saturday night a mother in a home on the west side hears a heavy thud, gets up, and goes into the room of her two daughters. Only one of them is breathing. Quickly she steps into the hall, stumbles, recovers herself and turns on the light. At her feet lies her other daughter, her throat slit from ear to ear, the blood gushing out and dripping down the stairway. Later, when she was telling her story to the officers, she said she picked up her daughter, carried her back to her bed, awakened her husband and called the police.

Stripped of its details, there's that story. Monday the police were without clews, and they stayed without them. The *News-Times* castigated the department and officials. Again Cooper comes back from police headquarters in a fury. He and Dick Jackson have both been working on the story. Dick follows Coop into the office, and sits down to write. Carl goes into another conference with the editors. I ask him about it, but he just shakes his head.

I write the notice of funeral arrangements with a giddy feeling of importance for being so near the covering of a murder. I tell Carl I think police would be more effective if they were appointed by civil service instead of by politicians. He tells me that, little as I know about newspaper work, I know still less about politics. I ask him again what those conferences are about, but before he can tell me, the W.C.T.U. president calls up and I take a story from her about liquor and sin.

Well, on the Saturdays we didn't have murders to distract us, we rejoiced at the Notre Dame victories, and finally the team got through the season undefeated and thousands lined the streets to welcome the champions back from their last game, which had been in California.

The elections, which the people, wrought up by murders, and football, had almost forgotten, were held, and one Democrat administration succeeded another. A promise of a shake-up in the police department was made. But when the shake-up came, it only amounted to shifting the officers around.

Almost before you could say *etaoin shrdlu* we had another murder. A white man found a Negro doctor in bed with his wife, and shot them. He gave himself up. The little news boys ran about the streets yelling, "Black and white murder, extra, extra!" The police were only slightly more bewildered by the murderer's confession than those of us on the staff. Why anyone would confess to a murder in South Bend we didn't understand. But it turned out that the man was slightly crazy, so that explained it.

We continued trouncing the police anyway, but no one was very exercised about it, since everyone was intent on getting ready for Christmas. I think South Bend people spent even more money on this lark in 1930 than they had the year before. Depression? It was still in the national news section for us. Our local columns were clear.

Snow was on the ground, but the office was warm, and we entered 1931 with the happy feeling that maybe South Bend was going to get through the depression with only a few minor burns instead of a holocaust. For we had basic industries; we had industries upon which were firmly based the American standards of living. And the word "bank" gave us only a comfortably secure feeling. And a job was something you got up in the morning to go to—not something you looked for. Oh, we knew there had been a crash—but for the most part it was in Wall Street and only our wealthiest people had been pinched in their personal speculations. We little people were snug and comfortable. We were, that is, until—

One Saturday noon, a group of the town's biggies came to see Mr. Stephenson and Mr. Huston. Everybody looked up and we stared at each other and said, "what now!" The faces of these men were as lively as those of ambulating cadavers and we knew something had happened and *that something* was no tea party.

The paper was ready to go to press. On Saturday the staff was divided, one group getting out the daily paper and the other coming in later to prepare the Sunday edition. We went to press early to get the desk clear for the big weekly issue. And when these men came in we just naturally knew that the front page was going to be torn up and the paper revamped for a new story. What was it?

A bank president had shot himself! I knew him. He

was about sixty, quiet, sensitive, a lover of art, a reader of scholarly books. He had an observatory beside his home, sent his sons to Harvard. He ought never to have mixed into banking in the first place. For several weeks a quiet run had been in progress on one of his banks. He had gone to Chicago on Friday to see if he could put through a deal to save the situation. He couldn't. Forces bigger than he nullified his life's work. He knew what was coming and he wanted none of it.

Here was the issue the visitors put up to the *News-Times*. Should we, as a newspaper, publish the fact of his suicide, or as guardians of the public welfare, should we say simply he had died? Better to forestall a crisis if we could. We chose to conceal the truth, but the other paper said he killed himself.

Monday morning the banks began to toboggan down their frozen assets onto the hard bottom of the depression. One bank, of which the dead man had been president, closed its doors. Panic burst upon the town like a storm, and the people, suddenly bereft of security, rushed through the streets like flood water, going from bank to bank, checking their money out of one and putting it into another, or renting safety deposit boxes, or taking it home to hoard. They collected in little groups to gossip and relate the hundreds of rumors sprung from fear. In the few weeks following, four of the six downtown banks closed or limited the amount a depositor might draw. A considerable number of the banks in the outlying districts closed permanently.

We didn't even try to relax after this news break. Every sheet from New York to San Francisco would rather have a local story on its front page than the Second Coming of Christ, Coop once told me. But the *News-Times* wouldn't—not in the winter of 1931. For the local news was as frightening as a clammy hand against your throat in the dark—men laid off at Studebaker's—men laid off at Bendix—more frequent stories of families on relief. It was like a death watch. Little businesses closed up and moved out, and their stalls stood vacant. Here and there whole buildings towered empty, their windows staring. Advertising volume in the paper fell off, and we in the office had our salaries cut. The murders, relieved only by the temporary intercession of football and elections, had keyed us up to top-screw pitch. And now the strangling tentacles of the depression plucked our nerves. We were frightened, and chafing at our fears. So we were all glad when the paper once more began to nag and worry the police about South Bend's unsolved murders.

It was while this was going on that I was assigned to cover the spelling bee. I worked at this afternoons and evenings, but during the mornings I was just a plain obit reporter and I could not shake entirely free of the emotional fringes which had us tied up in knots.

Therefore on that Tuesday afternoon when a plane flying over Kansas exploded in the air and carried Rockne down to his death I was as stunned and horrified as everyone else. For seconds that seem like hours we stand staring at each other. Rockne! Is it true? Our first knowledge of it is phone calls from people who heard the flash broadcast. To the composing room—get ready for an extra; to the office boy—call Coman,

106

Chester, Cooper; to Ahearn, get long distance; to Smallzried—go to the morgue and get all the Rockne file.

Give us murders, suicides, depressions; give us dopey police departments—but not this. Rockne—Rockne is dead!

Sometime later, Carl Cooper got a scoop on a follow-up of the Rockne story. A University of Notre Dame priest had testified in a Chicago murder case identifying the killer of Jake Lingle, a *Chicago Tribune* reporter. This priest, so the story ran, had booked transportation on the crash plane. At the last minute he had to cancel his reservation, but Rockne, who was going to Hollywood to make some movies, offered to take it. Coop had it from government agents working on the case that the gang to which the Lingle killer belonged had put a bomb in the plane to get the priest. Notre Dame officials, for some reason I never knew, were furious with us for printing the story and called us "scavengers who ate out of garbage pails." If that story is true, and there's no doubt about the government men telling it to Coop, the gangsters were never caught.

Rockne, you will remember, was buried on the day before Easter. Sunday was a beautiful, warm spring day and I somehow felt life would relax. I went to church all dressed up in new clothes and my family and I took a drive in the afternoon and looked at the St. Joseph River flowing gentler than sweet Afton, and the little willows putting out their lacy green leaves. The air, the colors, and the fragrance were so soft I could almost forget my responsibilities as spelling-bee editor.

Cooper had advised me to take it easy, and I tried to follow this advice. About the middle of the week I began looking forward to the Notre Dame Lawyers' ball and thinking what I'd wear. I didn't even bother to read what I'd written, much less the editorials aimed at the police department for not solving crimes. I couldn't understand why we kept rapping the police so, when the murders dated back to the autumn. I asked Carl about it, and he was about to tell me when the phone rang and he had to answer it.

The ball was on Friday night and it was great fun, as things of that kind always are. It was nice to relax, and I was sitting in a restaurant afterwards holding hands with my escort, waiting for a hamburger with pickle and mustard, when—yes, you've guessed it. This week of quiet was too good to be true. One of the waiters came to our table with his eyes bugged out a foot and said, "Hey! You're a reporter, ain't cha? Well, there's just been another murder!" A man named George Perry had been shot from ambush near his home in the northwest section of town.

We went in search of the place and found it, and there were lots of police cars around and we couldn't get in, even though I said I was a reporter. I can see the detective's point. Covering murders in evening clothes is hardly to be expected, and after all, I hadn't actually been assigned to it. (I thought I never would be sent on a murder story and I wanted to be, sooo bad.)

Next morning, Saturday, good old Saturday, Frank Ahearn was plenty excited. Police, of course, were without clews, but we weren't. Some months back an internal revenue collector in Chicago, a woman, had been in Springfield, Illinois, and had won $50,000 playing faro with three strange men. When it came time to pay off, one of the men says to her, "Now, we'll pay you, but we want to know if you could have paid us if you'd lost." So she says, "You wait here," and she high-tails it back to Chicago and gets a couple of friends who can raise $50,000 in cash (and this late at night, mind you), and back they all go to where the three men are waiting. So the men say, "Try it again?" And they do, and you know the rest. The woman and her friends practically had to hitch-hike back to Chicago. She came to South Bend and identified George Perry as one of the three men who had "swindled" her out of $50,000. And we wondered if George, in his turn, had left his cohorts in the lurch and taken the dough, and if they, in their turn, had got even with him.

We spent several days on that theory, and then one day Coop comes in and there's another private conference and the *News-Times* all but puts up a whipping post to flay the police alive for not solving this crime.

On a Friday night one week later, the chief of police went into his office and sat down. I remember that office. I'd seen it when Ahearn, unable to find a copy boy handy, had sent me to get police news as it was being written by our boys in the city hall press room. The office was a cubbyhole really, with its clock, roll-top desk, and a couple of chairs. It was quiet, stealthily quiet there, that night when the chief went in. Perhaps the ticking clock struck a rhythm with his thoughts as he sat with his elbows on the desk, head bowed in his hands. Perhaps his thoughts began, "To be or not to be—"

Damn politics and jealous detectives. What chance does a man have? (Whether 'tis nobler in the mind to suffer the slings and arrows of outrageous fortune—) The *News-Times* and its editorials: what's wrong with the department? What's wrong? What's wrong? (—or to take arms against a sea of troubles, and by opposing end them?) Crime and murder and butchered bodies of young girls and the hulking corpse of the slain gambler. If I could talk, could tell what I know, if I—(and by a sleep to say we end the heart-ache and the thousand natural shocks that flesh is heir to—) He took out his gun. (To die—to sleep.)

Saturday's paper blazed with the story of this suicide, and a recapitulation of the crimes and frustrations that had led the chief to take his own life.

I got hold of Cooper that afternoon and I said, "Now listen, let's go have a glass of buttermilk and you tell me what this was all about."

"Well," says Coop, as we sip our refreshment, "the police know who killed the little child, and the girl on the west side, and George Perry."

"Cooper!" I gasped, "why in God's name—"

"The police," he continued, "could not get a confession. It is not the place of the paper to get confessions or to indict criminals. We did what we could. We never let up."

"Who did it?" I asked.

He told me the stories, but names he would not tell me. "You're a little gal, and it's not wise for little gals to know too much about bad mans," he teased me. It is not my business to get confessions or indict criminals, either, so I let it go there. As far as I'm concerned the whole thing is buried with the late chief of police.

So there it is—five murders, two suicides, Rockne, four banks closed, salaries skidded to half what they'd been. But there was the championship team at Notre Dame, too—and the spelling bee.

That's what it is to report news at the crossroads of America.

CHAPTER VI

Hell's Bells

IF LITTLE BO-PEEP didn't look after her flocks any better than the pulpit shepherds do theirs, it's no wonder she lost them. For, though sheep are traditionally good-natured and easily led, even they make some minimum demands on their keepers. Wasn't it Milton who delivered himself of the opinion that there were preachers who "for their bellies' sake, creep and intrude and climb into the fold"? And then he added, "The hungry sheep look up and are not fed, but swollen with wind and the rank mist they draw, rot inwardly."

Well, Milton said it better than I can. However, I was church editor once, and I can feel like Milton, even if I can't swear like he could.

It was the autumn of 1931 when I was *promoted* to the job of church editor. (If a reporter says he was promoted he means that somebody was fired and he has been given more work. If he says he got a raise, he's just plain lying.) Church news included the reporting of a Sunday sermon in each Monday's paper, accounts of special holiday services, the meetings of various young people's groups, ladies' aid quilt shows, revivals and conventions.

I mention conventions last, but it should have come first. For I had hardly wiped my nose and started to make a file of the ministers' names and phone numbers when the Methodists took off and celebrated the centennial of Methodism in St. Joseph County. South Bend, being county seat, was the natural location for the festivities.

Now, I think it only fair to tell you that when I heard the news of my "promotion" I affected not to care very much; I tried to behave with the aplomb of a star reporter assigned to a Paris beat—what was Paris more than just another place to such a creature? But had I actually been sent abroad, I could hardly have been more thrilled. I felt that I, like Lazarus, had been raised from the dead, so long had I been writing obituaries. I, at last, was a general news reporter.

Therefore, when the Methodists announced their centennial plans, my new life bloomed like dandelions. It was my first convention. Let my colleagues on the staff kid my promotion—it is I, and not they, who am going to sit in session with so cosmopolitan a body as the World Board of Methodist Bishops.

For four days I practically live in the First Methodist Episcopal Church following my Bishops faithfully, looking, listening, anticipating something tremendous. I rush into the office during the morning and tell Ahearn

to save some space for me, run up to the church and go
from meeting to meeting, learning significant facts about
the heathen, like: "It's not hard to save souls, but it's
difficult to keep them saved," and then tear back to the
office and write about four thousand words which is
cut to half a column.

Jay Walz, whose experience and work is a couple of
steps above mine, looks over at me from his desk and
says sympathetically: "You're getting your baptism by
fire, aren't you? Don't you think you'd better have
some lunch?"

I stare at him with amazement. Does he think anyone
covering a convention can actually take time out for
eating? "I'm afraid I'll have to get back," I say, as
though explaining something to a child. By the time I
have finished writing about the morning session it is
time for the afternoon program to begin.

It is after hours when I get back to write up the
"P.M." meetings. I sort over my memoranda: money
and membership was discussed, committees appointed,
and the Rt. Rev. E. L. Waldorf (of Kansas City, not
Astoria) had reported on a visit to South America:

"Protestantism is getting strongly entrenched in
Latin-American countries. Especially in the Argentine
there are evidences of a growing self-consciousness on
the part of the Methodist group."

Right there I pause. What's happened? The glitter
which surrounds my World Board of Bishops seems to
have dimmed a little. I remember that as a child I had
the idea Jesus Christ was watching over me. Supposing
He is, I think. I wonder what His reactions are as He

peers over my shoulder and reads that the Methodists of Argentina are self-conscious.

Well, mine not to wonder why. I paste the sheets together, toss them into the copy basket, go home to powder my nose so I can return to the church in time for a dinner meeting. Making up for my lack of lunch I have four helpings of chicken and biscuits, coffee and pumpkin pie. Feeling more like a Roman than a Christian I settle back to hear what the Rt. Rev. Charles Wesley Burns, Bishop of San Francisco, speaker of the evening, may have to say. Following his introduction a dramatic hush falls over the audience. He rises, makes his acknowledgment to the master of ceremonies, opens a little case and takes out a pair of spectacles. "I have here," he says, "a replica of the spectacles belonging to John Wesley. The originals are in a safe in Los Angeles with a pair belonging to Francis Asbury and one which belonged to Bishop McHenry. I like to think of John Wesley wearing them and looking into the future of this movement he had started. For Methodism was a movement and not a church when it began."

And then follows a long oration on the character, thoughts, and hopes of John Wesley, with digression into the hopes of the Methodist Church. At one point the bishop says, "—as long as there is a Ladies' Aid, there will be a Methodist Church, and as long as there is a Methodist Church, there will be an Eighteenth Amendment in the Constitution." (I have heard since that the Eighteenth Amendment was repealed. But if the Methodist Episcopal Church has disbanded and left the Ladies' Aid in the lurch, it has not been brought to

my attention.) I take enough notes to make a roll of—
oh well, never mind. Anyway when the editor sees it all
written up—six pages—he shakes his head and says, "You
could have written the Life of Christ in half the time
and space."

After this, I feel a little let down. Perhaps the World
Board of Bishops are not going to take any tremendous
steps, after all, even though they have surveyed the
ground through John Wesley's spectacles. The third
day crawls by and my chief thought is that I'm not going to have my usual Sunday morning sleep. I have to
get up early enough to breakfast with the Rt. Rev.
Edwin Lee, Bishop of Singapore and the Orient, who
is to preach the morning sermon. He will give me the
gist of his talk and I won't have to go to the service. He
tells me some of the difficulties a missionary in the
Orient must face. There are so many religions to cope
with, Buddhism, Brahmanism, Confucianism, fire worship— Fire worship! The words electrify me! For only
a few days ago I had been gossiping with the cafeteria
manager at the Y.W.C.A. about that group's study of
comparative religions. "They're doing Zoroastrianism,"
she said. "What's that?" I asked. She shrugged as one
who could take the Persian Messiah or leave him alone.
"Fire worship, I gather." I stored this fact away with
others I never expected to use again. Blandly I look up
into the bishop's eyes. "You mean Zoroastrianism?" He
drops his hand to the table. "Yes! How did you know?
Never have I met a reporter so well informed on religion." I flee before he can question me further, and
write my final story of the convention.

In due time the bishops evacuated South Bend and returned to the world. I was left for news with the St. Joseph County Ministerial Association, and I didn't expect much of it, and I wasn't disappointed. It met every Monday and seldom provided me with anything more than a paragraph of resolutions which filled in at the bottom of my obituary column. But we were, after all, in a depression, a time in which church people are diffident about making news. The clerics were hard put to know what to do about it. If they questioned the wisdom of the social order they offended the deacons, elders or vestry, who were the business men of the community and the principal contributors toward their salaries. And if they didn't question it or at least make gestures of sympathy and assistance, they drove away in disappointment the little man who had lost his job and sat in the pew wondering how he was going to pay his wife's doctor bill when the baby came.

What will they do, I ask myself as I sit in session with the ministers in their meeting rooms at the Y.M.C.A. The pastor of one of the Methodist churches gets up to have his say: "I have been accused of being a Communist." He walks around his chair and leans on it. His voice is hardly more than a whisper. The men of God are stirred from their apathy. They look at the speaker, anxious and embarrassed. "The Communists," he continues as his brethren flinch at the word, "are the only people I know who are dying for what they believe. Communism is not a political party. It is a religion with martyrs and leaders. When I look into the faces of my people today, I know I can no longer comfort them with the hope of a better world to come. I can only urge them to a better world in the present. I *am* a Communist."

A recognized religious leader in the community, a Communist! That was news. I hurried back to the office and wrote about half a column. But my nose for news had betrayed me. The story was cut to a paragraph. One of the editors explained to me that it was a policy of the paper to ignore the publicity-seeking efforts of the Communists.

Now, I seldom engage in a fight in which I am licked before I start. But this was too much. "Publicity?" I am incredulous. "He didn't do this for publicity. He had tears in his eyes when he spoke."

"I know, I know," comforted the editor, mockingly. "Now go over to your desk, little girl, and write your obits."

Obits, indeed! This called for thinking. I went into the johnny, lit a cigarette and leaned against the washstand. This was the first time I had ever disagreed with the policy of the paper. To act as though you could remove a fact by denying its existence! Supposing the Notre Dame football team went onto the field some afternoon and said to themselves, "We'll surprise the coach. We'll play as though the other team isn't there. All they want out of this game, anyway, is the publicity." Folly, folly!

I didn't care that the paper was against Communists. What bothered me was the fact that it wasn't going to mention the word "Communism" in my article at all. The Rev. Dr. C. spoke. That's all that was to be printed.

I knew the admission on the part of this clergyman that he was a Communist was news and I knew the other paper was going to print it. It wasn't fair to our subscribers to keep this fact out of the paper. I began to think about other things. This seemed to me to be a lot less like editing a paper than censoring it. I knew that if the government issued an order forbidding any reference to Communists in the news, editors would one and all cry to high heaven about the loss to Americans of their inalienable right to a free press.

Well, if I didn't like the policy of my paper I could quit. As I stood by the dirty washstand in the john, seeing but not noticing the spilled powder, the grimy soap stains, I knew I was facing a choice—the choice every reporter has to make sooner or later. The paper was bigger than I, and I had to be "with" it, or I had to get out. Shall I get out? The thought made me tremble. I needed those dollars—few as they were—in my weekly pay envelope, but more than that I needed and wanted and loved my job. I couldn't get out, not if I were that mythical millionairess, Mrs. Van Astorbilt, herself. So I stubbed out my cigarette, combed my hair and—went back to my desk to put in my day's calls to the undertakers. My paper, r. or w.—but *my* paper.

One day when I pass the courthouse, returning from a Ministerial meeting, I see the remnants of torn banners and standards. "Down with," I read, and "basket plan." It's the reliefers, I know. They have been complaining because the trustee is giving them baskets of food instead of scrip to buy the kind of food they want.

When I get back to the office I learn there has been

a "riot" and Stella Machulies has been arrested as a Communist leader and thrown into jail. "Riot!" I say, and one of the desk men says, "Yeah. They got together to pop off about the basket plan and the police went over and broke it up. They took five or six of the leaders, including your Stella, off to jail."

My Stella. I remembered her perfectly. I had interviewed her a year or two before. She was not going to jail then, but to the Wisconsin University Summer Labor School. I ran pictures of her working over clothes to wear, saying how grateful she was for the scholarship which made her summer school possible—the first university schooling she had ever had. For Stella Machulies was what the Y.W.C.A. called an Industrial Girl—she had a job in a factory in the west end.

In Stella's interview, she had said to me, "If you do not have an education, you do not live—you just exist." Because she believed that so intensely she had tried out for one of two scholarships given each year by two socially prominent women's clubs. These scholarships were not designated, so nobody could say which club assigned which one. But Stella was so smart and so promising that Wisconsin had in its turn granted her a second scholarship to the Vineyard School in New York. And after that, both groups had tried to claim her for theirs.

So she was in jail, that alert, bright-eyed girl who had wanted to get herself an education so she might live. I went to my desk and called the president of one of the scholarship clubs. "Stella Machulies," I began, "is in jail." "Oh, my dear!" cried the president. "Thank heaven it was not *our* group that gave her her summer in Wisconsin. A little education sets these people up so!" I called the other president. Same business. I couldn't spit, because only the men did that, and anyway the gaboon was over by the city editor's desk and I might miss it.

"Well," I said finally, in that tone of voice which implies that if you live long enough you always come out right, "I guess the Communists are news today."

The desk man looked up at me with a "Won't dumb dames ever learn?" grimace and said, "The police are news for breaking up the meeting."

"I suppose you're going to say that the man who thought up the basket plan is also the one that sent the police," I replied. I knew him. He's one of those professional taxpayers that obstructs every worthy enterprise a city plans. I'd rather live in hell with any one of the nine thousand families who were on relief in South Bend than be caught dead up yonder with him.

The Communist pastor went to call on Stella while she was in jail and reported his visit to a meeting of the Ministerial Association. I was barred from it, but eavesdropped anyway. He said he asked her if there was anything she wanted and she said, "Some soap." As I went back to the office I thought about this visit, and longed to write it. There was something about it—about the girl who wanted to live, and the man who respected her because she was willing to die—something about his wanting to help her, and her being beyond anything he could do save bring her a chip of soap, that touched me all the way through. But—their humanity didn't count. They only wanted publicity.

This clergyman was relieved of his pastorate, which paid him in the neighborhood of four thousand dollars a year, and was sent to another one which pays about half that. In case you think I am unduly impressed by Communists let me point out here that Dr. C. could have kept his mouth shut and stayed with his high salary. It's his indifference to money that impresses me, and the strength of his conviction. Stella got sixty or ninety days, I forget which, and Benedicite! The Communist threat to South Bend was over.

The holiday church pages were a great trial to my belief in God and man. At Christmas and Easter the paper gave a full page to running accounts of the special music and sermon topics for the gala services. It is quite a job to make up these pages, so before the occasion I send a card to each minister and ask him *please* to have his notice in ten days in advance. Slowly they dribble in, but never are they all in by the date set. Those that are late just aren't published.

Comes Christmas Eve and also an angry shepherd of one of the Evangelical churches. I hear him as he stalks up the stairs and when I see his wild and distorted face, I know the worst has happened. "Where is my notice?" he bellows at me.

"You didn't get it in in time," I reply meekly. (Blessed are the meek—)

"It's sheer partiality." His voice is raised to such a pitch everyone in the room looks up. "You got the Presbyterian in, the Catholic, the—"

"And they got the information to me on time." I'm less meek. After all, why do I want to inherit the earth as long as special services have to go with it?

"I'll—I'll," he's spluttering.

"Tell it to Mr. Ahearn," I say. "He's the editor."

"I'll tell no one. I'll denounce the *News-Times* from my pulpit on Christmas Day." He runs down the stairs.

How I envy his congregation. Oh come all ye faithful to hear the *News-Times* denounced. And she brought forth her first-born Son, and wrapped Him in swaddling clothes, and laid Him in a manger because there was no room for them in the Inn, and there was no room in the *News-Times* for my notice. And the wise men came bearing gifts, but I have only blame to bear the *News-Times*. And the angels sang peace on earth, good will towards men, but not towards the *News-Times*. Hallelujah, hallelujah, hallelujah!

The Episcopal Church, to my way of thinking, has more to offer than the other Protestant churches. It has a liturgical service and if you don't like the sermons you can always go to an early mass. The Rev. Dean L. C. Ferguson, of St. James Church, however, was sometimes witty in his sermons and I liked to hear him. I remember once when he was discussing the custom of fasting before Communion. "If it makes you ill," said he, "to go without your morning coffee, by all means have it. God never meant for you to make a scene in church."

As for the Roman Catholic Church, what is there to say? They have 2,000 years of tradition and bingo one night a week. The priests were congenial and co-opera-

tive and if I were to omit the entire list of Catholic services from a holiday page, they would not have acted as
disgracefully as our other Evangel did. (But, boy, would
my editor have raised hell!)

The fact about priests, which often distresses the
Protestant clergy, I discovered, is their business ability.
You almost never hear of a Roman Catholic church
being in debt. And with good old bingo as a pillar in its
structure, why should it be?

The Ministerial Association, made up of Protestant
clergy, became very exercised about the influence of
bingo in the community. For not only were there the
parish recreation centers, there was more horrid naugh-
tiness, abetted, no doubt, by the public taste which had
been maddened by these games of chance. There were
bank nights at theaters, horse books, pin-ball machines
and gambling casinos. The Association started a campaign against all gambling in the city. It made headlines
for many weeks and the ministers were at last able to
bask not only in their publicity, but also in the self-
righteous glory of being a moral force. They were able
to shut off the livelihood of people they didn't know,
who weren't in their congregations, to close places where
they had never been and where their congregations
didn't go—they didn't, of course, try to close the bro-
kerage houses, for the more affluent members of their
congregations did go there.

My quarrel with this burst of self-conscious virtue on
the part of the ministers is its selective quality. For they
had turned a deaf ear to any number of opportunities
for doing a constructive good. I remember Judge Dan

Pyle had asked their co-operation in the matter of re-
habilitating young girls who for one reason or another
were haled into juvenile court. The judge explained
that the girls were not being held for sexual delinquency,
but sometimes for petty stealing, or playing hookey,
because of abuse by drunken fathers, or because of the
lack of parental guidance in broken homes. Perhaps the
ministers would ask the women of their congregations
to take these girls in as wards. As it was, the girls were
put in the county jail with prostitutes and often suffered
morally as a result. But they weren't bad girls. They
simply needed a helping hand.

But the Association let this matter drop. A gambling
crusade is more spectacular. If the girls go to the devil,
they at least cannot blame their fall on the drugstore
candy punch board.

Among the Jews there was one leader, Rabbi William M. Stern, who brought to my attention the sermon
topic for one of his services—a book review of Eugene
O'Neill's *Day Without End*. I attend and am held for
a moment by his query, "Isn't there a worse sin than
sexual immorality? Who is the greater sinner, a man
like Samuel Insull, who rooks millions of people and
sends them to poverty and suicide, or a man who is once
unfaithful to his wife?"

As a rule I was spared the ordeal of attending revivals
conducted in various tabernacles. The traveling evan-
gelists would come up to the office and bring their sermon topics along for publicity. And this was given
without comment. Some eager scholar ought to do a
Ph.D. thesis on those topics. One, I remember, was

"The Biggest Liar in South Bend." I could think of several candidates and the next morning I called up the regular pastor of the tabernacle to find out who had come out ahead. It turned out that the biggest liar was the man who says, "There is no God."

Once, however, I was sent to cover an evangelistic meeting because it was being conducted by a preacher-lawyer who was the son of one of the local clerics. He had gained some sort of fame for defending a Methodist Bishop's son in a trial in the West. His topic was to be "The NRA: the Mark of the Beast." I sat near the front of the church. I looked at him and he looked at me. He was a heavy set individual and perspired freely during an hour's fanatic oration. I remember that at the close he asked for prayer. To my surprise the congregation slid from pews to knees and turned around. Then the evangelist came from behind his pulpit and while the men and women were weeping and sobbing in hysteria, he made indecent gestures for my benefit. I left in a rage and complained to my editor, who said, "Give the son of a bitch a paragraph." And a paragraph he got—on the back page with a B.F.C. (This, in case you don't know, is a one-line head in bold face capital letters, the same size as newspaper type.)

After months and months of listening to the faithful shepherds preach to fewer and fewer people I am brought to the conclusion that the Presbyterians have their Calvin, the Methodists their Wesley, the Lutherans their Luther, the Catholics St. Peter and the Virgin. Jesus Christ has clearly come out on the short end of Christianity.

I called this chapter "Hell's Bells" thinking to point out how feeble their tinkle has become. But on second thought I believe I should have entitled it "Obituary." For I am reminded of nothing so much as a family quarreling over the legacies of the dead.

CHAPTER VII

Teched in the Haid

WHEN I SAY THAT I am in favor of legalizing the mercy deaths of idiots and imbeciles, I know I shall stir many people to resentment. Nevertheless that's my stand, and I'll tell you why.

After I had been on the paper a few months and convinced my editors that I could run a typewriter and compose a simple English sentence, I felt that I deserved to be assigned a feature story, and I asked for it. I might say I asked for it and I got it, since the two are not always the same thing.

An assistant to the township trustee complained to Mr. Huston that seven feeble-minded children had been refused admittance to the state home in Fort Wayne, Indiana, because St. Joseph County had already exceeded its quota; that three insane men were in jail awaiting admittance to the state institution in Logansport; and that five women were being kept in a private institution at public expense until such time as there was room for them at the state hospital.

My assignment was to find out why these people were being denied state care and what should be done about it. The only thing I was sure of was that I didn't know. While I was sitting at my desk wondering whether I should be civilized and write my feature after the manner of Alexander Woollcott, or whether I should be a little savage, like Pegler, I heard a familiar voice say, "On your way. You can't find out anything here."

So I said, "Yes, Mr. Ahearn," and departed. Now when you are sent out on a news assignment you're told where to go, for the first step of your story at any rate, and I found it a little inconclusive just to be sent outside, as it were, and told to get the facts. Where to go? Well, not to the library. This was no matter for theory. I decided I would call on the township official who had made the complaint, a decision I ought to have made in the first place without a moment's hesitation. But a young reporter has to learn from his own experience. No one tells him these things.

"Would you like to visit one of the homes?" he asked, after I made myself and mission known to him.

I nodded. From that time on, although he never actually took my arm, I felt as though I were being propelled through a ritual. I walked one step ahead of him, and fairly rapidly too, to avoid the double catastrophe of having him step on my heel and throw me on my face.

That was the first part of the ritual. The second part was getting the car started. He was a short man and rather heavy set. He had to arch his back and stretch in order to reach the starter and each time he did so he emitted an anguished grunt.

"We're going to a home, miss," my informer said as we drove off, "where there's a feeble-minded child. She ought to be in Fort Wayne. There are two other children in the home and this little girl disrupts the morale of the whole household. She can't care for herself at all and the other children are suffering from neglect because this child takes all the mother's time.

"It's a grave problem, I tell you, miss, with all our state institutions crowded. These feeble-minded children should not be allowed to remain in the family, and there's no place else to take care of them. It's the same way with the insane. We need a detention home."

Now, my knowledge of how to go about getting a story may have been scant, but I had learned how to be hard-boiled. When a politician suggests the city or county buy something, you are supposed to look around and find out what he has to sell. I decided this man had a house that wasn't paying him anything and he was going to drum up a little public sentiment and unload it. His next sentence practically convinced me.

"I mean we need to build a home, or buy one of the big vacant houses on the market now so those people may be cared for while they are waiting for admittance to state institutions. The burden's too great for a family. You'll see."

He stopped the car in front of a small frame house and we got out. A thin, worn woman with straggling hair opened the door and admitted us. Once the door was closed the hot stench of urine was almost suffocating.

"We want to see the little girl," my companion said. "This is Miss Smallzried from the *News-Times*. She's going to help us."

This last piece of information came as a surprise to me. I stared at the trustee and at the woman and I knew that I had been wrong about him. He was in earnest about doing something for these people, and not trying to fatten his own purse. No human being could commercialize such desolate misery. I was almost on the point of apologizing to him when the woman, who had been regarding me eagerly, said, "Oh, I do hope you can help me."

Two little girls literally clinging to their mother's skirts, their dirty dresses not concealing dirty underwear, yellow hair falling in thin strings about their faces, stared at me with undivertable directness. The mother brushed their hands away and motioned for us to follow her. When she turned her back I looked around the room, which was dirty and unkempt. Springs had worn through the leather davenport in spots, the rug we stood on no longer bore a recognizable pattern, such portions of chairs as could be seen beyond soiled clothes and newspapers thrown over them were all of different design, and I guessed they were the gifts of relatives.

We went into a small bedroom where the blinds were drawn, and the woman pointed to a tiny figure on the bed. The little girl lay on her belly and looked up at us, and the daylight from the living-room windows shone through the doorway upon her face.

"There you are, miss," my companion said.

The words "She's going to help us" came into my mind again. The child's eyes, fixed upon me so intently, had nothing in them at all. That stare might have clung to me forever, but it would never have conveyed more than my animal shape to the child. And I knew that if I returned to that home every day for a year, she would be no nearer recognizing me at the end of the time than she was that very moment.

She began to cry, and following her example the other children set up a whimper. I was distressed and wanted only one thing, and that was to get out of the house as soon as possible. Turning to the woman I said, "I'm sorry. I don't know what I can do, or how soon anything can be done."

I was not, after all, a social worker. My duty was to present the facts, and faced with a situation demanding sympathy and help, I felt a mingling of horror and resentment. I was all ready to give up the business of writing features and go back to obits.

Once outside I took a deep breath of the clear winter air. As I exhaled, my escort said, "I know how you feel, miss. It's an awful situation. You don't know the difference it will make in that household once we get the child in an institution. The mother isn't shiftless. She'd keep a house as neat as a pin if she had the chance. And I'll tell you something else. Her husband is threatening to leave her. Says she don't make a home for him."

In spite of the fact that I was in no mood for levity when I got back to the office, I couldn't help smiling at my earlier concern over my choice of style for my feature. I knew now that the style I wanted was Fannie Hurst's.

I reported the incident to my editor, and a sort of gleam came into his eye. "You take tomorrow off and go down to Fort Wayne," he said. "Interview Mc-Gonigle at the Home for Feeble-Minded and get everything you can. The State Legislature is going to convene pretty soon, and we'll dump this business in their laps."

I don't suppose any reporter is often seriously tempted to hug a city editor, but I came as near it then as I ever was. Not only was my Sunday feature growing up, but I was getting what was as good as a holiday with it. My father was working in Fort Wayne, and Mother, Ellie, and Mary would drive down with me and Dad would blow us to a swell dinner. The lark was certainly on the wing as far as I was concerned. Besides that, my feature might make the front page. I wanted desperately to get a page one spot.

Next day when we arrived Ellie chose to go through the Home with me, and Superintendent McGonigle, informed previously of our coming, greeted us very cordially.

In the hallway several of the inmates were gathered and they hailed us with giggles and delight.

"They think you've come to stay," the superintendent said with a smile.

Although this mistake was as much at Ellie's expense as mine, she chose to have a laugh at me. Before showing us around, Mr. McGonigle took us into his office for a preliminary chat. I told him the situation in St.

Joseph County and said the paper wanted to present the facts, and hoped the result of the article might be an appropriation from the State Legislature for additional provision and aid.

"I hope you accomplish that purpose," our host said. "We certainly need it. The problem of your county is a state problem and not yours alone."

Then in a few words he gave us the reason for the acuteness of the whole situation. A feeble-minded person, with few exceptions, has the same life expectancy as any other person. Therefore, once he is admitted to an institution, he is there for life, and that sometimes means as much as forty or fifty years.

"For example," he continued, "this home was established in 1888 and some of the people admitted then as children are still here. We have a capacity of 1130, and a population of 1591. Of this number 1322 are more than sixteen years old.

"We can admit a child only when someone dies, or an old person is transferred to his home county Infirmary. This doesn't happen very often because the Infirmaries are crowded, too."

He said that very few, about three out of each one hundred, ever become insane, and that the care given in the institution kept the patients healthy and prolonged their lives.

Then he took us around. When we went into the training rooms where the inmates were gathered for instructions in sewing and other handicraft projects, they made a fuss over us and told us Santa Claus was coming. Instead of being depressing it was heartening because their happiness was apparent and their easy equality with each other spoke volumes for segregation and institutional care. My revolt, arising from my first experience, began to wear away.

As we were walking down a hall, Ellie asked, "Where do these people think they are?"

"Oh, they think they're at boarding school," he replied, "or college."

(Wellesley, Smith, Vassar? Harvard, Yale, Princeton! I meditated on prospective topics for their Ph.D. theses. And I don't mean to say I was making fun of the inmates, either.)

From the teachers I learned that the feeble-minded are divided into five groups of which morons, imbeciles and idiots are three. I don't remember the other two. The types are separated and taught by classifications. The upper groups, the staff doctor told me, are conscious of the mental discrepancies of the lower types and endeavor to aid in teaching and taking care of them.

The more competent ones were trained for domestic service, in the case of women, or for gardening and farming, in the case of men. The feeble-minded are especially adapted to outdoor life, and the residents of Fort Wayne make use of their labor.

The doctor told us only twenty per cent of the feeble-minded are born of feeble-minded parents. Sterilization, therefore, is only a partial answer to the problem of prevention. But it is worth making mandatory, however, for although feeble-minded children may be born of normal parents, a normal child is never born of feeble-minded mother and father.

When we visited the dormitories we were appalled to find that the beds were less than twelve inches apart. A person had to move sidewise to get into bed. It meant that a fire would bring incalculable tragedy.

I wrote my feature, emboldened enough by the work I had done to discard the models of the literary great and venture upon a style of my own. At that I had to rewrite my story only twice. And it had at least one thirstily appreciative reader when it appeared in print. I think I could still quote it verbatim.

But just the same there was a little flaw in my purple patch. I made out a happy case for the segregated. But I did not and could not point out at what cost to the public this happiness is possible. That is not the business of the reporter. I couldn't say then that the care which brought these unfortunate human beings from their appalling childhood to their appalling old age preserved nothing worth preserving. I couldn't say that Indiana's taxpayers dug down into their pockets for thousands of dollars to give idiots a happy life, while sane people suffered and died. I couldn't say that if the children in the county who were waiting to get into the institution could be painlessly removed, their families would regain status of equality with their friends and neighbors and not be ostracized or gossiped about as "queer." I couldn't describe the lives of people who had money enough to keep their imbecile offspring at home. I knew of such cases. I knew the morbidity, the hysteria that such a situation can breed, when a family's interests are all conditioned by the abnormality, and life gradually grows unbearable. I had talked with a wealthy woman who had built a chapel in her home where she could spend her life atoning for the birth of an idiot son. For hours every day she was on her knees, crying, "Forgive me, God!" Her husband, feeling less conscience-stricken, went around glibly speaking of his holy wife and—pinching young girls.

No—I didn't say any of these things, for I was a reporter, and not an editorial writer. I wrote what I saw. My job was to furnish the picture which would play on the heartstrings of the public. Ahearn had said we would dump the problem in the laps of the legislators, and so I got the facts. Awhile ago, when my minister friend said he was a Communist, I had learned that what I thought was nobody's business but my own. So I came back to South Bend knowing my convictions on the subject of mercy deaths were so much dead sea fruit.

The story was not front page news but it was sufficiently interesting to warrant a follow-up the next Sunday. I went around to the public officials to find out what they thought should be done about the situation as it affected South Bend. For the most part they were pathetically glad to call the attention of the solid citizenry to the handicaps under which they labored, and were about equally divided on whether to get a detention home in the city or put pressure on the Legislature for more money.

One man I talked to, a city pediatrician, stuck his thumbs in his vest armholes and with his eye on probable publicity, proceeded to get off the subject. "I can no more approve of segregation for the feeble-minded than I can approve of fresh-air rooms for children in the public schools."

Since fresh-air rooms were a pet project of one of the socialite clubs, I asked what was wrong with them.

"Think what it does to the child to be segregated from his classmates," he said. "And it's all done to gratify parental vanity. Cripe! A family has a baby, and if it hasn't doubled its weight in six months, like the government book says it should, they come running around to me, yelling their heads off."

I quoted this in my story and would have had some fancy follow-ups on it, too. But about this time an internecine socialite warfare broke out in town which was to take the greater part of my time for several months. So I left the doctor to ponder over the folly of government baby books, unmolested and unprotested.

I allow sympathetic readers, however, to imagine my pride when the State Legislature voted a quarter of a million dollars a few weeks later to relieve the situation. Since there must be idiots, I suppose it's better for them to be happy and well-cared for than miserable and neglected. I had done a little tugging—whether the direction was forward or backward I suppose not I, or anyone who reads this page, can say. I can revise an old proverb and comfort myself with the reflection that sufficient unto the day is the labor thereof.

CHAPTER VIII

The Greatest of These—

I'VE ALWAYS LOOKED at my job as reporter of the welfare agencies (a part of general news) in the light of what St. Paul had to say to the Corinthians about charity. "And now abideth these three: faith, hope, and charity; and the greatest of these is charity." As I always do when I first hear a thing, I believed that. But now I am amazed at the innocence of St. Paul, and would give any amount up to a nickel to know what the Corinthians wrote back to him.

At the same time I was made church editor I was also given the South Bend Community Fund, Inc., and its member agencies to cover. These include: the Red Cross, Y.W.C.A., Camp Fire Girls, Boy Scouts, Visiting Nurse Association, Children's Dispensary, Salvation Army, Orphans' Home, Epworth and St. Joseph Hospitals, Associated Charities—I can't remember them all. Then there was the central office of the Community

Fund itself where the money raised by an annual drive was taken in to be redistributed to the member welfare groups.

As a sort of starter let's play you've taken me by the hand and are going to go around to visit the agencies with me in search of some news for the day.

The first stop is the Red Cross. I never shall forget it. There is a new secretary there, Miss Toots we'll call her, a very attractive woman with a young face and an engaging smile. She glibly tells us how many thousands of dollars the Red Cross brings into the community each year by helping the war veterans get disability compensations, and we write it down, and have her picture taken, and make out in the story that the county debt will practically be paid off with the swell work she's doing. (I was too new to realize that the secretary whose place she took had really done the job, and this new gal had walked into it to take the bow. Don't ask why. That's just the way things happen. But being philosophical is no help in this job.)

Well, it's only natural that as we drop around every morning, we become better acquainted with Miss Toots, and pass the time of day with her, as much of it as we can spare anyway, and talk about life, love and birth control.

"Birth control!" she ejaculates in an emotionally stifled voice. "I certainly don't believe in birth control. Why, a family might have six idiots and the seventh child would be a genius."

We ponder the life of a family with six idiots, and mentally argue that the pride of giving birth to a genius

140

might be one that the parents of six idiots would be willing to forego, but we just smile and bow our way out.

Then one day we go and find that Miss Toots has her jaw all strapped up, and the whole side of her face resembles a July sky clouding up to rain. She tells us a fancy story about tripping over the electric refrigerator cord and falling into a set of dishes, or something similar, and we resort to making mental notes again, this time thinking that a picture of her now would carry a lot more human interest than the first one we printed.

When we get back to the office the city editor, hard-boiled citizen that he is, greets us with a devilish gleam in his eye and says, "Was there anything unusual about Miss Toots today?"

We get that having-been-played-for-a-sucker-again feeling and reply, "Why, her face is all strapped up as if maybe she closed a door before she was all the way out. Why?"

"Haw, haw," says the city editor. "She was out with her boy friend last night and he beat hell out of her. Some women love it."

And shortly there is a new secretary at the Red Cross.

Now we'll drop over to the Y.W.C.A. and see what's going on. There's a new secretary there too, in fact several of them, because four secretaries resigned all at one time. I don't know just what the scrape was, because women are kind of hysterical at times (the same as men are, I might add) and you don't always get the straight of the story.

As we enter, the new secretary is standing with her back to us talking to the desk secretary, and we listen because you get some of your best stories this way.

"We've got one room here for transient women," the new executive is saying in a firm voice, "and this woman stays three days. I told her yesterday we couldn't have it. We are not giving free room. And she left as mad as could be. And last night she called me and said, 'I'm in a house of prostitution. That's what the Y.W. C.A. has driven me to.' And I said, 'I don't believe it. There's a depression in that business, too.'"

Our laughter announces our presence. We are introduced to Miss Upanatem, chat awhile, and get whatever there is—a panic of a story about a new typewriter someone has given them.

Our next stop is the Camp Fire Girls' office. You can see by now why one gets so hollow-eyed working on a newspaper. It's the excitement of charity beats. I would have you remember this visit, for it has a moral attached to it. Before we left the office, the city editor told us a story had come in over the wire service that Camp Fire Girls were to be permitted to wear shorts instead of bloomers, and he wants us to arrange a picture. So when we get down to the inner sanctum of the Camp Fire honor system (right hand and two fingers raised) we ups to Suzy, the secretary, and tells her as much. She laughs us away (she's a charming creature, really) and assures us that until she has confirmation from the New York headquarters, we cannot have our picture. The city editor is plenty sore when he finds this out and swears through his teeth that he will have a pound of flesh off the secretary if it's the last thing he does. Months later Suzy, who has been separated from her husband for some time, decides to get a divorce, and naturally does not crave much publicity. But alas for those who do not co-operate with the press (that's the moral), she gets her picture in the paper, headlines and everything. So there.

On our swing back we stop at the Anti-Tuberculosis League, and Irma Collmer, bless her heart, has a really good story for us, page 1, section 2. The doctors of St. Joseph County have just defeated a bill to bring all Indiana T.B. hospitals under state control. Had the bill passed, state instead of the county taxes would have supported the institutions, and since St. Joseph County could afford a really good hospital out of its own funds, the medicine men were not interested in a state scheme. We go back to the office wondering how the poorly supported hospitals in southern Indiana are feeling, but our thoughts, of course, are not headline stuff.

Once back, we look over the phone calls that have come in since we left, make our call-backs, and then start to write. Remember now, we have also to write the obituaries, the church news and other assorted items, as well as the news we have picked up on our morning jaunt. It is eleven o'clock by this time and we have to have all copy in by twelve-thirty, and we will be interrupted a time or two before we finish. But when we are caught up we may go have a sandwich and a cup of coffee and a cigarette. So life is not without its little pleasures, even if lunch time is only half an hour.

Now, here is a tip to the cub. Never saunter back

from lunch as though you were through for the day. Instead, rush in, sit down to your typewriter and begin typing furiously, "Now is the time for all good men to come to the aid of their party." While you are typing this you can make plans for the afternoon, like catching up on your correspondence, and considering what you will write for a Sunday feature, or, perhaps, attending a matinee. When your plans are made, get up and hurry out again without attracting the notice of the city desk.

That's what we should do. In our case while we are typing a letter to Della Tilman to find out the Wabash news, Mr. Ahearn looks over in our direction and says, "Oh, Miss Smallzried, what are you doing?" and being caught off guard, we merely look up and say, "Huh?" and that not being the right answer, he says, "Go out to the Orphans' home with Johnny [the photographer] and get a picture of a new nursery they got out there. We'll use the story Sunday." Although our plans for the afternoon prove slightly miscalculated, there's something in not having to sweat for an idea for the Sunday feature.

You should have seen the Orphans' Home nursery. I don't know what Gloria Vanderbilt had that those orphans haven't. Several play rooms, well stocked with toys, a kindergarten room, sunrooms, all new beds, baths —everything to make an infant's life one shriek of joy. We took a number of pictures, among them one of Billy, who was a very attractive youngster, not quite a year old, born of good, unmarried parents. After it was over Johnny still had a load for his camera, and so, in a spirit of play, he took a picture of me in the doorway of the nursery.

Then I went to the superintendent, Mr. Bowen, for some statistics for my feature. (Did you know that seventy-five per cent of the "orphans" have both parents living, twenty per cent one parent, and only five per cent both parents dead?) He told me about the adoption program and it was while we were discussing it that I got one piece of information which I regard as the killer-diller of the day. It was about a family who had seven children. And a very poor family it was, too. And all the children were placed in the Orphans' Home because the parents couldn't take care of them properly. Each month the mother and father came to visit the offspring, and since the children were attractive, it happened that each month there were adoption papers for them to sign. They made their marks without question or emotion, and on their various return trips never asked about the children who had been adopted. Never one single question! Came the day when every one of the seven children had been adopted. As they signed the final papers ma looked at pa, and pa looked at ma, and then they both looked at the superintendent, and pa says in a hearty, proud voice, "Well, we'll have another one for you, 'fore long."

When I got into the car with Johnny to drive back to the office I said to him, "It's just things like that that make me think maybe I'm the one who's crazy." And Johnny, who was a recent father, didn't have anything at all to say. I spent some little time on the story (which with the picture brought more than 100 requests for

Billy's adoption, or about one from every thirty sub-scribers), and Johnny went into the darkroom to do the developing. He was quite a while, too. Finally he came out, drying his arms, and with a quiet grin on his face. He took several wet prints over and laid them in front of Frank Ahearn, and says, "Isn't that a cute little fellow? He has red hair and is bright as a button. Here's a picture that should interest you, too. I saw this girl lurking around the door of the nursery, and since her hair is kinda red I just wondered—"

My ears heard the last and my feet got me over to the city desk in record time. Why hadn't Johnny told me about this gal? I could hardly wait to see her. I heard Frank's laugh and when I peeked around his shoulder, there was the picture Johnny had taken of me. But it ain't so, people, and I can prove it. Me and more than 30,000 others can account for every minute of my time from 1929 to 1936.

So much for the organized charity administered by paid workers. But there's another sort of charity, the vol-unteer kind. That's the charity which provides Sunday society sections with pictures of lovely ladies wear-ing orchids for the benefit of the Fund for Superannu-ated Doormen. These good ladies serve without recom-pense as directors on the boards of welfare agencies, and the publicity they get in the Sunday sections has noth-ing to do with the case at all!

I am sitting at my desk writing a notice that the executive committee and board of directors of the South Bend Community Fund, Inc., will meet in the evening. The executive committee includes the secretary who collects the pledges made each year in the fund drive and redistributes them to the member agencies, and six or eight business men of the city who "volunteer" their services. It's the duty of this committee to survey the welfare picture and make suggestions for its improvement. The board of directors is composed of two members from each agency board, and their business is to be skeptical of the suggestions made by the committee and vote down undue interference.

Names. I had read the names of these men and women in the society column. I was beginning to meet the persons who went with the names. I felt a rising tide of self-importance. I knew the big-shots, and the big-shots were beginning to know me.

While I sat there at my desk letting this fact crystallize in my mind, the Rev. Fred H. Koehnemann came up the steps. Mr. Koehnemann was pastor of the Immanuel (German) Methodist Episcopal Church. He was a short, rather stout man, light hair, blue eyes. He always had an expression of tolerant faith. I noticed this about him, but not much else. I didn't listen very hard to what he was saying and when he set a toy wheelbarrow down on my desk I looked up at him in utter astonishment.

"I'm sorry," I said. "I'm afraid I didn't get what you were saying."

So he explained it to me again. There were a number of old men in the city, transients in a sense. They didn't have any families, any homes, any work. With the help of a patron he had opened a shop in the basement of the church, "The Friendly Workshop." He wanted me to put a notice in the paper that some of these men would call at homes and ask for waste materials, scraps of wood, spools, tin, cloth, etc. These they would make into various products, toys, stools, tie racks, shelves. Then they would take them around to the homes and sell them. He had brought the wheelbarrow along as an example of the type of thing they planned to do. I said, "O.K." and wrote it up without a second thought.

My mind was on the glamorous welfare directors. That evening I went to the meeting of the executive committee and the board of directors and was allowed to wait in the hall until it was over. Then I was given a typewritten report of a proposal to merge two of the fund agencies, the Children's Dispensary and the Visiting Nurse Association.

Next morning I showed it to Mr. Ahearn and Mr. Huston and Ahearn said, "Holy Mackerel!" and Huston said, "That's a good story. They tried to do it once before and failed." And they took the story away from me and gave it to John B. Chester, one of the ace reporters, to write.

I had a fit of sulks because I was afraid it would make the front page and I had been itching to have a sensation of some kind there for months. But it only made page 1, section 2, where my stuff had been printed lots of times.

Next day, however, Ahearn said to me, "Now, Miss Smallzried, I want you to stay on that Dispensary row. There's a lot of good stories in it and it's up to you to dig 'em out."

I said, "Yes sir!" And then went back to my desk.

Row? What row? I felt pretty miserable. Here goes my job, I thought. I hadn't sat there very long (no one ever just sits in a newspaper office for any length of time), when Mr. Huston called me.

"I've just had a phone call," he said, "from a woman who tells me Miss D. has just resigned as secretary of ——" He named one of the leading welfare agencies. "You will find the president of the —— board having her hair done at the Harper Shop. I suggest you go get the story on it."

Well, I found the president all right, and she couldn't have been more surprised at a Visitation from the Lord. "How did you know I was here?" she cried.

"Oh, reporters find out those things," I replied. "I came over to get the story on the resignation of Miss D."

"Why, I just found out myself twenty-five minutes ago! How did you—"

She had telephoned it to another member of the board from the beauty shop. A friend of the paper overheard her and told us. I was plenty thrilled at having her buffaloed and never told her a word about how I knew. I just acted as if I was psychic.

The important thing was not the story of the resignation. It was that, her hair being down, she told me a lot of other things. She was all hot and sore at the executive committee of the Community Fund for proposing the merger of the Children's Dispensary and the V.N.A.

"It won't work," she said. "The Dispensary doesn't want the V.N.A. and the committee has put both organizations on the spot!"

"How?" I asked.

"Well, the Dispensary refused to do it once before. This time the committee brings it up without consulting either agency and puts it in the papers. You know how women are. The Dispensary is going to refuse to do it, not for administrative or financial reasons, but because their board members just don't want the V.N.A. board to merge with them. And everyone will know that, and the V.N.A. board is going to be mad, because they are in the position of being turned down on a proposal of which they were not a party. And all the other agencies will fly at the executive committee for backing down under the wrath of the Dispensary board. Mark my words."

So, Ahearn wanted me to dig out some stories, did he? Here was a fight, not of my starting, but I could keep it going because the situation was a natural. The Dispensary board members were the social cream. The V.N.A. board members were cream, too, but of a thinner variety, so some people said. (As far as I was concerned they were champagne.) The Dispensary board couldn't dream of letting the V.N.A.-ers elbow themselves into the top bracket via anything so easy as a merger. *And*, the V.N.A.-ers, having been turned down once, were touchy and resentful—as if they wanted to belong to the old Children's Dispensary anyway! They would be tail to nobody's comet. I began to see new vistas to glamour as I sat down to write my first story. I said that a prominent social leader confidentially predicted the failure of the proposal and condemned the method of the executive committee in bringing it up without consulting the agencies involved.

My second story was a formal statement from the Dispensary that they regretted very much the action of the committee. They could not agree to the merger as they had no room in the Dispensary building for an enlarged program including the V.N.A. This story they stuck to in spite of the fact that they had a whole section of their building vacant. When it was suggested that they offer this space, they countered with the fact that they were some time or other going to use it for a children's hospital. (To the best of my knowledge, the hospital is still waiting to be born.)

Then I began to call up members of various welfare boards and the social workers and asked them what they thought. They didn't think much of it. Their objections were various:

"What I can't understand," said one woman, "is why the committee favors the Dispensary with the largest budget of any group, and then kicks them in the teeth with this merger business."

"It seems to me," said another, "that the overlapping charge is pretty weak. The committee says these two agencies are doing the same work. That's ridiculous. The Dispensary is taking care of crippled and handicapped children. The V.N.A. sends its nurses out to indigent homes to care for the sick. I'd like to know what's back of it all."

"Listen," said a third, "those men had no authority to do this. They can't force the issue without the backing of the other agencies. And they'll never get it. How does the Salvation Army know but what in another two weeks they'll be asked to merge with the Boy Scouts? That committee will back down and like it. Men who won't take no for an answer are in books, not on community fund groups."

But nobody mentioned the Children's Dispensary board's blackballing the V.N.A. board.

As predicted, the executive committee fell before the verbal onslaught of the women and in a few weeks dropped the urge to merge altogether.

But men are hard to convince. Whether it was a face-saving gesture I don't know, but in a few weeks the fund's committee turned up brightly with a proposal to merge the summer camping program of the Camp Fire Girls and Y.W.C.A. The Camp Fire Girls were operating in the red and the men thought the "Y" could help out. I heard about this before the "Y" did and called the general secretary.

"I guess the Camp Fire Girls are having a little trouble meeting expenses with their camp," I say.

"Yes?" says the secretary.

"And," I continue, "the executive committee is going to ask the 'Y' to combine with their camping program to help out."

"Is it, now?" explodes the secretary. "Well, you can tell them we'll do it when they make the Children's Dispensary merge with the V.N.A."

The executive committee began to blame me for a lot of its troubles, although, God knows, even in my dullest moments I would not have thought up measures they proposed. I didn't have to worry about my job, because the more people hated me the better I was liked around the office. But I was nourishing a grief—a private one that I wouldn't have had my colleages know for the world. It was about all those people on the boards—those big-shots I had looked forward so eagerly to knowing. The new Corinthians. I licked my wounds in private, ashamed of the naïve vulnerability which had laid me open to them.

Day in, day out, reporting was a jumble of obituaries, church news and accusations hurled at each other by the upper ten via the columns of the great free press. If it hadn't been that we were in the midst of a depression and I was daily going to poor relief headquarters and looking at the bread lines, I might have forgotten the poor, for whom the executive committee and the board members labored and wept.

There was one thing that touched me in a way I couldn't explain, and that was the recurrent visits of Mr. Koehnemann with his news items on the Friendly Workshop. One day he told me the men had formed an organization, the "What Would Jesus Do Club." They would meet once a week, sometimes for lunch. It was a sort of Rotary Club on a poverty-stricken scale. They had guest speakers, discussions, travel talks. Of course the name of the club gave rise to many an office jest, but just the same there was something about it that I couldn't put my finger on, and I was uncomfortable when it was laughed at.

It wasn't until I was flat on my back in the hospital with a combination of surgery and overwork that I learned the facts about the Workshop. Mrs. Frank Hering who (with Mrs. Howard Woolverton) did more good work with less publicity than anyone else I knew, had set it up on her own. No boards of directors, no community fund committees, no social service workers —and, aside from the tiny paragraphs on the men themselves, no news.

I remembered seeing those old men, their eyes wet with the infirmities of age, their hands slow, their clothes ragged and dirty. In the basement of the church they worked over the discarded waste materials, happy at having a job to do—the What Would Jesus Do Club laboring as carpenters.

It is no accident that I did not mention Mr. Koehnemann in my chapter on the clergy. He belongs apart with Mrs. Hering in an account of something which I suppose there is no room for in this book—that thing which is the best of good natures and is called charity.

CHAPTER IX

Come, Let Us Reason Together

(AUTHOR'S NOTE: All names marked with an * in this chapter are fictitious.)

The club house was crowded. Women were collecting in little groups in the club parlors instructing each other as to the two slates. Women were filing up and down the stairway to the second floor where the voting was going on. Women were checking over the registration lists, then driving off and bringing in those members who had not yet cast their ballots. Women were tiptoeing in and out of the auditorium where the program was being given, dutifully allotting a little fitful attention to the singer. Candidates were nervously eying each other. Mrs. Henry Warner Kieth*, president of the club and automatically retired at the end of a two-year term, went from group to group, relieving the tension here and there with a gracious manner which never seemed to desert her. The odor of perfumes was mingled with that of wet rubber and furs, for it was a snowy January day. The mothers' department of the club, taking advantage of the full attendance on election day, was holding a bazaar in the foyer to jack up their treasury.

Elsie*, a sort of Queen Mary turned career woman, was society reporter for our opposition, the *Tribune*. The last of a good, though not prosperous family, she was a paid-up member of the club and had much power in the social underground. She bustled up to Mrs. Lathrope*, who was standing on the stairway. I couldn't hear what she was saying. Her demeanor, however, was that of a woman who has been shortchanged at market. Mrs. Lathrope's eyes opened wide and then narrowed as she hauled off and slapped Elsie hard enough to shuffle her bridgework.

I ran out of the club house and back to the office. I didn't want to get mixed up in anything.

"Gee," I said, trying to get my breath, "Elsie got slapped."

"Slapped!" cried Ahearn.

"Umm-humm," I said. "She's been supporting Mrs. Mirage* for president of the club and she went up to Mrs. Lathrope, who's on the other side, and said something controversial, I guess, and boy! Did she ever get it!"

Carl Cooper looked up. "What those women need is a good man. A good man could break up their meeting any time."

"You haven't taken sides, have you?" Frank wanted to know.

"Course not," I said. "I told them I was a reporter first and a friend afterwards. And anyway I'm not a paid-up member of the club, like Elsie. She thinks if Mrs. Mirage wins, she'll get a lot of scoops over me, because she's helped in this election."

I went back to the club house that night to find out who had won—the elections I mean. It was ten o'clock before all the votes were counted. Mrs. Mirage had come out ahead by a margin of twenty-eight. Although the elections were held in mid-winter the administration didn't change until June. So I had six months of grace before the new officers and Elsie began to gang up on me. Or so I thought.

The president-elect began her pre-administration activities impartially enough. She invited Elsie and me to be her guests at a preview of the Hoosier Art Salon and a reception for the artists held in Mr. Vincent Bendix's Chicago home. He owned the old Potter Palmer mansion at the time.

I stick pretty close to Elsie, so she won't get anything I don't. We go from room to room, have tea together, are properly impressed with the artists, and finally stroll into the ballroom where the program of the afternoon is given.

To enter the ballroom we cross a dais at the side on which are standing two old chairs belonging to English kings. I am about to sit down in one, when Elsie gives me what Dickens called, in caps, "A Look." We step down onto the floor and walk around the room inspecting the tapestries in a collection said to be the finest in the United States. I gaze at them with a "time marches backward" feeling—five, six, seven hundred years. Here-is history as well as craftsmanship. I think of the elaborate processes of making and dyeing the thread, of the painstaking years of weaving, of the scenes themselves, victories in battle and victories in love. Ah, what a room!

My rival and I sit down on a couple of folding chairs and I look up at the crystal chandeliers and think about the Nineties, and wonder what their gaiety had that makes it remembered with such nostalgia. Elsie leans over and whispers, "I'm getting the biggest thrill out of being here. Mrs. Palmer was one of the famous hostesses of the era, you know. Can't you just see Grand Duke Boris striding down those steps?"

I look over at the dais, but see nothing save the chairs which belonged to English kings. But I do not need Grand Duke Boris. I am happy with the chairs and the tapestries. I think of the human transactions they have looked down on, and I am moved to my own dreams. In a moment I hear Mrs. Mirage's voice—she is talking about the program for the afternoon, and I come quickly back to the moment, interested to discover what the event is for which this setting has been provided. "I am going," says Mrs. Mirage, "to give you a pianologue reading of *Madame Butterfly*."

That night at supper Mrs. Mirage suggested to Mr. Bendix that he open his South Bend estate to a tea which the club would sponsor. The women could sell tickets and make a lot of money. Mr. Bendix, gentleman that he is, agreed. The date was set for a Saturday in May.

It was during the preparations for this party that Mrs. Mirage made her first misstep. I learned that after asking me to come to the estate at half-past three in the afternoon to get some publicity pictures, she had invited Elsie and her photographer to come at four. This difference in time meant Elsie was to have something I wasn't to know about.

So on the way I say to Johnny, "Stall around. I want to see what it is Elsie's going to get that I'm not."

The estate is a lavish affair in the heart of South Bend's most exclusive residential section. It is one city block wide and two city blocks long with a high iron fence around it. The house, a chateau, is in the center, and before it are a large reflecting pool and terrace. Johnny and I go to the pool to take the pictures. Amateur dancing groups from the city's academies pose for us. They are more eager than graceful, and stand on first one bare foot and then the other while Johnny stalls and stalls.

Shortly after four o'clock Elsie and her photographer arrive, and so do a dozen of the town's junior socialites all dolled up in afternoon gowns and picture hats, looking lovelier than God's own angels. So that's it, I say to myself. She's to get society while I get a lot of overweight adolescent Pavlowas. Not much!

I go up to the girls, and they say, "Hello, Kay," and I say, "Hi there. How about posing for me when you're through here?" And they say, "Sure."

Elsie turns several shades redder than the azaleas surrounding the terrace and says, "Indeed, these girls will not pose for you! Mrs. Mirage promised me I could have them exclusive for Sunday."

I acted not only as though she weren't there, but as though I had never even heard of her. "I'll meet you over on the other side of the reflecting pool," I say to the girls, and they smile.

Johnny and I walk over and throw ourselves down on the grass to enjoy the sun. I can't hear what Elsie is saying to Mrs. Mirage, but I gather from the violence of her gestures that it isn't small talk. Pretty soon Mrs. Mirage begins to walk toward us. The place of our retreat is several gazelle leaps away from the scene of battle, and it takes the little lady a few minutes.

"Kay," she says slowly as she approaches, "I've promised those pictures to Elsie. I thought you could use the dance groups this Sunday and the girls the next, and vice versa."

"I'm sorry," I say, "but we won't use them after the *Trib* has had them. I'm afraid we'll have to take their pictures today. Elsie can have the dance groups, too, if she wants them. That's all right with me."

Mrs. Mirage trudges back to convey this piece of information. It seems logical enough to her that if I am willing to waive my "scoop," Elsie should be willing to waive hers. I watch the pantomime as Elsie refuses, and the president-elect, shaking her head sadly, again sets out to see me. I wonder if she has corns and begin to pity her. She asks me if we can't do it the way she has planned and I tell her no, if I don't get those pictures I'll be fired for not doing a good job. I suggest that she let me take them, and then she can come in and talk to my city editor and ask him not to use them. She agrees to this, but is doubtful. "I wonder if it's going to be like this all during my administration?" she asks. "I didn't know a club president could have so many troubles."

Needless to say, we used the pictures, and the story of the battle got out, and that part of the club which had been against her in the election took my side and called me to tell me so.

The tea was referred to by my colleague in the society department as a gala occasion. Socialites of the first, second and third divisions dressed up and wandered over the estate to their hearts' content. Miss Margery Maxwell, Chicago Civic Opera star, was the hit of the program and sang the "Indian Love Call" for me both afternoon and night. Oh, warm spring night, fragrant flowers, silken gowns, murmur of voices, shining silver tea service, sandwiches of caviar, tiny cakes with whipped cream—what a story I shall write of you! Who thinks of the poor, the ragged, the ill-fed on the other side of the city?

Well, the poor do! I got back to the office that night to find all hell broke loose.

"Write the story of your life, Smallzried," Ahearn barked at me. "Pour it on 'em."

"I mean to," I said, a little indignantly. "What's all the excitement about?"

"Nothing, nothing," Ahearn replied indulgently, "the unemployed have just bombed the Bendix factory, that's all."

"How many dead?" I asked eagerly, wondering which of the official hostesses would be first to send flowers.

"Nobody dead. Now, sit down and write your story."

Oh, lovely unemployed, to provide the climax! While South Bend society strolled the luxurious Bendix estate Saturday night at the outstanding social function of the spring season, the desperate unemployed fought back. A bomb tossed at the plant wrecked a small section of it. Damage was slight—except to the self-esteem of those who were at the party.

Club women thrive on publicity, and therefore, in cities where there is more than one newspaper, they take care to treat both alike. All stories are released to each paper at the same time. A good scoop on club work is practically unheard of because the reporters themselves respect this sacred rule. But I had been (and still was) a general news reporter. Although I hadn't let Mrs. Mirage know it, I was plenty sore at the tea-party picture business. So I bided my time until one hot August afternoon. The club was going to open its season in another month. What if I could scoop Elsie on the biggest club news in South Bend? What if I could get hold of the program and committees for the whole year! It had never been done in the history of the town, but there was no law which kept me from trying.

I called on one of the women who was friendly to me, but not to Mrs. Mirage. Yes, she told me, the programs for all nine departments as well as the general club, and the entire committee lists, were all made up.

They were at the printer's where the yearbook was published. I went to the printer's with all the dignity I could muster. "Are the proofs ready yet for the club yearbook?" I asked. "Just a minute, ma'am," the man said, and went off to get them. I held my breath. Suppose one of the women would come in and catch me. I watched the door. I watched for my proofs. I stood up on my toes and back on my heels. Why didn't he come? If I got caught—but I didn't.

Back to the office I went. It was after hours but Ahearn was still there. I told him about it. Even he was excited. "It'll raise an awful stink," I said. He looked at me. "That's what you're for." I was too thrilled to wonder what he meant by that crack.

I spent three days eating and sleeping in a hit-and-miss fashion waiting for the Sunday paper. In my lead paragraph I had boldly declared that this information was an "exclusive" for the *News-Times*. Suppose Elsie did get hold of it? I didn't even dare let anyone else on the staff know what I had.

Well, I needn't have worried. It was around nine-thirty Sunday morning when Mother got me out of bed to answer the first telephone call.

"Yes?" I said.

"Kay!" wailed a voice. "How could you do this to me? Where, where did you get that information?"

"It's a legitimate scoop, Mrs. Mirage," I said. "I'm sorry if it embarrasses you, but I can't tell you where I got it."

"Embarrasses me! Elsie has called me and she's so

angry! She—she says she'll never print another line of club news."

"Oh, nonsense," I said. "She'll print your news all right. She'll have to. Her boss will see to that."

"I don't know what I'll do." She refused to be comforted.

So I told her to call Mr. Ahearn and complain to him about me and she said she guessed she'd have to. I sat down to doughnuts and coffee and had a mouthful when the phone rang again.

"Congratulations," said a hearty voice. "You got South Bend up this morning earlier than it's ever been up before."

"Oh, hello, there," I laughed. I recognized the voice as that of a woman whose good looks had led me to use her picture a number of times. "What do you mean, I got them up early?"

"Why," she said, "that story. Everybody's calling everybody else. I've had six calls asking me if I saw it, and all the lines of the people I want to talk to are busy."

"Good," I said.

"Good!" she repeated, coming back with an old one, "Hell, it's perfect."

I decided I'd better call my city editor and let him know the storm was breaking, but he had already had several calls.

"One of the women said you promised you wouldn't print any more stories without their permission," he said. His voice was not pleasant to the ears of one whose coffee was getting colder by the minute.

"She's crazy as hell," I said firmly. "I don't make promises and *you* know it."

"All right, Kathleen." He never called me Kay. "It was a nice piece of work."

I heated the coffee again and poured it. The phone rang.

"This is Mrs. Featherskull*," a fluttery voice informed me. "Kay, I want to ask you something in confidence."

I took a sip of coffee. I had learned my lesson, and moved my breakfast to the telephone stand. "O.K.," I said.

"Well," her voice was pitched low enough for a deathbed confession, "well, I've just read your story and my name has been omitted from one of the committees."

I swallowed half a doughnut whole. Good God, had she read through six hundred names to find hers?

"I wondered, Kay, if the person who gave you those names had left me out on purpose, or if I've hurt your feelings and you left it out, or if it is just an accident. I've certainly never meant, Kay, to do anything—"

"Really, Mrs. Featherskull," I assured her, "I know it must have been accidental. No doubt the proofreader, in going over the names hurriedly, missed yours. I'll tell you what, when your program comes up, I'll use your picture."

"Oh, Kay, dear, I didn't mean—I—"

There, my friends, on *that* Sunday morning, was a crisis. Had I received any calls when the Bendix factory was bombed? Oooh, nooo. What's a wrecked plant and hungry people compared to the glory of revenge and the glamour of having your name in the paper? And that revenge was not necessarily my own triumph. For in settling an old score I had gratified all the women who were opposed to the present officers of the club. Anything they could do to embarrass the administration was gravy on biscuits for them.

One afternoon after the club season had opened, a friend drew me aside. "The cast for the operetta has been chosen. You know the director—"

All's fair in love, monopolies, and newspaper work. I called the director and said, "The music chairman said you have the operetta all lined up. I wonder if you can give me some dope on it."

The music chairman had said it, probably, but not to me. She was a henchman of Mrs. Mirage. Anyway, the director gave me the whole thing, cast, story, music, curtain! I ran it with some pictures of the cast that I dug out of the morgue.

I went to the movie that night to escape the telephone reaction. The next day, however, I saw Frank Ahearn bounding over in my direction and I couldn't tell from the look on his face whether it was good news or bad. It was a brand-new expression.

"You have just received the highest compliment ever paid a *News-Times* reporter," he said.

I began to assume my "I only did my duty" air when he saved me the trouble of bringing it to full flower by saying, "I have just had an anonymous telephone call from a woman who said, 'I recommend that you fire

Miss Smallzried. She is causing confusion and dissension in the town and is doing the *News-Times* no good!' "

Someone told me afterwards a club chairman had made the call. I don't know and I don't care. I had something bigger and more important ahead of me than the jittery local women, for I was to cover the convention of the Indiana State Federation of Women's Clubs, to be held in South Bend.

I went to see Mrs. Keith to get the particulars on this event. I don't remember now whether she was county or district president, but at any rate she was the local head of arrangements.

She explained to me that a federated club belonged first to the county federation, then the district, then the state, and finally to the General Federation of Women's Clubs. Indiana, being longer than it is wide, was divided geographically into north and south. The state conventions were held one year in the south, then in the state capital, then in the north, then in the state capital, and then in the south again. All this seemed important, so I asked, "Why?"

"Well," said Mrs. Keith, "when the meeting is in the southern section, naturally more women attend from there than from the northern part of the state. So a southern candidate is likely to be chosen president. The convention cities are chosen to keep the offices balanced between north and south. Half the officers are elected every other year, and a president is never chosen when the meeting is in Indianapolis, but always when it is in the northern or southern sections."

"Why don't you run for president?" I asked her. She

seemed to me to deserve it. I never heard her say a bad or catty thing about anybody.

She looked at me for a minute as though only the young could be so ignorant. Then she explained that before you could run for a state office, you had to serve an apprenticeship. I repeat all this because it brought out a very startling fact about the mechanics of the federated clubs. There are two slates at the state convention. The opponents for the office of president had been about twenty years preparing for it, having come up as department chairmen, club officers, club presidents, county presidents, district presidents and state officers. Then they could run for state president. Following the state presidency the retiring officer is automatically a member of the General Federation board of directors. If she's clever and gets herself appointed to important G.F.W.C. posts and elected to the lower offices, she may in another ten years get to be national president. It was my turn to look astonished at Mrs. Keith.

"Gee," I said, "it takes a woman longer to work herself up to the top post in the General Federation than it takes a man to work himself up to the presidency of the United States."

Before I left she gave me a copy of the "Convention Call," a bulletin sent to club women before a get-together to give them an idea of what's awaiting them. The theme of this convention was "Come, Let Us Reason Together."

Well, the candidates and the delegates reasoned with each other for a couple of days, and the upshot was that the woman from the northern part of the state was elected president. All the women who hoped she would name them to important state chairmanships held a Halloween party for her afterwards at which they told fortunes and giggled and squealed like co-eds. I stood in the corridor and looked into the room and listened. "I see you speaking before large groups of women—and wearing many gardenia corsages—and your picture will be in all the papers—" Fortune! Huh! That was no prophecy. That was futile fact. I went down the corridor to the headquarters of the defeated candidate. She was there weeping in desolation among her wilted flowers. To have gone twenty years, building up, making friends, serving apprenticeship, only to lose out in the end! For her it was tragedy, and she couldn't try to make a come-back, because others from her section were pushing on towards their candidacy two years later. Candidates sometimes are chosen for as long as fourteen years ahead.

With all I knew about women, however, I was not prepared for the General Federation of Women's Clubs' convention held in Detroit in 1935. I registered at the Statler Hotel and then I went in search of the two national candidates, Mrs. Roberta Campbell Lawson of Oklahoma, and Dr. Josephine White of Ohio. I wanted to interview them. Mrs. Lawson acted as though she had come to Detroit for the sole purpose of meeting me, but Dr. White put her hand to her head and said, "Oh, my dear, I don't know when I'll ever have time to be interviewed." When a club woman turns down publicity you know she's got a real problem on her mind.

This election was going to be a close one, and the delegates got pretty excited. They tore up each other's banners, hurled accusations of all kinds, moved from one table to another because they wouldn't sit with supporters of rival factions. Whenever you saw two women together one of two things started: a fight or a campaign song.

This business of singing created a real stir. On the night before "play day" (play day must have been thought up by one of the members who had a sense of humor; it comes before election day) a big meeting was held at the Masonic Temple, and five thousand women were present. Various state groups lifted their voices in song, proclaiming musically:

> Oh, Mrs. Lawson, we love you.
> Oh, Mrs. Lawson, we love you.
> Oh, Mrs. Lawson, we love you.
> It is evident
> You'll be our president.
> Oh, what a grand event.
> Oh, Mrs. Lawson!

Or, "Oh, Dr. White," etc. I made these words up, but the originals followed this pattern. In the *sängerfest*, the West Virginia primadonnas, by intention or accident, were snubbed and not asked to sing, and so play day began with a grudge fight which had been gathering steam all night. I forget which side the West Virginia group was for, but anyway, all the people on that side took up the snub as a personal affront to their candidate. The plans for play day were privately revised to include a little mayhem. All went well until the rival groups found themselves on board a boat which was to take them for an outing on the Detroit River. Then the playing began in earnest. They played at thinking how to get even with each other, and I don't know who thought up the idea first, but finally one group heaved the "buckeye" souvenirs of Dr. White overboard, and the other side tossed the "tomahawk" (or whatever) souvenirs of Mrs. Lawson into the river.

And after that the club officers had the nerve to ask the reporters why they made club women seem so ridiculous in print!

When the General Federation of Women's Clubs with its 2,000,000 membership exerts its influence in a worthy cause (I'm sure there is one, somewhere) I shall be glad to eat crow for any tiny part I've had in making them seem "ridiculous."

CHAPTER X

A Cat May Look at a King

FOR THE PAST FEW YEARS just about all the books written by reporters have been those of the foreign correspondents. And I've enjoyed reading them. But I keep wondering why reporters on this side of the water don't confess. It can't be because life is dull. I know better. Practically everyone says to me, "You're a reporter! Reporters lead such interesting lives." And it can't be because we don't see and meet celebrities, because we do. Just look:

THE PRESIDENT AND MRS. FRANKLIN D. ROOSEVELT AND PARTY

Once when I got tired being a reporter (I, too, have my foolish moments) I went to St. Mary's College as publicity director (see: "Sex Appeal from a Convent"). I'd been there about a month when Easter vacation came

up and Sister Maria Pieta told me she had arranged a
week's educational trip for students to Washington and
New York. Did I want to go? There was a bargain rate
and I counted my pennies. I could make it.

We arrived in Washington on Easter Sunday morning. The girls and nuns got off the train outside the city
to go to Communion at the Franciscan Shrine. I went on
into the capital thinking I'd hear mass in the Episcopal
Cathedral.

My thoughts were more on my own gratification than
on the Holy Day, I think, because I meant to go to
church with the President. And it didn't occur to me
that a President would go to any place less magnificent
than a Cathedral. I called a cab.

My grandmother has warned me from time to time
not to talk to strangers or cab drivers, because if a cabby
discovers that I'm just a young girl trying to get on in
the world, he may kidnap me. Ellie always figures if I am
kidnaped I'll be sent back, all expenses paid. However,
I honor my grandmother's fears by behaving circum-
spectly, and it is only with the greatest reluctance that
I reveal my destination.

But I am glad the drivers' grandmothers have not
warned them against women, for even if I don't talk
to them, they do talk to me. And on this day my chauf-
feur informed me as we passed St. Thomas's Church,
"There's where the President's going." So I said, "Let
me out."

I went to a side door in a manner which indicated
my family name had been on a pew in St. Thomas's for
at least three hundred years, but even so I was stopped.

"Where's your ticket?" the usher inquired. I didn't have any. I went into a corner of the vestibule and sulked. But wait—

Around to the back door I went. I had a press pass given me by the police department of South Bend which admitted me to police lines and fires. I got it out and flourished it before the guardian of this entrance. "Where's the press section?" I figured he'd see the word "Press" and stand aside, but no! He took the miserable thing away from me and read it through. "Now isn't that nice?" he said in a voice whose tone I did not feel was properly Christian. "Fires in South Bend!" I began to back away, but I could hear him muttering, "South Bend, South Bend!" as though it were the name of a particularly smelly fish. "You'd better go around to the front door," he called after me.

When I got to the front door my wits really clicked. Even if my pass only admitted me to home-town fires, I was a genuine enough reporter. So I plunged through the crowd and plucked the lapel of the chief usher. "Where's the press section?" I inquired in a tone of voice which implied if I was kept waiting another minute, it would be a sorry day for St. Thomas's.

"Oh, a lady reporter!" he exclaimed. "You'll want a seat near the front. Colonel Van Schuyler, escort this lady to a pew up front." (I'm not kidding. The head man really was called Col. V. S.)

I felt like a movie queen going to my own première. I had arrived a little ahead of the President, and kept turning my head around so I wouldn't miss him. And I

didn't. In he came with Mrs. Roosevelt, the late Louis
McHenry Howe and other members of his party. They
sat two rows behind me and I looked at them and I
thought, "How big he is, and what nice eyes she has." I
thought of handing a little note back to them and asking
for an interview that afternoon. But I was afraid some
secret service man might shoot my hand off at the wrist,
and after all, I would rather have my right hand than an
interview with the President.

PRESIDENT ROOSEVELT (SOLO)

On December 9, 1935, the University of Notre Dame
conferred honorary degrees upon the President and a
representative of the Philippine Islands. The occasion
commemorated the independence of the Islands. The
University was very interested in the grant, its officials
feeling that the action established the first Christian nation in the Orient—a nation whose population is pre-
dominantly Roman Catholic.

Although I was publicity director at St. Mary's when
this occurred I returned to my Alma Mater for the day
and was assigned the job of writing high lights for the
News-Times. Once again I was a roaming reporter. If
the opportunity presented itself I meant to get a few
words in private with the President.

I roamed up to the press section and watched the secret service men go through the equipment to be sure
an assassin wasn't in hiding, over to a crippled children's
sector to get their reaction, queried some of the big-

shots, and finally sat down to listen to what the honor guests had to say. I took a few notes to intersperse in my high lights.

Afterwards the President was so surrounded with big-shots I couldn't even attempt to see him, so I went in search of a press party instead. I didn't find it, but I did find some reporters coming from it, and they offered to hold another one especially for me. By the time I got back to the office I felt well consoled for losing out on the first party.

I examined my notes. I puzzled over them. As far as reading them now was concerned, they might as well have been written in ancient cuneiform. And besides, I felt dull. I sat down to my typewriter and began to transcribe my quickly clouding memories of the occasion. When the paper hit the street, the Philippine representative was quoted as saying wise words about national economy and "unearned excrement." Carl Cooper, whose respect for pomp and ceremony was flatter than a cop's feet, comforted me by saying, "Don't worry, Kay; you weren't so far wrong at that." But I was glad I hadn't interviewed the President, because my account of it might have caused an international incident.

Amelia Earhart

It was a big day for me when Amelia Earhart came to town, because the number one spot on my list of outstanding women was all hers.

I found her in her hotel room, seated in a big chair, her feet drawn up, one hand clasping her ankles. When the photographer came in, she didn't budge. She just held up a hand in greeting and let him snap the picture. I thought of the preparations club women make for getting their immortal beauties recorded on photographer's paper.

Elsie was there asking burning questions, like what did she think of club life. I stretched out on a bed and ate some of the candy the management had given her, waiting for a chance to get a word in edgewise. Finally I said, "There's one thing I want to know." And she grinned and said, "Only one thing?"

"Well," I said, completely captivated by her informality, "I meant one thing about you. I read in the paper some months back that you were at the White House, and you and Mrs. Roosevelt took a moonlight flight all dressed up in evening clothes. I like impulsive jaunts, and I'm curious to know what led you to risk getting grease on your Sunday best."

"It was after dinner," she replied, "and there were going to be some movies. Mrs. Roosevelt and I had seen them, so we decided to take a flight over to Baltimore and back instead."

"Just like that?"

She smiled and nodded. There, I thought, must be the only job in the world more fun than reporting.

Later in the day I attended a tea given in her honor, and I asked her to autograph the print our photographer had made. It is the only copy in existence and I cherish it very much. When she was ready to leave the party I asked her if she would like me to drive her back to town, and she said, "Gee, that would be swell if you would." Then she said, "Do you have any pockets? These chocolate brownies are awfully good and I thought maybe you'd stuff a couple in your pockets for me." I did. On the way back to the hotel I offered her the brownies and she told me she would eat them that night while she was driving to Toledo. She got out of the car and walked into the hotel.

Let Dorothy Thompson have her interview with Hitler. He was making history. Amelia Earhart was making friends.

ABBÉ DIMNET

You can take it for granted, unless otherwise stated, that most of the celebrities I mention were in South Bend for programs sponsored by one or another of the various local women's clubs.

In addition to covering the lecture, I usually interviewed the speaker either before or after his appearance on the platform. I almost didn't interview Abbé Dimnet, because his talk had been such a disappointment. But orders are orders and I went around to the hotel to see him.

When I made my acquaintance with him he said, "Who ees thees woman that runs the program?" After a few minutes I knew he was talking about the program chairman, so I explained her activities.

"Do you know," he said, his voice incredulous, "that she ask me to talk down to the audience? Just before I went on the stage she tell me to talk *down!* I get out there and do not know what to say."

No wonder his lecture had been disappointing! It was no good my trying to tell him that she was a club woman with a weakness for giving twilight teas at which a coterie of friends talked about what they did not read—i.e., literature. It was no good my trying to tell the serious little Frenchman anything at all about the genus American club woman. But I thought about her as I walked back to the hotel. I think she defined herself better than I can in a question she put to

VICKI BAUM

I went to Mrs. Mirage's residence where Frau Baum was being given lunch. Only the hostess, guest, club program chairman and myself were there.

Madame Chairman was cross-examining the writer a question a minute, and I just listened. There was a dramatic pause as the older woman prepared to glean a bit of terribly vital information. "Tell me, Frau Baum," she said earnestly, "do you think we have culture in America like you do in Europe?"

Oh magic word! Hitler, Mussolini and Stalin, you have culture. Treasure it, or our club women will take it away from you. Frau Baum looked at me, at the hostess, and at her interrogator. She was almost too embarrassed to speak. At last, the color rising in her cheeks, she murmured, "Oh, yes. Yes, I am sure of it."

Later she escaped from her inquisitor and revealed herself as a witty, good-humored conversationalist. When the photographer came to get a picture, she gave me a large purse to hold while she posed. When I returned it she smiled and said, "My husband calls this my midwife's bag."

GLENN FRANK

"America's Hour of Decision" was the topic of Mr. Frank's lecture in South Bend in March of 1935. He was president of the University of Wisconsin then, and not chief platform writer of the Republican party. And I guess it was a good thing, because if I read the criticisms of the New Deal right, one of the chief targets is the power of the president as opposed to that of congress. I quote Mr. Frank: "We must stop the inexpert intrusion of the legislative group into the intricacies of the administration. That is the price we have to pay for a democracy instead of a dictatorship." If that sentence says anything it says that by taking the power away from congress and giving it to the president we can have a democracy instead of a dictatorship. And the Republicans have been saying just the opposite since 1933. Of course, at the time of this lecture, some people (was Mr. Frank one?) thought he might be candidate for the presidency.

SHANE LESLIE

Some celebrities would be better off if they had the ability of Indian fakirs to toss up a rope, climb it and vanish at the end of their lectures. As far as I'm concerned, Shane Leslie is one of them.

The first time I heard Mr. Leslie I was a reporter gone highbrow and studying creative writing in Sister

M. Madeleva's class at St. Mary's College. The noted Irish critic and author was a guest lecturer at the University of Notre Dame and made weekly visits to St. Mary's. I was respectful in my account of his first informal talk. I quote Mr. Leslie on an incident that impressed me. He is referring to his student days at King's College, Cambridge: "Two other boys and myself who were interested in poetry knew that Cambridge had no memorial to Shelley. We decided to make the University a present of a Shelley manuscript. Not knowing quite how to go about it, we advertised in the paper for one. We did not know of the rarity or the value of what we asked for, and the whole incident is rather like a story-book romance.

"Not long after the advertisement appeared we received a registered package from Liverpool. In this was Shelley's diary written in Rome and the original manuscripts of three of his poems. There was a letter from the woman who sent them saying that Shelley had presented them to her grandmother and she wanted to be sure they would have a good home. The price was ten pounds, or fifty dollars. We heard from a collector that he would have given 5,000 pounds, or $25,000, for the diary."

Shortly after this I went to St. Mary's as publicity director and had the opportunity to know Mr. Leslie better. I received a note one afternoon informing me that the Irishman would like to go horseback riding Sunday morning with Miss Margaret McCoy, drama instructor; Miss Bridget Cunningham, a faculty member from Oxford, and me. Both girls were my own age and we were good friends. Mr. Leslie had spoken to Bridget several times, making much of their being from the other side.

I was the only member of the party to have a car and I picked up the group and drove to the stables. After the ride was over, Mr. Leslie paid one dollar for his own horse. The girls had brought no money, not expecting this denouement. There was an awkward pause and then he said, "I'll stand you, Bridget." Fortunately I had a couple of good American bucks in my purse and I paid for Margaret and myself. The next time we heard that Mr. Leslie wanted to go for a Sunday morning canter, we were busy.

G. K. CHESTERTON

I am mad about paradoxes and once bought a complete set of Oscar Wilde to satiate my passion. If I had not been still paying for the books when I discovered G. K. Chesterton, I would undoubtedly have bought his complete works, too. Mr. Chesterton came to Notre Dame as guest lecturer. It was during my early days as a reporter, and I was not trusted with the assignment of either interviewing him or covering his lectures. But I did get passes to hear him.

The night I attended he was talking on the folly of attempting to found a code of ethics on the science of physics. He said: "Because you believe the world is based on circles or triangles, it does not follow that you will not steal your neighbor's wife—or even his umbrella." He was a great huge man who had to sit down when he talked because his excessive weight tired him when he stood. He chuckled frequently and always seemed on the point of rolling off his chair.

While he was there Sinclair Lewis received the Nobel prize, and John B. Chester was sent to find out what Mr. Chesterton thought of the judges' decision. I remember his saying that the strength of Sinclair Lewis' writing was the fact that, although he found the faults, errors and hypocrisies of the life around him, he never suggested any panacea for them.

When he left Notre Dame he said either in a lecture or in writing that South Bend was a Polish peasant town full of high-class middle-class people. This offended the citizenry and some women retaliated by reporting that he ate the crumbs off his vest when he was out to dinner. Only one woman, Mrs. H. Russell Stapp, had the wit to retort, "Better be high-class middle class than middle-class high class."

One-Eye Connolly

At one time South Bend sports followers were enthusiastic about the future of a Negro boxer named Redman. He was a local boy and his promoters had visions of his winning the heavyweight crown.

One-Eye Connolly, famous for crashing gates at events of importance, heard about him and stopped off to look him over. Part of my job at the time was to drop in to the hotels and look at the guest list for the day and that's how I discovered Mr. Connolly was in town.

I had a very nice talk with him and asked what was the first gate he ever crashed. He said: "When I was a boy, I got a big kick out of circuses and fairs, as most boys do. I wanted to go to a county fair in my home town, but I didn't have the money. I hung around the gate until I discovered that if you had anything to enter in the exhibits you got in free. I went across the road to a cemetery and took a bouquet off one of the graves and told the attendant I wanted to enter it in the cut flowers exhibit. I not only got in free, but took a prize with my entry."

Olsen and Johnson

Now, in some autobiographies, especially the memoir type, the author leans heavily on the chance acquaintances of a lifetime, and makes out that Premier Laval never so much as peeped without consulting the tell-all-er first. I hope you don't think I'm doing that because if you asked any of the persons mentioned in this chapter if they knew Kay Smallzried, they'd all say, "Kay *who?*"

All of them, that is, except Olsen and Johnson, of *Hellzapoppin* fame. I owe my friendship with this famous comedy team, not to a feature I wrote about them for the paper, but to the fact that my father has known Johnny Olsen since he was in knee pants and worked at the Big Four railroad yards. For Uncle Ole was a Wabash boy.

Several times when Ole and Chic were playing South Bend the family and I went on parties with them afterwards. One time we took over a big room in a speakeasy

in the west end of town. There were about thirty people there, Ole's mother and sister, Chic, some of the
cast and some guests I'd invited. All during the evening
the two comedians saw to it that everyone had a good
time. More beer—more sandwiches—will you dance with
me—did you hear about—would you like—

How vastly different they are from those celebrities
who step down off a lecture platform and wait for their
public to come up and gush all over them! I think a
comedian gets his first thrill (whether on or off stage)
out of making people laugh, his second out of reaching
the top of his profession, and his third out of the money
he makes.

Olsen and Johnson have no off-stage sensitive souls
that yearn to do *Hamlet*. They have a conviction of the
worth-whileness of fun. And I'd be glad to be one of
their stooges any time.

Charles "Buddy" Rogers

The day I interviewed young Mr. Rogers I looked
like a fugitive from a rummage sale. I had on a black
dress, black sweater that was too big for me, black hat
that had blown on my head off the street (I couldn't
have bought it), and black flat-heeled shoes. It was Saturday and I never made myself beautiful on that day,
because I wasn't supposed to be sent out. I just did a
few telephone calls, some proofreading, and thought
about what I would wear dancing that night.

So when Frank Ahearn told me Buddy Rogers was
in town for the Kansas-Notre Dame game and to go in-

terview him, I wanted only to jump into my own grave and pull the dirt after me.

But I went, and found the ex-movie star and orchestra leader was a regular fellow. He is a Kansas alumnus and was looking forward to the game with all the enthusiasm of a sophomore halfback who's made varsity.

I asked him about his preference for girls and he said, "Well, she's a blonde, a brunette, or a redhead, and I suspect she's in South Bend, but I haven't found her."

Naturally I'll always think that if I had worn my $9.95 copy of Schiaparelli maybe his ideal girl would have been in South Bend. But I daresay Mary Pickford feels differently.

CARL SANDBURG

It was during my first year on the paper that Carl Sandburg came to town to lecture. I had been an admirer of his since I first read poetry and when I heard he was coming I knew I just had to go to see him.

I hadn't been trusted with anything save obituaries at this time, so I asked for an afternoon off and Mr. Huston wanted to know, "What for?" I told him to hear Sandburg and explained all about it.

When the day came I was told to cover the lecture, and this made me happy and frightened. It had never occurred to me even in my most self-congratulatory dreams that I would be asked to write it up.

By the time I got there I could only sit on the edge of my chair like a photographic subject of the '90's who had her skull clamped in the cameraman's head-brace. I listened to his reading and singing and after it was over I went up and asked him to say something. That was my idea of interviewing then. He smiled and said, "I'm an old battle-scarred interviewer myself. I worked on the *Chicago Daily News* for many years. But you don't need me to say anything. Your story was all out there on the platform."

I felt embarrassed and rebuffed. But it was no time to think about my feelings. I hurried back to the office and (aided by a couple of poetry books I brought from home) I wrote my story. Among the paragraphs of my account:

"Swaying slightly as he read, placing the proper intonation on the crisp phrases of modern poetry, he easily reached his audience."

I finished with a little biography from my Untermeyer book and in my final paragraph referred to Auslander and Hill:

"They speak of the quiet smoothness of Sandburg's poetry, his understanding of the oppressed, his sympathy for the misunderstood. No other words could describe it better."

My face was hot and my hands cold when I turned the story in to the city desk. I tried to think of things to do so I could hang around and watch the face of the city editor when he read it. But he went out to dinner and there was nothing for me to do but wait for the Sunday morning paper. Great days! I had a by-line and my story was just exactly as I had written it.

When I went down to work Monday Carl Cooper said, "That was a good story."

Hervey Allen

The only author I've heard talk shop, except Mr. Huston, is Hervey Allen. I met him at a tea given by the late Professor Camille McCole, when he was at the University of Notre Dame.

I liked Mr. Allen because he wasn't patronizing. His easy manner and conversation indicated that we writers had our problems.

"I usually go into my room and sit down for an hour or so to think the thing out. All my characters appear to me as they would on a stage. I see them; I hear them talking. When I write I even delete some of the things they say. I may write ten pages at a time or work days on two paragraphs.

"My wife typed my manuscript (*Anthony Adverse*) for me, being the only one who could transcribe my writing. She returned the manuscript and I rewrote it. It was rewritten four times and proofread eight times."

And this with 1,224 pages!

I've remembered these things and tried to see my characters and hear them talking. But I think it must be easier to do that in fiction than in autobiography, because my characters are always quarreling.

Edna St. Vincent Millay

When I was fourteen years old and a freshman in high school, I picked up a copy of *The Dial* one afternoon shortly before art class was to begin and sat down on the steps leading into the room to look it over.

I saw a poem: "What lips my lips have kissed and where and why, I have forgot—" I read on and then re-read it. Edna St. Vincent Millay. Who was she, any-way? She certainly did know how a person felt. I called for some of my friends and they clustered around and I read it aloud.

Well, fourteen, fifteen, sixteen, twenty-three, twenty-four, twenty-five. I was still reading Miss Millay. *Fatal Interview*—"I know my mind and I have made my choice." For better than ten years I had been asking myself what she was like.

She was going to read some of her poetry at a lecture in Chicago, and I made up my mind to go hear her. She came onto the stage wearing a long green velvet gown and a black velvet cape. Hearing her read her own poems I realized meanings in them I had not known be-fore. I decided to go back stage when it was over and meet her.

She was refusing autographs when I arrived, and was ready to go out the door. I said, "Miss Millay." She turned around and looked up at me for a moment (my big moment), and said, "Yes, my dear."

I didn't know what to say. What do you say when you're face to face with the idol of your adolescence? "I wanted to meet you," I said, "to see what you were like."

She kept a perfectly straight face, her expression kind. She took my hand, "Won't you walk out to the car with me?"

So I did, and told her she had been a dominating in-fluence in my life for so long I had come up to Chicago from South Bend to sort of prove to myself that she was worth it.

"How far is South Bend?" she asked.

"Ninety miles."

"I didn't dream anybody would come from anywhere to anywhere to see me," she said.

"Well, I would and I'm glad I did," I said.

She squeezed my hand and smiled, and her car drove up. I felt about her as I had those long years before when I first read the sonnet. Miss Millay is the only celebrity I ever met about whom I didn't write for the paper. I couldn't do it because it was too personal a thing. Meeting her hadn't happened to "Nobody." It had happened to me.

CHAPTER XI

$0,000 Reward for Information

(NOTE: Because the criminals involved in the story of this chapter are, insofar as the author knows, at large, names marked with an * are fictitious.)

Before I enter into the serious and pertinent matter of this yarn, which has to do with a kidnaping, I want to pause right here and ask a question which has been bothering me for some time.

Why is it that in kidnapings where a ransom is involved, women are never the victims? Wealthy men and the children of wealthy parents are snatched from their homes, but never a wealthy woman. Or I'll say hardly ever, in case there have been one or two which escaped my notice.

We can remove from our discussion the instances of child kidnaping, because these crimes invariably are the result of one man's effort. It is obvious that the lone kidnaper would rather take and then murder a defenseless child than risk a biting, scratching, screaming woman or a two-fisted man.

But the kidnaping gang? That's a different story. Let's pretend we are sitting in with the boys while they plan a snatch. Of course, I've never really done it, so some of the details may be a little off. Still, I'm willing to bet that, since they never take women, their conversation goes something like this:

"Jeez," says the cross-eyed member of the gang, "here's a good prospect."

He has opened the evening paper to the society section and is closely inspecting a picture of Mrs. Ritchbitch*, chairman of the St. Moneyplease* Hospital board. She is in evening clothes and the poor fellow has mistaken a mole on her plump and shapely bosom for a costly jewel. The others look over his shoulder.

"Naw," says Algy, "we don't want to get mixed up wit' no dames."

"Why?" asks the c.-e. member. He's a sentimentalist at heart.

"Listen," says Percy, "dames is trouble. I knew a girl once in Tuskaloosa. I blew her to a two-dollar steak and 'en she drops me for a guy wit' coily hair."

"An' besides," says Aubrey, the brains of the gang, "no guy is goin' to pay $50,000 bucks to get a woman back. Not even his mudder. Let's get her husban'."

There you have it. Kidnapers are misogynists who feel that no woman is worth the price they ask. And that is not very flattering to us women, however relieved we may be.

It may be argued that I am needlessly flippant about a

serious crime. Certain aspects of the only kidnaping case I personally observed and worked on, however, set me the example.

I call the South Bend snatch the first of the modern crimes of this type because it happened in January 1932, because it attracted national headlines, and because following this crime, kidnaping became a regular feature of the news, with cases in Chicago, St. Paul, Hopewell, N. J., Arizona, Washington and other sections of the country. Kidnaping is still too frequent in the news, and some of these crimes are yet unsolved.

This January morning was clear and warm and I turned my face to the sun and walked slowly to the office so I could enjoy it longer. When I arrived and reached the top of the stairs I knew I had stared too long at the sun. Ahearn was an optical illusion. No matter where I looked, there he was.

"Smallzried," he barked at me as though I'd been there for hours, "get the file on Wilburforce *."

"Which Wilburforce?"

"Homer."

"Dead?"

"No, kidnaped."

"Good Lord!" I gasped.

Homer Wilburforce was one of the leading industrialists in South Bend. I hurried into the morgue and pulled out the file with his pictures, some of his wife, and some of their only daughter, together with such news stories as they had provided. There was one on the enlargement of his plant, another on his civic activities, several items on his wife's good works. I took these and put them on the city desk. I knew better than to ask Ahearn to tell me about it then. We were readying an extra.

"Write a sketch of his wife." Ahearn didn't look up at me, but started at once to place the cuts I had brought him on a dummy front page for the composing room.

I was too curious to settle down. Before I could write a word I would have to know something about it. The office boy was taking a handful of copy to the composing room and I followed him. He'd know more about it than anyone else.

"Tell me what happened," I implored him.

"Well, he was kidnaped last night for $50,000 ransom. That's all I know."

I leaped up the steps into the editorial room and started for my desk. I was disappointed. I wanted to know "whodunnit." But for that matter, so did the police.

"Where's that sketch, Smallzried?" Ahearn yelled at me.

"Coming up," I said.

"Where's Pete?" He's referring to the office boy.

"Composing room."

"Well, call the press room and ask Cooper and Jackson what the hell."

He means to call the city hall, ask for the press room and demand of Cooper and Jackson why they haven't yet brought their stories in. And they haven't because they have only been at police headquarters about fifteen minutes. Ahearn knows this but it doesn't make any dif-

promise was, her husband would be set free. She was told to turn the car around, go home, and not notify the police. She complained that she would be unable to turn the car on the narrow, dark road, so the kidnapers did it for her and started her back in the right direction.

As she came to an intersection in South Bend, she stalled her car, and having by this time relaxed from fear to the point of hysteria, she lacked the physical coordination to start it again. A policeman (and where were the police when they drove through town the first time?) noticing her, walked over to ask if anything was the matter, and Mrs. Wilburforce told the whole story.

She had been given a ransom note which said she would receive no further instructions. By noon the next day she was in a state of collapse. The paper said representatives of the family indicated it would be impossible to raise the $50,000. The same intermediaries between press and family also said Mrs. Wilburforce would not drive out to deliver the ransom money as directed.

A second story said the Secretary of State, a South Bend man and friend of the family, had a corps of state police coming into the case. A third story listed other members of the Wilburforce family and their positions in the community. The news accounts were rounded out by my sketch of Mrs. Wilburforce.

Centered in a box near the top of the page was one of two superb human interest stories printed in connection with our kidnaping. And yet it was written without subjects, predicates or adjectives. It was a list of "public spirited citizens" who were putting up good money as a reward for information leading to the identification, capture alive or dead, etc., of the kidnapers. A total of $8,525 had been posted when the paper went to press. The smallest donation was $25 and the largest $2,000 with other amounts ranging between the two. That $25 subscription will be discussed in just a moment. First let's look at the larger sums.

What, specifically, do they represent? There were several matters of private and public concern involved, it seemed to me as I thought about it. In the first place, consider the individual donor.

"My God," he thinks as he sits at his desk, looking with a frightened and possessive glance at his luxurious office—that office whose safety has been at least vicariously threatened. "They might have got me. Poor old Wilburforce. It's awful. Such things oughtn't to be allowed to happen. And I'm going to do my part. Supposing they had got me! Where were the police? We've got to put a stop to these things. Why just supposing— me! Money can't buy— Now let's see, how much can I afford to give?"

And he reaches for the phone, calls the paper and has his name put down for however many dollars he feels he can spare. After all, business isn't so good, and it was Wilburforce they got. He's done his part. He feels somehow comforted and secure. (And besides, his name will be in the paper.)

So much for the big sums and the big name givers. The $25 was sent in anonymously and because of its small size I am inclined to think its subscriber was some- one who either honestly wanted Mr. Wilburforce to be returned, or whose civic interests outweighed his personal lust for notoriety. For a man who can give $2,000, $2,000 is easy to part with. But your $25 man has parted with money he could use to help pay for his wife's winter coat or to have his tonsils out.

The second thing in regard to this reward or any other reward which strikes me as being downright shameful is the admission that the police department is either unable to cope with the job or else is too indifferent to try unless there's a bonus for its efforts. Why else is a reward offered? The fact of the matter is that it's cheaper to give rewards in an emergency than to pay sufficient taxes year after year to provide satisfactory salaries for policemen. Rewards seldom have to be paid, but taxes always. Just the same, I thought, as I ordered a second hamburger, I'll bet these men wish now they had let the city council raise salaries instead of cut them in the last budget.

The third thing this little human interest story pointed out was this: if it hadn't been a Wilburforce who had been kidnaped, no money would have been put up. I remembered all the unsolved murders I described earlier and I knew that not one dollar had been offered towards encouraging the solution of those crimes. Putting justice on a pay as you go basis creates a situation clearly out of place in a democracy.

At last I brushed the crumbs off my lap and went back to the office. This was one day when it was as much fun to work as theorize, and trading my thoughts for action was no chore. I found that the *News-Times* had its own plan of action. Mr. Millis was explaining that it had to be a long premeditated job, because the

199

kidnapers obviously had to be thoroughly familiar with
the setup of the Wilburforce household. They had to
know their victims were at the Hamiltons'. The ransom
instructions made it plain that they knew Mr. Wilburforce owned two cars, since Mrs. Wilburforce was told
to drive toward Chicago in the one they were not using
the night the crime was committed. Therefore, Mr.
Millis reasoned, the kidnapers (who couldn't possibly
be South Bend people) would have to have moved to
the city two or three months before and settled down
to a study of the life and habits of the man they elected
to snatch. So he got a list of all the families who had
moved into town since the preceding November. (Don't
ask me why it takes two or three months to find out
where a person lives, who his friends are, and what
kind of cars he drives—that was Mr. Millis's worry.
And, of course, nobody asked him why he thought the
gang would register its entrance into the city. We were
only reporters and we did as we were told.)

The staff was divided into groups of two and three
and told to go to the houses in which the new families
were living, and make notes of anything suspicious. I
drew as my companion on this man-hunt, Mrs. Millis,
wife of the publisher.

All afternoon we drove from house to house, visiting
everything from brothels to respectable homes of new
business men. I did the door-knocking while Mrs. Millis
waited for me in the car, a little distance away. I began
by explaining to the people who answered that I was
selling magazines, but soon changed that story to taking
an unemployment census. This gave me more time to

look around. There was one house about a mile from the Wilburforce residence which seemed to me worthy of note. No one was home, but I looked through the windows and saw a shabbily furnished living room and bedroom combined. Dirty dishes on the kitchen table indicated several persons had been eating at the same time. I turned my report in to the "chief" when I got back. I'll never know, however, whether or not this was the habitat of kidnapers, because—

About 11 o'clock that night, almost twenty-four hours to the minute from the time he was kidnaped, Mr. Wilburforce walked into his home unharmed.

The press was not admitted to see him, but his attorney gave out the following statement: Mr. Wilburforce was all right; he had been blindfolded the entire time and had no idea what his kidnapers looked like or exactly where he had been; he knew it was near Chicago, because he had been freed on the outskirts of Michigan City (about forty-five miles from Chicago in Indiana) and had taken a South Shore train back to South Bend; $50,000 ransom had not been paid; there was no statement on what arrangements Mr. Wilburforce had made with his kidnapers to gain his release; since he had been *blindfolded the entire time he would never be able to identify them in the event of their apprehension.*

The next day we carried the second of our human interest stories. But it was not in a box on the front page. It was a little paragraph trailing the main story and it said only, "Messrs X, Y, Z, and others who offered rewards for the apprehension of the kidnapers have cancelled their donations." I stared at it, and then I laughed.

So there it is. Who cares now whether the kidnapers are brought to justice? I was fit to burst with congratulating myself on my original analysis of the reward motives. Wilburforce was back safe and sound and they could pocket their reward money and the police could go rock on their fallen arches.

Why wasn't it just as important to capture the criminals after Wilburforce got back as before? It was a mystery to me and a funny one. I said to Cooper, "What's the idea anyway?"

And he said, "Huh! Putting up that money was just so much horse collar!"

Horse collar—the other words for it are baloney, tripe, or—just plain publicity.

CHAPTER XII

Shake Down the Thunder—

IN THE OFFICE

IT IS LATE SATURDAY AFTERNOON and little newsboys are running about the streets of South Bend yelling, "Notre Dame beats Georgia Tech; A's win." We can see them from the windows of the editorial room. We can watch passers-by stop, get a pink sheet and part with their pennies, hurrying off without so much as a glance at the *News-Times* building. For the paper-buyer the big presses, the littered editorial room, the whole complex of planning and doing housed in our building do not exist. He has the late sports edition, and so far as he's concerned, it might have been spontaneously generated. He doesn't care.

We, inside, hear the newsboys crying their papers, but, unlike the passer-by, we know all about those pink, folded squares, because we made them and got them out there on the street. It's been a wild afternoon. Ahearn should be dead under his desk, but he's bawling out the society editor and screaming, "Where the hell's Jackson? Smallzried, where are those cut-lines?"

Jackson's whereabouts may be one with the secret of the Sphinx, but Smallzried, exhausted from running copy two hours straight for Ahearn, is trying to sneak out for a coke. I don't want to settle down to write cut-lines for a quilt show picture. I want to go over to the Greek's and think about the afternoon. But Ahearn has nailed me. Nevertheless, as I write about the prize quilt, I do do a little thinking, for these game Saturdays are a thrill that no amount of experience lessens.

I'll never forget my first autumn on the *News-Times*. The Philadelphia Athletics and the Chicago Cubs were battling out the World Series. Notre Dame was playing its usual headline schedule, with a team that looked like (and proved to be) of championship stripe.

It's noon of a fine fall Saturday and I'm having a bite early so as to be back at the office by one o'clock. We have a three-point program ahead of us: one, to get a play-by-play account of the Notre Dame game; two, to get a play-by-play account of the World Series; three, to get our pink sheet with this information on the street ahead of the *Tribune*.

When I walked into the office I noticed a new man in the sports department. He had iron-gray hair and wore glasses, so he was removed from any romantic speculation. He was sitting in front of a typewriter and near him was a telegraph instrument board. I walked up to it and gave a couple of experimental taps. To my surprise it twerped back at me. The man laughed.

"You've just insulted the operator at the other end," he explained. Then he began to jiggle the little lever up and down. After a minute there was a reply and he looked up at me and said, "You're forgiven."

I glanced around the office to make sure Ahearn was out and wouldn't scream at me for bothering the help and then I said, "I just work here, and I wonder if you would mind telling me what this is all about."

So he said he was from Western Union and he was going to take a play-by-play account of the Notre Dame game via dots and dashes from the little mechanism. He would be up each Saturday the team was out of town.

Satisfied with this explanation I went out to the composing room to get a drink. I say "out to" for this reason: the *News-Times* had two buildings, one housing the business offices on the first floor, the editorial room on the second floor and the engraving department on the third. The second building had the press room and circulation department on the ground floor and the composing and stereotype rooms on the second. The buildings were separated by an alley, but there was a little bridge connecting the editorial and composing rooms. Near the door of the composing room was a drinking fountain where the water was always running and always cold, and that's why I went out there for my drink.

I am giving you this physical setup so you can better understand the arrangements during the climax of the afternoon. When I stood after taking my drink and looked around I saw the composing room was pretty busy. Walter (It-can't-be-done) Worth was giving lots of orders, and Ross Fankboner was carrying galleys of type from one place to another, and the linotype machines were all busy, and Art, the printer's devil, was pulling one proof after another.

"Why are you so busy?" I asked Ross. "I thought you took it a little easy after the paper's out."

"We're getting ready for the pink sheet," Ross replied.

"Pink sheet!" I said. "Why, you only make over the front page for that. It won't be out for hours yet anyway."

"I know," said Ross, "but today the World Series and Notre Dame are both going on and we want to get out ahead of the *Trib*."

Then he showed me the preparations. Two heads had already been set in 8-96 (eight columns wide, ninety-six point type); one read, "Notre Dame Downs Georgia Tech," and the other read, "Notre Dame, Georgia Tech Tie."

"But supposing Georgia Tech wins," I said.

"You don't suppose that if you live in South Bend."

"But they might," I objected, "and then you would be held up while you set a new head."

So he showed me that by picking up the letters which spelled Notre Dame and those spelling their rival's name, you could switch their positions and inform the public of an unthinkable catastrophe: "George Tech Downs Notre Dame."

There were two other heads set in 6-30 ital. (six columns wide, thirty point size italics) which read, "A's Win Again," and "Cubs Trim A's."

A tall skinny man, whose name I've forgotten, was leaning over the empty form which was to hold the pink sheet type. He blocked off the space for the heads and then cut the lead rules to make up the column widths. There was also a space blocked off for a picture. This would be a piece of leg art, I knew. For some reason the pink sheet was supposed to appeal to the baser nature of man so the picture on this page was always of a beautiful girl showing her legs.

While I was thinking about this I heard Ahearn taking my name in vain so I rushed out, jumped up the steps and into the editorial room. "Yes, sir."

"Get your work done," he said simply.

I was glad I had worked the evening before, because I didn't have much to do, and once I was finished I could roam around the office and see how the games were coming along. I wrote a few P.T.A. stories of meetings to be held the coming week, checked the undertakers, wrote an advance notice of the "Feast of Lights," a Hebrew holiday, a notice on a Woodmen of the World meeting. With the exception of the cut-lines, which I decided to write later, I was all caught up. I looked around.

Tom Coman, Ahearn and the Western Union man were grouped around the telegraph instrument which was jabbering like mad. Bobby Hoenig, Jack Ohnemus and Pete, the office boy, were hanging over the teletype machines which were going full blast. These devices were modern magic to me. They stand about waist high and look like safes with slant desk tops. In the slant part of the top is a glass through which you can read reports as they are automatically typed on a roll of yellow paper. In the level part of the top is a slot through which the paper slips as it is turned up from the roller. This paper you tear off, and presto! There is the news of the world. The sending stations are located in key cities like New York, Detroit, Chicago, Washington, and as the stuff is typed by the staff men it comes over the wire and is printed in local offices by the teletypes. We had three or four of them in a little cubbyhole at the same end of the office as the entrance to the composing room.

I tossed my news accounts into the copy desk basket and went to see what the teletypes had to say.

"FORTY THOUSAND FANS TURNED OUT THIS AFTERNOON TO SEE THE THIRD GAME OF THE WORLD SERIES, NO ONE SERIOUSLY BELIEVES THAT THE CUBS WILL PULL THEMSELVES OUT OF THEIR FRENZIED DISORGANIZATION AND GIVE THE ATHLETICS ANY COMPETITION. BUT THIS IS THE SERIES AND THE FEELING PERSISTS THAT YOU NEVER CAN TELL."

Hoenig and Jack Ohnemus, the telegraph editor, were writing sub-heads for the baseball game and getting the box score sheet ready. Jack also had to separate other news from the mass of baseball dope—for other things do happen on this Saturday afternoon when fast curve pitchers and fleet halfbacks fight for supremacy on the front page.

The office boy had already begun to run copy on the

World Series and I said to Ahearn: "I'll be stooge for you, so Pete can carry the baseball copy." To my surprise he agreed.

The Western Union man was listening to the little lever jiggling up and down, and writing, "Fifty thousand fans, all players in good shape, weather clear, starting line-up." Tom Coman took this bit of information and wrote three leads: "Notre Dame took another hurdle this afternoon in its march to a national championship, its first in five years. Fifty thousand fans saw the fighting Irish down Georgia Tech in the second battle of the season."

The other two leads read: "Fifty thousand fans saw an early season upset Saturday when Georgia Tech's Engineers defeated a touted Notre Dame team." The other lead substituted "tied," for defeated. Coman was batting for Don Trenary, the sports editor at the time, who was away covering the game. Trenary's account would be telegraphed in after the game for Sunday's paper.

When Coman is through with the lead, Ahearn takes the second sheet of paper from the operator, who types on small half sheets and uses a fresh one for each play. Ahearn reads through it, makes a few pencil marks on it and hands it over to me. I read it as I walk to the composing room. "Notre Dame won the toss and chose to defend the south goal. Georgia Tech kicked off and Marchy Schwartz returned the ball twenty-five yards. First down and ten to go on the Notre Dame 37-yard line."

On the little bridge between the two rooms I meet

Pete. "How's the game coming?" he asks. "Notre Dame first and ten on their thirty-five-yard line," I say. "How's the series?" "No runs, no hits, no errors, first inning."

Back and forth, back and forth for two hours, something like fifty trips. "Wow!" screams Ahearn and everyone knows that Notre Dame has a touchdown. "Ho-ho!" Bobby Hoenig hoots and you know that the Athletics are probably throwing bats instead of balls at the Cubs, in a generous effort to let a Cub reach first base.

It's the last few minutes of the last quarter, and the last half of the ninth. The baseball people are making a relay from the teletype to the composing room, with Ohnemus at the machine, Coman just outside, Elmer Danch midway between Coman and Hoenig, who is at the door of the composing room. Pi Warren is out there supervising the work of King, the compositor on the series, and the business of making up the page. I pick my way through this relay team and get Ahearn's copy to another operator, Mabel, who has been setting the Notre Dame game play by play.

Jack yells, "Hartnett up"; Coman, "Hartnett up"; Danch, "Hartnett up"; Hoenig, "Hartnett up." King sets, "Hartnett up."

There's a pause and then "He fans!" "He fans!" "He fans!"

"Root up." "Root up." "Root up."

"Out to Cochrane," and so on for the last few seconds.

"Yea!" yells Ahearn.

"Hot damn!" say I.

"Eee-yow!" Holland screams.

Schwartz has cut loose with a fifty-four-yard off-tackle run. Our yells drown out the relay team.

"It's over," shouts Jack.

"Over"—"Over"—"Over!"

"The gun!" Ahearn jumps up.

I run out to the composing room and find the page form being wheeled into the stereotyper who makes a cardboard impression of the page by shoving a roller over it. Then the next man takes this mat, fits it into a semi-cylinder form, and pulls a lever adjusting it to the boiler. The molten lead flows down and makes a second impression. This is run through a trimmer and then sent down the dumb-waiter to the press room. I don't see it, but I know the men down there will fit it onto the one vacant roller of the press and start things going.

Now I hurry back to the front window of the editorial room and lean out. We all do. Which will be on the street first, our pink sheets or the *Trib* green sheets? There goes our press! Thud, thud, thud!

"Extra, extra—Notre Dame wins!" Forty little boys come pouring out of the alley waving the pink sheets, and nary a scrap of green paper in sight. "A's and Notre Dame win!" they shout.

The A's and Notre Dame, hell! The *News-Times* won by full five minutes.

In the Town and on the Field

Notre Dame football is not a game played on eight or nine Saturday afternoons each autumn. Not exclusively, that is. It is played by thousands of downtown quarterbacks every day of the week, every week of the season, including September and spring practice. All this vicarious participation is the incubation period which brings the enthusiasm for the home games to its full flower. The people of South Bend look forward to their four home games like a drunkard does to a new quart. And when the season is over, they feel just as forlorn as the drunk does when the bottle is empty. Honestly, when Southern Cal beat Notre Dame after that string of eight victories in 1938, I felt as bad as if Mother had kicked me in the teeth on Christmas morning.

Now why should I care whether Notre Dame wins or loses? Why should you care, for that matter? The chances are that unless you are an alumnus of an opposing college you are rooting for the Irish. I've only met one person in my life who was consistently opposed to Notre Dame and she was a sore-head who hated all winners. But even *she* wanted to know if I could get her a couple of tickets to the Army game.

One autumn Jimmy Costin, sports editor, asked the Rev. John F. O'Hara, C.S.C., then president of Notre Dame, why the college didn't sell the broadcasting rights to its games. "Notre Dame fans are everywhere," Father O'Hara replied and went on to say that, such being the case, the school did not think it fair to limit broadcasting to a few stations. Altruism or not (I've told you in another place about the business ability of priests), that is the college's stand.

I mention this story because of the president's remark

that Notre Dame fans are everywhere. I know what he means. I haven't been all over the United States, it's true. But I have been in a number of representative towns in the Middle West and East and never yet have I spent a night in a strange place without hearing some fellow rooter walking down the street whistling, "Cheer, cheer, for old Notre Dame." Who is this man? What's Notre Dame ever done for him?

"Everybody rides a winner," explains a friend of mine. "That's why Notre Dame's so popular." But that doesn't hold water. The Irish haven't had an undefeated season since 1930. Other colleges have. Our whistler in the dark might better have given out with "Hail, Minnesota," or "Hail, Pitt," or, seeing that these two schools are at the end of their undefeated dynasty, "Hail, hail, the gang's all here."

Notre Dame has two sets of alumni, those who went to school there, and those who didn't. It has the nation lining up at the ticket office because a man named Knute Rockne could play his game the Friday before the whistle blew instead of the Monday after. The people around South Bend call the Notre Dame stadium the "house that Rockne built." In reality every stadium in the country was put up by Rockne. He gave a nation something to do over the week end besides change its brand of cigarettes. He knew that people didn't want to rest their throats come Saturday, but indeed, wanted just the opposite, to yell themselves hoarse. Mr. Hutchins, head tournament jouster for Chicago, can talk all he wants to about scholastic philosophy and ten cent football. He just doesn't know human nature. If my

seventy-nine-year-old grandmother thought anything
was going to happen to those Saturday afternoon games,
she would skin one of the *Three Little Pigs* with her
bare hands, blow up its bladder, hand it to some 170-
pound youth and say, "Take this and run like hell with
it."

She argues that's the only signal a team needs, and
there is at least one ex-Notre Dame player who agrees
with her. A story is told of Joe Savoldi, famous full-
back on Rock's last championship team. He was fast on
the field, but slow on the signals. Once in the huddle he
listened patiently while Frank Carideo called the play
and finally when he was good and mixed up he said,
"Oh, never mind the signal, Frank, just give me the
ball."

I don't suppose I could tell a Rockne story you
haven't heard ten times over, but there is at least one
Layden legend I want to repeat. This young man de-
votes a lot of his practice sessions to fundamentals,
teaching the players to block and tackle and to hold a
football. After all, the best halfback in the world won't
get far if the line falls apart like a moth-eaten blanket,
or if he dribbles the ball when he's past the line of
scrimmage. In 1935 the boys were in a dither over their
game with Ohio State. They didn't want to be razzle-
dazzled off the field and Layden drilled them hard all
week long. But that first half! Notre Dame was terrible.
It was perfectly plain that Layden was going to have
to talk long and loud to them during halftime period to
spark the dramatic drive that means victory. The coach
was not caught short with something to say. He went

into the dressing room, looked at the boys and said, "Well, we lost the first half. Now let's go out and win the second." That's all he said. Andy Pilney knew what he meant, however. It was the fourth quarter and the score was—but never mind. I'm drooling worse than a sports editor. But it's just this something, this eternal quality that makes you want to tell again its already twice-told legends that makes Notre Dame every sports fan's Alma Mater.

When Notre Dame opens its scholastic year in September, there is a sudden leap in the circulation of the *News-Times*. Football fans in all sections of the country want their dope straight and hot from the Notre Dame locker room and Jim can give it to 'em. His stack of mail includes letters from nuns and business executives, housewives and career women, factory workers and WPA crews, invalids and jailbirds, grandfathers and high-school jitterbugs.

Every Sunday morning during the football season the account of the Notre Dame game is the front-page banner story, win, lose or draw. And all my family (with the rest of South Bend) make a dive for the paper to read about it, notwithstanding the fact that they have either seen it, or heard the broadcast, or have read the pink sheet play by play. You would think we had been waiting on tenterhooks to find out how the game ended. That is the true Notre Dame fan spirit. The Smallzried family have been football enthusiasts since long before Rockne's day. My Dad took me to see the old Wabash Athletic Association semi-pro team play on Thanksgiving when I was only five years old, and we built fires around the side lines where we were standing to keep warm. We were used to getting in a stew about football. But once we moved to South Bend our earlier enthusiasm seemed about as animated as that of a walking typhoid-fever patient.

When the paper comes out on Monday night it is hours before anyone knows what is on the front page. What has the sports section to say about the team? What injuries were there? What does Coach Layden say? How did Southern Cal, the next opponent, come through its Saturday game? Has Layden a halfback in hiding for the coming Saturday when the Irish will battle the Trojans?

The office, the town, the school, the fans of the nation gird themselves up in preparation for the outstanding game on the home schedule. I enter into it on Tuesday when Ahearn assigns me the job of a daily story on arrangements for handling the crowds, notables coming to town, special trains.

Day by day the story grows longer. Postmaster General James A. Farley is planning to be present, also Fred Fisher of "body by Fisher," a trustee of the university. A group of fans in Denver, Colorado, have chartered one of the streamliners and will be on hand. Forty-three special trains will steam into the city, not counting the South Shore electric contingent which will bring Chicago rooters. There will probably be thirty or more of these cars.

Take a walk through the town any evening during the early days of the week and you get the impression that the merchants are going to abandon the place. The windows are all vacant. But stick around, and about Wednesday you will see the window decorators, cheeks flushed and eyes bright, arranging in one unique fashion or another, autographed footballs, trophies, blankets, pictures of Rockne, Layden, Jones, pictures of the team. The Retail Merchants' Association is going to give a prize for the best window. One of the men's shops lays a miniature playing field in its window and sets in mounted pictures of the individual members of the team in formation.

Thursday night the paper carries dismal stories from the coaches of both teams. It's just too bad about them. You get the idea that the Nine Old Men are coming into town to play the local post of the G.A.R. There's one man, however, who is honest in his predictions. That's the mathematical wizard who figures the percentages of all the football teams in the country for those demon bettors of the football pool. He says Notre Dame will win. Armed with this listing the sporting citizens of the town make their way to the hotel cigar stands and pay one dollar for a little card on which are printed the names of ten teams and their opponents. If you pick four winners correctly you get five dollars; five winners, fifteen dollars; six winners, twenty-five dollars; seven winners thirty-five dollars; eight winners, fifty dollars; nine winners, seventy-five dollars; and ten winners, one hundred dollars. The bettors have a short time to dream about what they will do with their ill-got gains before the upsets that happen on Saturday.

Friday Ahearn says briefly, "Give us a color story and get everything in it." Only twenty-four hours un-

til the kick-off! Oh, boy, that story almost writes itself.
The town has more color than a skyful of rainbows.
Meat and food trucks run about the streets delivering
huge, unbelievable orders to restaurants, night clubs and
hotels: thirty thousand steaks, four or five thousand
chickens, thousands of bushels of peas, potatoes, carrots,
innumerable baskets of mushrooms, onions, lettuce, case
after case of steak sauces and catsup. Those throngs that
storm the city are going to be plenty hungry after the
game. It's the one day of the year when South Bend is
stocked up with more beer than there is in Milwaukee
and more liquor than there is in Louisville. The motion
picture houses announce billings of four bell pictures
and the night spots are to have special floor shows with
entertainers from Chicago. A big name orchestra will
be in town at the Palais Royale. The South Bend Country Club will have a special program for local society
and their friends and guests from other cities. The society pages are filled with news of visitors and parties.

And Saturday! Well, I feel sorry for the people who
live in New York or Chicago and have never experi-
enced the cohesion of the home town in the grip of a
football Saturday—the sun hanging up in a deep blue
sky—the streets lined with flag poles flying the colors of
Notre Dame and Southern Cal—hawkers standing on
street corners selling pennants and little gold football
pins—other men along the street crying, "Yellow and
white 'mums, buy a mum?"—everywhere you look cars
with the license plates of other states jamming about the
streets—and drunks—my God, the drunks!

In the office the preparations are made about the same

way as for the out-of-town games, except that we will
not have a Western Union man. Instead, Bobby Hoenig
will put on a set of earphones and take the game as it is
told him over the telephone on a special line we have to
the stadium press box. Dutch Hennings loads up his
camera bag and I start telling him about 10 o'clock in
the morning not to go without me, for I am to write the
color story on the game for Sunday's paper. His assistant, Devon Beuhe (pronounced bee-hee, believe it or
not) is also to go, and in addition to Jim Costin, two
other members of the staff, one to telephone the game,
and the second because every member of the staff gets
to see one game during the season. I was allowed to
choose which one I wanted to see. I don't know why
unless it was because I had been there so long.

And what does Saturday show at Notre Dame? For
one thing there is the debris of a huge bonfire where a
pep session was held the night before. Father O'Hara,
Coach Layden, the captain of the team, old grads, representatives from Southern Cal, all rallied 'round to
send the spirits soaring. Up went the flame thirty feet
into the air and the sparks shot over the heads of the
crowd and settled upon them like the inspiration of the
Immortal Rockne.

What a contrast on this Saturday morning when the
team goes quietly to Mass and invokes the blessing of
God on their efforts for the day! What a contrast between these young men whose names are on the lips of
a nation, and those other youths housed just a few rods
away who are unknown and unsung, for whom the
men's fashions in *Esquire* mean nothing! They are al-

ready wearing black. They chant prayers instead of football yells. They are studying for the priesthood.

But on this day we pass by the seminary and make for the cream-colored oval of the stadium. The gates of the modern Valhalla are thrown open, and the players, like so many fine gods, take the field. Fifty-five thousand spectators swarm about the giant bowl to find their places. Crawling along the highways leading to the field of battle come more and more cars, moving and stopping and turning to the shrill whistles of scores of policemen.

The teams line up and fifty-five thousand hearts skip a beat as the ball is kicked down the field, and twenty-two young men in gold silk pants and gold helmets go into action.—Well, I guess you can carry on from here. Who is there in this country that hasn't gone out on a Saturday afternoon to freeze, and drink, and scream at a football game? Multiply it all by twenty and it's a Notre Dame football game.

There are one or two more things, though, that I'd like to tell you about. The Notre Dame stadium is built right up to the playing field, instead of having a cinder track around it as most stadia have. For this reason it seems smaller and more chummy than the huge bowls. The sod on which the boys play came from Ireland and was given to the University by an alumnus named Cartier.* That's the setting for the ceremony between halves as the bands of Notre Dame and its opponent

* It seems I'm wrong again. I found out later that Cartier did give them the sod, but it didn't come from Ireland. I liked the idea so well, however, that I thought I'd let you believe it a moment before you looked down here to find out it ain't so.

come onto the field to play and salute each other. Then, as a memorial to Rockne, the Notre Dame band plays "Ave Maria," oh, so softly, and fifty-five thousand people stand silent as death itself while the music floats up beyond the flame-colored ridge of the stadium into the blue sky—the students, the fur-coated women of the boxes, the Boy Scouts, the priests, the fans, the drunks who will later be swearing and fighting each other—all are united in this perennially moving homage. Then the drums and horns blare out the transitional, tum ta dadada daaa—and thousands of voices sing out:

> Cheer, cheer for Old Notre Dame—
> Ring down the echoes cheering her name—
> Send a volley cheer on high—
> Shake down the thunder from the sky.
> What though the odds be great or small,
> Old Notre Dame will win over all,
> While her loyal sons are marching
> Onward to Victory!

Game's over! The throngs descend the hill into the town, to eat, to drink, to listen to the special entertainers, to dance, to revel.

And what revelry it is! I have to work that night, and I sit in the office and smoke and listen to the police calls on the radio. What's this? "Car number four, calling car number four. Proceed to the Oliver Hotel. Man throwing lighted matches out the sixth-story window. That is all."

That is all, indeed. The drunk tosses his lighted

matches, but in his happy intoxication they are beacons, torches, and conflagrations. Good old Rock! Good old No'er Dame! The game is over. The high spot in his year is past, but, as his last match goes out the window, the glow surges over him and warms him to the heart. Today—he has fought with the gods!

CHAPTER XIII

Classic and Regular Features

BY THIS TIME you are probably aware of the difference between a feature story and a news story. But since this chapter is going to deal with features I'll make a brief distinction to keep the matter clear.

When I wrote a paragraph saying Mr. and Mrs. Harold S. Vance had given a therapeutic pool to the Children's Dispensary, that was a news item. When I visited the Dispensary, got a picture of some children in the pool, described methods of treatment, the kinds of cases helped, the number, and so on, that was a feature.

Some features grow out of news stories and others grow up by themselves. In a general way features have either a human interest or informative value, sometimes both. I liked to write these stories because they gave me a certain opportunity for creative work and often led me to unconventional places and people.

For instance, I doubt if I ever should have gone to the Gay Nineties Bar if there hadn't been a crippled drummer playing in the orchestra. Someone tipped me off on his story and I went to see him.

The Bawdy Nineties Bar would have been a better name for the place. It was located on one of the main downtown streets and its windows were flush with the sidewalk. To insure the patrons of some privacy the glass had been frosted in a fence-board pattern. The entrance was center front and set back a little. Its panes were frosted, too. In other words if you wanted to know what the place was like you had to come inside.

I had asked one of the boys on the staff to make an appointment for me, and also to be there when I went. This was not arranged because I was afraid of being mistaken for a painted lady, but because I had heard that the subject of my interview was shy, and I wanted him to feel at ease. I knew the reporter was a friend of his.

So, when I arrived I was surprised to find nobody at all in the place but the bartender. I sat down at a table and looked around. There was sawdust all over the floor except for a small space in front of the orchestra stand, which was located in the window. Pictures of women in various states of undress adorned the dirty walls, and everywhere there were cardboard plaques bearing sentimental or suggestive mottoes. The lights were so dim that if you looked at any one thing for any length of time it went black before your eyes. The bartender came over for my order. "I'm waiting for friends," I said.

He eyed me a minute. " 'Re you from de *Noose-Times?*"

I nodded.

"Then they're waiting for you in de press room."

Press room! I picked up a handful of sawdust and sprinkled it on my head—ashes of repentance for my ignorance. This was a refinement I hadn't been told about. Sure enough, there was the boy I had asked to meet me, also a reporter from the *Trib*, and a couple of floosies. The room was bare except for a large round table and a number of chairs. Suspended from the ceiling was a light with a green shade. The proprietor had fixed it up so the boys could come and play poker and drink. I don't know why the girls were there because, as I said, the room was bare except for tables and chairs. My friend ordered a beer for me and told the bartender to tell Gene Daniels I had arrived.

Pretty soon he came in creeping on all fours, for his condition made it impossible for him to stand. I shook hands with him when he was introduced to me, and he climbed on a stool beside me where he sat in a crouched position, his head and shoulders just visible above the table. He had as alert a face as I've ever seen in my life. His head was large, oval, and well shaped. His hair was light brown and his eyes dark blue. He moved his head with quick rapid gestures when he talked. I liked him at once.

The conversation was general at first, about the weather, some drunks who got in a fight the night before, a funny story that was going the rounds. Finally I said, "You used to be an auto racer, didn't you?"

"Yes," he nodded his head vigorously.

And that's where my story started. He had been speed-crazy as a youngster and had taken to the dangerous profession of auto racing. His career was brief, however, because on a California track, as he was rounding a bend, the car leaped into space and came crashing down, itself and its driver both wrecked. He was months and months in a hospital—mending and being mended. The verdict: he could never walk upright again. He couldn't even sit very long at a time. He tapped his fingers on the bed. What to do? A set of trap drums was the answer.

So Gene stayed independent and made a good living. He asks nothing of anyone except not to feel sorry for him. He told me one thing I found extremely interesting.

"A few years ago," he said, "I went to Notre Dame with some South Bend friends of mine. We came into the church during service and no one paid the slightest attention to me. They didn't stare at me or inconvenience themselves for my benefit. I was so impressed by their manners I joined the Catholic Church."

The final accomplishment Gene had reached in the reorganization of his life was—driving a car. He loved to drive and he could do it safely.

I sent the photographer to get a picture of Gene at his drums. He stretched out on a little bench when he performed, but he was so clever you didn't notice.

Well—row, row, row your boat. Pull into shore, pick up a feature, and be on your way again. The day after I made Gene's acquaintance I was in an antique shop learning about silver. Julia Holmes had become something of a specialist in this field and sold quantities of it to our best families. I learned that Georgian silver is solid, but Sheffield is plated over copper. The latter is much more garish and ornate than the conservative Georgian. I heard a very good joke on a popular socialite in connection with her silver and I passed it on to Do Konold who used it in her column. The lady was entertaining at a cocktail party and took occasion to display her Sheffield ware, explaining the plating process. One of her guests, inebriated beyond the point of proper interest in things cultural, examined it carefully and then said, "Y'know, if you hadn't told me, I'd never have known the difference."

Some features come up every year, and that little item about the man or woman who "sees the first robin of spring" is one of them. I think, thanks to Frank Ahearn, that I wrote the first-robin-of-spring-story to end all such items.

It was a bleak *November* Saturday afternoon. My desk phone rang and I dutifully answered, *"News-Times* editorial department, Miss Smallzried speaking."

"Now listen," the shrill voice of a female admonishes me, "I've just seen the first robin of spring, and I've been waiting for years to see the first robin of spring so I could get my name in the paper, and you are not going to keep it out now because I saw a big fat robin in the yard, and my name is Mrs. John Doe, and I live at 618 Elm Street, and I want you to put it in the paper, and I'll look for it tomorrow morning, and if it isn't in I'm going to stop the paper!"

"All right, thank you," I said. I feel as if I had walked smack into a fireman's hose going full stream. I must have looked dazed because Ahearn asked me what was the matter and I told him.

"Write it just that way, Miss Smallzried," he said.

And I did, and I thought that would put an end to our ornithology correspondents who keep a weather eye on our feathered friends for the shameful purpose of exalting themselves in the public prints. But no! When that season of the year which had always passed as spring until Mrs. Doe moved it up to November came around, telephones in all parts of the room began ringing as the open season on the first robin started.

Once while I was assistant society editor in addition to being general news reporter, I was assigned the task of writing a feature story for the front-page society section about Mrs. Roosevelt. To my way of thinking there was no excuse for this story. She had not been in South Bend, wasn't scheduled to come and I had never met her. But we were going to print her column and this was a piece of "subtle" promotion. I went through the files, gathered up some news items about her, and strung them together in an effort to show that she was an active, human sort of person who enjoys life. I quote from this story:

"When you fit together these stories about Mrs. Roosevelt, and read something of what she says, you find that she is 'adequate to the situation,' not overdoing formality until you are stiff beyond a recognition of yourself, nor so familiar as to be unworthy of regard, but, in the phraseology of the society editor, Mrs. Roosevelt is 'delightfully informal.'"

In order to give this story some excuse for being in the local paper I said in another place:

"South Bend, along with the rest of the nation, has learned to look for the delightfully homey stories of the social regime in which friendly and easy naturalness seem to have displaced the pomp and rigorous splendor and decadent values of days gone by."

If anyone asked me now what I meant by "decadent values" I couldn't tell him and I'm not sure I could have said when I wrote it. From this point on the whole story grew *delightfully* worse. Oh well, I had to learn to write sometime and I also had to write what I was assigned, but I'm sorry I had to practice on Mrs. Roosevelt because I admire her very much.

Some of our best feature stories are side lights on the weather. Freak storms, hot spells, blizzards—all bring their share of news, features, and pictures. One spring the wind pulled itself off Lake Michigan and swooped across northern Indiana at better than sixty miles an hour, and while that's not a hurricane, it ain't creepin'. The next day we had a story on the thousands of dollars' damage done to orchards, vineyards, barns, etc. But the apéritif had to do with a little girl five years old.

Shortly before the blow came up, she had to go to the potty and skipped lightheartedly to the outhouse. While she was there the wind came along like a sky plow and lifted the outhouse, youngster and all, and blew her along. Ma and Pa were inside looking out when this happened and when they saw the johnny take off without benefit of so much as a streamlined propeller, Ma fainted and Pa lit out after it running and stumbling across the fields just as worried as he could be, because he was a Republican and heaven knew when the WPA would get around to put up a new one for him. The wind carried it along for about two miles and set it down neat and careful. The little girl burst out screaming her head off from fright, but otherwise all right.

I have seen young girls studying to be "journalists," whatever that is. It certainly isn't anything spoken of with respect around a newspaper office. The earnest pupils figure they will write literary criticisms which will set a new standard in the world of letters, or that they will be sent to cover perfectly shocking murder trials. I ought to know what they think, because I thought the same thing without ever studying at all. What a lot of these youngsters don't find out until it's too late is that "journalism" is a classroom term for newspaper work, and I do mean work. Consider the day Frank Ahearn looked over at me and said, "Miss Smallzried, take a photographer and go find the hottest place in town."

You say, "What's that girl crabbin' about? Lookin' for hot spots ought to be fun, what with night clubs, grill rooms, drinks on the house, floor shows—"

Listen. When I get that assignment it is mid-afternoon and it is 104 in the shade. God knows how hot it is in the sun. Nobody in their right mind would try to find out. It is a day when the asphalt on the street is so soft your heels sink into it when you step on it, and if you spit on the sidewalk it goes "pssst" with the heat. It is one of those days when you wake up in the morning wet with perspiration and you stay that way all day long. And it's been like that for days and days. Everytime I walk across the street to get a coke I get a new crop of freckles just from that few seconds of sunlight. Night clubs and floor shows indeed! When Ahearn says to find the hottest place in town, he means it literally. This will be my Sunday feature with pictures.

I told Jo Crabill I wouldn't be able to go swimming at the Country Club with her. Every now and then I got the idea that I could have a life of my own and do things like other people did, but Ahearn had a sixth sense about this and never failed to hand me an assignment that would take the hours in which I had wistfully planned to do other things.

The Great Elmore was practicing dart-throwing in his studio when I found him and told him what was ahead of us. "What does Ahearn want that kind of a story for?" he asked. "Nobody cares about that."

"Well, whether or not they do doesn't concern us," I said. "We're going to find out about it, anyway."

So he gathered together a bag full of equipment and we started. I noticed a traffic cop standing at a street intersection, puffing and sweating and looking very uncomfortable. "Wait a minute," I said. "I'll ask him how he feels."

He took his cap off when I approached and mopped the head band. "Pardon me," I said, "I'm a reporter from

The *News-Times*, looking for the hottest place in South Bend."

"I thought reporters knew where those places were," he said.

"No, I mean 'hot' as in weather. I wondered what you think of this corner."

"Lady, you wouldn't want to print in your paper what I think of this corner this afternoon. You try the kitchen in one of the hotels. That ought to be a hot job."

It seemed like a good idea so I told Elmore we would go to the Hotel LaSalle and have a look around. I informed the publicity man there of my wants and he took us to the kitchen. At least I think it was the kitchen. It was long and narrow and full of steam and I was conscious of shadowy figures milling around and voices speaking to me as if from the other side, and what with the heat it seemed like the wrong side.

"How hot is it in here?" I asked, ducking a tray load of dishes that loomed out of the mist, supported by a hand attached to nothing I could see.

A mustached head appeared very close to me and breathed hotly on my cheek. "Chicken à la king is to-morrow," it said. "Veal cutlets are on the plate lunch tonight." I stared miserably into the sad brown eyes of the apparition and wished I could find Elmore. The head looked startled and said, "Oh, pardon me. I thought you were the steward," and disappeared.

"It's a hundred and six," a voice to my right said, and the full figure of the chef was visible.

"Do you mind it?" I asked.

"Not very much. We're used to it. If you want some place really hot, why don't you try a laundry?"

I groped my way to the door and found Elmore sitting at his ease in the air-cooled dining room.

"Can you get a picture of that?" I nodded towards the kitchen.

But he wouldn't try. He said if the newspaper business was going to want pictures of fogs he guessed he'd enter the ping-pong championships.

We stopped at a laundry and I explained to an office girl that my mission in life was to find the hottest place etc. She seemed a little dubious about whether or not the laundry would want that kind of publicity. I tried to tell her it was to be all very gay and funny, just a playful effort on the part of the paper to prove it wasn't the heat but the humidity that made people so uncomfortable. She had her own ideas about newspapers, however, and was determined that what I really meant to do was to reveal the abuses foisted upon the poor girls by the management, a sort of "girls faint in sweat shop for four dollars a week" sob story. She agreed reluctantly to escort me into the plant. The heat was thick and damp and did seem worse than that of the kitchen. My guide wouldn't tell me how hot it was and I asked one of the girls surreptitiously but she didn't know. She said, "It ain't so bad. If you want to find some place really sizzling, why don't you go to de foundry at de Oliver Woiks? Me brudder's dere and he says it's so hot he puts on a sweater when he leaves so he won't take cold."

By this time my dress was clinging to me like a shady

lady's nightgown. My nose was shiny and my forehead damp around the edges of my hair. My feet hurt, too. And in addition to my personal discomfort I couldn't see any angle to this story. I began to suspect I was in the grip of a frustration nightmare and no one would wake me up.

We climbed into the car again and as I sat down on the thick, woolly upholstery I knew that was the hottest place in town. I also knew Ahearn would not let me get away with a story like that. I looked at Elmore with envy. Was he mopping his brow? Was he cursing? No! He looked at me calmly and said, "Now where?"

"Oh, let's go to de woiks," I said. "De woiks" are more formally known in South Bend as the Oliver Chilled Plow Works. I suppose the plant is fifty years old or so, and has been making farm implements for the nation during all that time. When we reached the foundry I knew I had discovered what we were looking for.

It was too hot to think, almost to hot to see. Gasping and shielding my head from the demon heat of tons of red-hot coals being poured from one huge receptacle into another, I walked over the cinder floors which felt warm through my shoes. Crinkly air shimmered up from tracks upon which miniature cars were running back and forth. Men stripped to the waist, dirty and sweaty, were putting things into and taking them out of red furnaces and somewhere molten metal was being poured. Nothing made any sense to me and when I found out that this was a process of "chilling" plows, I felt vastly worse. The temperature was 112 to 115 degrees and it was true the men put on sweaters when they walked out into what had seemed up to now a hot day. Elmore set up his camera and took some pictures of the machines and crews.

The grime and dust of the foundry settled upon my white clothes and limp features and when I got back to the office I looked as though I had been dragged by the hair over miles of soft coal. I sat down at my desk and typed:

"So you think you're hot, do you! You ought to be ashamed of yourself. Sitting there on the veranda drinking ice-cold lemonade. Why, I can tell you of places—"

And then I told them. Sunday Ahearn played up the story on Page 1, Section 2, with a big picture of the foundry workers, and four or five column headlines, and my own by-line. It went over big because everybody thought it was so original. And, of course, down in my heart, I have to admit that if Ahearn had sent anybody else on the story I'd have sulked for a week.

During the time I was assistant society editor, and later, women's page editor, I wrote more feature stories than at any other time in my career. I had to write human interest yarns for the news sections as well as the women's section. I thought up my own ideas for the society page and as I reread them now I wish I had it to do over again.

I find one with the heading, "Where Is the Man Who Dares Ask for Hot Biscuits?" This was a brief essay on breakfast, its pleasures and dangers. I quote:

"There is one factor, peculiar to breakfast alone, that

235

plays an important part. You are of course in that delightful state of transition between sleep and consciousness. There is a sort of vagueness about it, like there is about Peggy Hopkins Joyce's third husband."

I well remember when I wrote that. I thought I had hit the bull's-eye in giving vagueness its ultimate definition. And even as I look at it now I don't think it bad. If you can identify the lady's third husband with any certainty, walk up and shake my hand. I'd like to know you.

One time I got hold of a page from the diary of Abigail Foote, a resident of Connecticut in the year 1775. I don't remember where it came from but it provided me with a better than average space filler for the Sunday soc. page. I wrote:

"She had about as much chance to lead a frivolous life as a missionary in Africa. Take a long breath and read this excerpt telling of her daily work:

" 'I mended mother's riding hood, spun short thread, fixed two gowns for Welshe's girls, carded wool, spun linen, worked on a cheese basket, hatcheled flax, pleated and ironed, read a sermon of Dodridge's, spooled a piece, milked cows, spun linen 50 knots, made a broom of quinea wheat straw, set a red dye—had two scholars from Mrs. Taylor's—I carded two pounds of whole wool and felt nationally, spun harness twine and scoured the pewter.'

"There now! Who wouldn't feel 'nationally'?"

Jerry Holland assigned me a Sunday feature for a Christmas edition that I remember with extreme pleasure to this day. And if I do say it as shouldn't, it was one of the most successful stories I ever turned out. The subject was what the young lady expects for Christmas and what she gets. If ever I wrote an open letter to Santa Claus that was it and I stood over my family on Sunday while they read it.

I pointed out that what I expected was black silk underwear, and what I always got was a girdle with stays in it. I said what I wanted in the way of perfume was "My Sin," or "Night and Day," and what I got was deadly nightshade or tree of heaven or some other stinkum that made me smell like a dime-store counter on the loose. I wailed that I liked to read Aldous Huxley (this was before he went Christian mystic), and such was the state of mind of my relatives that they remembered me as they had last seen me when I was eight years old and dutifully persisted in sending me copies of *Little Women*, so that I could now supply every boy and girl in the public school system with the book.

This diatribe had some effect at home and I got my black silk underwear (in addition to the girdle). I was so enchanted with it that I bought myself a black satin dress with a cream lace yoke, so the black lace of the undies could show through. Some months later, in the middle of the summer, I wore the underwear without benefit of the girdle to a dance. I was too hot to be confined. When I undressed that night I discovered to my eternal disillusionment that my torso was blacker than Topsy's, and I was hours scrubbing my skin an inch at a time to restore its natural whiteness. Various members of the family came into the bathroom to watch. Ellie offered to buy me an ice-cream cone as consolation but all Mother could think of was getting me a summer girdle. Cooky, my grandmother, didn't know whether or not to laugh—she was afraid I would be dead of dye-poison by morning. Mary was the only really helpful one, and she scoured viciously at my back like a paper hanger taking paper off a wall.

Another story I enjoyed very much collecting and writing was a Christmas feature assigned by Ahearn.

"Miss Smallzried," he said, "go around to women of as many different nationalities as you can find and ask what the Christmas customs were in their homelands."

I telephoned the foreign communities secretary of the Y.W.C.A. and asked her to accompany me. As we went from house to house, calling on half a dozen or so women, I grew excited with the prospect of writing the story. The eyes of these women grew large and soft when I asked them about the Christmases of their childhood. The hundreds of memories the question evoked crowded in upon them and it was difficult for them to choose one from another. The magic of Christmas—its fragrance—the surprises—the food—the gifts—the anticipation—all these trembled in their voices as they talked. The French woman said, "Early Christmas Eve Mother held me on her lap and we looked out at the sunset and Mother said it was the reflection of the oven-fires in heaven where the angels baked Christmas cookies." And the Austrian: "The ringing of a bell awakened us and we went in to see the tree all lighted with candles and Santa Claus holding it up high. We each kissed his hand and then he tied the top of the tree to a ceiling beam and it hung from there." The Hungarian: "We spent

238

Christmas Eve shining our boots well and placed them outside the window and the next morning they were filled with gifts." The Polish: "My mother and father spread hay on the table in memory of Christ being born in a manger and the next morning we would hunt for gifts which were hidden in the hay."

I had a Russian, a German and an Italian Christmas, too. When I sat down to write I wanted to make everyone realize how personal and how deeply felt these experiences were—remembered Christmases, sadly sentimental and yet gay, too. I thought for a time and then I began it with a quotation from Sara Teasdale:

"Oh, better than the minting
Of a gold-crowned king
Is the safe-kept memory
Of a lovely thing."

This chapter could go on endlessly because I wrote lots and lots of features. I did one, at Mr. Ahearn's suggestion, on the factory whistles that blew in the morning. I went around to the various factories, examined the whistles, their construction, what made them blow, and so on. I got a corking good yarn out of my Studebaker guide. The whistle atop the factory is in three sections, graduated cylinders one above the other. Altogether, it stands around ten feet high and weighs more than a ton. Its appearance, however, is very deceptive. It looks small and light. I found out that the three sections enabled it to withstand the steam pressure when it was blown. If it were in one section—well! They once had a whistle all in one piece and they were proud of it and set it up with care. Some South American diplomats were coming to visit the factory and the management planned a special ceremony and decided to blow the whistle for the first time when the honored guests looked on. So they did it! And up went the five-hundred-pound whistle careening in the air like a paper kite over the heads of the astonished and horrified diplomats, and down into the asphalt street where it buried itself forever.

I learned a lot from running around after those features, the sort of thing I couldn't write, because nobody cared that the trials of getting the story were often as interesting as the story itself.

The purpose of local features is to make the subscriber feel the paper belongs to him and has the human, heartfelt interest of himself and his neighbor foremost in mind.

Therefore, if you have two white rabbits and later on something happens and you have more rabbits and—perish the thought—a BLACK rabbit shows up among them, call your paper. They will print your picture and the rabbits' picture and what you have to say about it. If the reporter is given to whimsy (as I was once when I interviewed bears at the zoo on spring's coming) he may even imagine what the white papa rabbit has to say about the black baby bunny.

CHAPTER XIV

While I Think of It—

I WANT TO SUGGEST that the members of the Schuyler Colfax chapter of the Daughters of the American Revolution be put in a prominent case in a good national museum.

Just offhand, the ladies might be offended if they chanced to read that statement, but I mean it sincerely as a compliment. For this group of South Bend women conducted their affairs with dignity and friendliness. Never were their elections like the hair-pulling brawls the club women staged. Never did they storm the office and demand the front page for their publicity.

I covered a state convention of the D.A.R. and it was conducted without a ripple of discord, and when it was over I received several nice letters thanking me for my work in connection with the event. Such unique conduct entitles the members to a pre-eminent place among the historical and sociological exhibits of our time.

Yes, I'm willing to give a little wee bit of an orchid to these women. But before I do there's something I'd like to take up with them.

The business of being a reporter is often the telling of how man, the rational animal, behaves in his irrational moments. The only difference between what I am writing in this book and what I wrote for the paper, is that here I can say what I thought of the people I wrote about. If I don't think much of them it is their fault and not mine.

I'll bet the down payment on an armchair radio-victrola that the church editor of Greeley, Colo., the club editor of Akron, the spelling bee editor of Detroit, the Soap Box Derby reporter of Atlanta, the obit writer of Houston, and the welfare agency reporter of Pittsburgh will pretty well string along with me in what I have said.

Now since the Schuyler Colfax chapter behaved itself rationally on all occasions, I almost left it out of this account. But the national D.A.R. has committed an act so foolish that I am brought to a new realization of the golden inoffensiveness of the South Bend women. I refer to the D.A.R.'s refusal to allow Constitution Hall to be used for a concert by Marion Anderson. I feel sure the local chapter would not have done this.

Had I been in the office the day that news came over the wire I should have held my nose and said, "What a bunch of stinkeroos." That is how we should have labeled the D.A.R. Other stinkeroos include sweaty wrestlers who participate in fixed matches, revival leaders, whining tax crusaders who want to cut the school budget, boy travelers who tell wonder tales, ward politicians, and in general the stupid idiot fringe of society. A wrestler would be a strange bedfellow for a D.A.R., however beribboned her buxom bosom might be.

Therefore, before I send my orchid to the Schuyler Colfax chapter, I would like to see them take up a collection and buy a spotlight to illuminate the 13th amendment of the copy of the Constitution in Constitution Hall (in case they have a copy there). And then let them open the doors and windows and let out the smell.

CHAPTER XV

Dillinger! Here?

(Note: Lest I libel the sport of kings all names marked with an * in this chapter are, insofar as I know, fictitious.)

One Saturday noon I went across the street to the Arcadia, ordered a sardine sandwich and a coke, and then opened a copy of *The Daily Racing Form*. Easy money is just as attractive to reporters as it is to prosperous people.

But no sooner had I found out that *Droopy Drawers* * was by *Slowfoot Sam* * out of *Despair* * than Bill, publicity man for the Colfax theater next door, came running in shouting, "Dillinger's just robbed the Merchants' Bank!"

I rushed back to the office, up the steps two at a time, and carried the word along—"Dillinger's just robbed the Merchants' Bank!"

Ahearn was standing in the middle of the room. Pete White, police reporter, was on one of the phones. Jay Walz was about to sit down. The society editor was cursing club women. But generally speaking the office was quiet and my message electrified them. Without changing his position Ahearn said, "Jay, you go to the bank. Kathleen, you go to the hospital. Pete, you go to the station."

I turned around and ran back down the steps and home for the car. Then I drove to the hospital, speed laws and traffic lights nonexistent. In less than five minutes from the time I had been sitting in the Arcadia I was looking at the blood-spattered emergency room of the hospital and taking the names of the casualties. Two bankers who had been used as shields were shot and injured, one policeman killed.

Back again at the office with my report, I got my next order. "You get the pictures of the bankers. I'll send the office boy for one of the cop."

I drive out to the country estate of one of the financiers. The family have gone off to the hospital and I have to haggle with the maid. She isn't sure the family would want me to have a picture and she doesn't want to lose her job over it. I tell her to tell the family I forced my way in and stole it. She brightens with relief and hands the picture over. I tell her not to calumniate me unless the family objects, but she looks so pleased with the story that I'm not sure she won't tie herself up and blame it on me. I'm in too much of a hurry, however, to worry about it. At the next house one of the children gives me a picture without any question.

Again I'm back at the office. My part is over for the present. The rush is on and it isn't long before the little news boys are on the street with the familiar "Extra, extra! Dillinger robs Merchants' Bank!"

We get a copy of the *Tribune* and to my chagrin I find, or rather Ahearn finds, that there was another injured party, an innocent bystander, who was taken to St. Joseph Hospital. I had checked only Epworth. After I've listened to appropriate descriptions of my shortcomings as a reporter I am sent out to get a picture of this man. For, of course, all pictures will be used again in the Sunday morning paper and the whole crime hashed over.

I haven't yet had an opportunity to read the story, but my business is to write for the paper and not read it. Who am I to indulge myself by reading the paper I work for? I'm off again, this time to the west side, for the innocent bystander was a resident there. He had been sitting in his car near the bank, or maybe driving past it, I don't know, when a stray bullet went through the windshield and grazed his cheek near the eye. When I arrive at his house all the neighbors on both sides of the street are on their porches shouting back and forth, or collected in small groups shaking their heads and fearing the worst. I am tempted to philosophize over the intensely human aspect of this scene. The women are in house dresses, and the men have on blue shirts, and the children are running around the street yelling and screaming and hiding behind their respective parents and playing at being Dillinger. The whole picture is one of human curiosity at its liveliest as it puts the incisors into catastrophe and chews it over. I get my picture from a tearful member of the family and am on my way.

I turned the picture into the city desk without much comment. I felt the boner I had made pretty keenly and never wanted to make cracks around Ahearn when I was in disgrace. So I sat down to write some exceedingly top-flight items on the Salvation Army, Camp Fire Girls, etc., which were awaiting my attention.

Johnny came back with the picture of the cop at long last, but in the meantime we had discovered that the officer we were backing was not really the one who had been killed. This was not my fault, however. The hospital had been mistaken and had given me the wrong name.

The office boy said, "Oh, God, and the mother of this one collapsed when I told her he'd been killed." The mothers of cops have their heroic moments, too.

By now I was good and confused about the whole thing and was reaching for a paper to find out what *had* happened, when Ahearn says, "Miss Smallzried, go out and interview the widow of the cop. Find out if she wants to raise her boys to be policemen."

Here was the sterling opportunity of my career. If I had a sneaking feeling that it was heartless to plague a woman about the careers of her children before her husband's body was cold, I suffocated it instantly with my pride in the assignment. Here would be a history-making human interest story, the like of which had never been written in the local annals. Let Ahearn bawl me out whenever he wished, so long as he gave me assignments like this.

I screwed up my professional sorrow air that I had acquired from long years of writing obits and went to the home of the officer. And there I found out that he wasn't married! I stopped and had a glass of beer on my way back to the office. My own disappointment was nothing to what Ahearn's would be. But at last I forced myself to go up and tell him. He said, "All right, forget it." But his face was a foot long. Had he known yesterday what was going to happen, he'd have made me marry the poor policeman, I'm sure. Ahearn was one to value a good story.

Before finishing my work I picked up a paper and read the story. "John Dillinger's gang Saturday noon held up the Merchants' National Bank and took $30,-000. One officer, John William Doe, was killed and three men shot. The injured are:" and so on.

The brigands had walked into the bank just before closing and announced from the center of the room, "This is a holdup. Everyone get down on the floor." The dispatch and finesse of the crime were responsible for its total success. After taking the money, they had forced two of the bankers to act as shields as they left to climb into the waiting auto at the curbstone. The traffic officer, seeing them come out of the bank, took his gun and rushed toward them and was dropped in his tracks. Of course the bandits made good their escape.

I put the paper down. There was some comfort in knowing that our bank was in good shape. Dillinger robbed so many in our district that when he passed up a town the citizens worried for fear their banks were wobbly and not worth the attention of really top-rank bandits.

Crime might be one of the nation's most costly problems. But not for me was sociological speculation. My lesson for the day was always to check both hospitals and to make a law that all cops should be married.

CHAPTER XVI

Hell's Half-Acre

ONE DAY AHEARN SAID TO ME, "Kathleen, go over to the Chamber of Commerce tonight and cover a butchers' meeting."

Now, how in the world are you going to classify a butchers' meeting? It's hardly news to anyone except the members of the trade and it doesn't come under the head of a human interest story. I had a number of such assignments outside any category the tradition of the fourth estate could give me. This bothered me and I wasn't happy until I thought up one of my own.

One of the boys would say, "What are you going to do tonight?" and there I'd be stuck with a butchers' meeting, a Billy Sunday revival or maybe the American Association of University Women's tax study group. So to keep the newspaper game on a glamour level I'd say of all the nonclassified subjects among my assignments, "I'm going to cover Hell's Half-Acre."

I want to mention here a few of the stories under this head, and also to include reminiscences I haven't been able to fit in any place else.

Let's begin with the butchers' meeting. I find myself the solitary female attendant at a lecture on what to do with a lamb that had been led to slaughter. I wrote the story in the dark days of the depression and my lead was:

"This is a story about lamb that has nothing to do with the March weather. It is a story of cuts that aren't spoken of in percentages. Lamb cuts!"

Then I explained that there was more to lamb than legs or chops, that there's the lamb neck (which makes a splendid casserole dish rightly done) the lamb shoulder (which makes a delicious mock duck) and also the cushion shoulder. Whatever epicurean delight it could be turned into I have long since forgotten.

The noisiest lecture I ever covered was given by Dr. W. T. Levitt of the Corning Glass Company. I was completely enchanted by it nevertheless and said so in these words:

"There wasn't much lecture, just actions, which you have always heard are more eloquent than words anyway. Right before your eyes Dr. Levitt made a chemist distiller's outfit with 'joints,' 'stop cocks,' tubes within tubes.

"In the first place, glass blowing is done to a terrific amount of noise. Dr. Levitt made a distinction between 'lamp blowing' and that done with a furnace. But lamp-blowing is not the making of chimneys for old-fashioned oid lamps. It means you melt the glass in an oxygen gas flame from a small jet.

"This gas under pressure makes all the noise. Once it's adjusted, you can take a glass tube in your bare hands, hold the part you want to melt in the flame until it looks like taffy. When the tube was red hot, Dr. Levitt started to blow the taffy-looking red ring.

"There you have it, noise, flame and the fashioning of glass shapes. It's a great spectacle."

I didn't always have to leave the office for these stories. Some days portions of the Acre would be brought to me. I remember the day a man came up the stairs with a phenomenon well wrapped up. He set it down on the city desk and proceeded with delicate care to unfold the paper. Although he hardly looked the part, we felt that he had at least a newly discovered Rembrandt or Stradivarius. Imagine our utter chagrin to discover that he was bringing, of all things, two mice caught in the same trap. And he wanted us to take a picture of him holding this atrocity, and run it in the paper! Ahearn wasted no time. He told him such a picture would have about as much news or human interest value as a dish of cold hominy. The man, his feelings crushed but his anger inflamed, seized his prize and stormed out of the office swearing he'd cancel his subscription to the *News-Times* and take the *Tribune*.

Truck gardeners are another hazard to the city editor's peace of mind. They dig up a turnip or potato that has a human form and come trudging in to claim their fame. The first one or two of these offerings were accepted because we liked to please our rural subscribers.

But it's like printing a baby picture. Hundreds more follow. So we made it a rule that the vegetable had to look like the President or Myrna Loy before we would print it.

There's no denying the fact that the more interesting assignments made routine work seem like wading in a creek after you'd been swimming in the ocean. Covering the Western Open Golf Championship practically spoiled me for an entire summer. My job was to visit with the wives of the golfers and write a daily feature about them, the while Jim Costin and Elmer Danch covered the tournament, and Dick Jackson wrote the side lights.

I met Mrs. Abe Espinoza, Mrs. Byron Nelson, Mrs. Harold McSpaden, Mrs. Jimmy Thomson and a number of others. I found them sitting under a tree knitting and talking about what their men liked to eat. I gave a separate story to Mrs. Thomson, because she is the former Viola Dana of the old silent days in the movies. She said she didn't regret a bit giving up her career to be the famous golfer's wife and that she enjoyed traveling around to country clubs where Jimmy played in tournaments. She looked forward to the day when they would be settled in one place long enough to warrant building their own home. I quoted her exactly in my story and the next day she looked me up to thank me for doing so.

Johnny Revolta won the tournament and I nailed him for an interview as soon as he came into the club house. He looked a little uncomfortable and said, "Well, do you mind waiting while I make a phone call?" I said no and he went off. When he came back he was all smiles. "I wanted to call my wife first thing and tell her," he said. His devotion impressed me and I made his call the lead of my story.

Before the tournament was over, I made the acquaintance of a local woman, Mrs. Joseph E. Neff, a meeting which both of us found advantageous. Mrs. Neff, who was chairman of the rules committee for the Women's Western Golf Association, had been holding golf clinics for women members of country clubs throughout the Middle West, explaining to players what they ought to know about tournaments, rules, and effective season programs. Because it was such a good idea, and because Mrs. Neff had had really astonishing successes, I thought I scented better than a local story, so I wrote to Grantland Rice, editor of *The American Golfer*, and asked if he would like an article on it and he said he would. I wrote one and got paid all of thirty-five dollars for it—and Mr. Rice gave me a by-line.

As a result of the story Mrs. Neff was invited to the Pacific Coast to hold a series of clinics. She was so good that even the men became interested, and a group of them in Portland asked her to go over a course there, which was laid out so badly it couldn't be played with any fun. She made ten or a dozen suggestions for changing it, and the men adopted every one of them.

As I look back at this assignment I remember it with the greatest pleasure. But I did get one awful case of sunburn out of it. My arms were so blistered and drawn up that I couldn't straighten them out for a week.

When I was working both in society and general

news I discovered a "double play" on the part of a publicity chairman that gets the record. The Woodmen of the World have five branches of women's auxiliaries, and each branch has a particular function of its own. I had been printing small items about their activities for more than a year, when I took over society. The first morning the publicity chairman called me and gave me a report for the club column. Later in the morning when I had moved over to my news desk she called again with the same item.

"Why, you just gave that to me an hour ago," I said, "for the society page."

"Yes, I know," she replied, "but this is for the news page with one of those little headlines."

I protested. "We don't publish the same item twice in different parts of the paper."

"You've been doing it," she informed me. "The national lodge is giving a prize to the local group that gets most publicity and I've been calling each department up there for some time now. I want to get the prize."

"You've got it already, as far as I'm concerned," I told her. "I'm sorry but from now on you can have your items on the society page, or in the news section, but not in both."

She thought this over for a moment. "Well," she said, "I'll have them in the news section because those little headlines make them look longer."

It's just things like that that made me—oh well. Let's talk about something else.

One of my pet stand-bys was the St. Joseph County Medical Society. South Bend has more than its fair share of able physicians and surgeons. Probably one of the best-known members is Dr. A. S. Giordano, clinical pathologist for the South Bend Medical Laboratory. He received recognition for his work in isolating the Malta fever germ. He is also secretary-treasurer of the American Pathologists Association. The laboratory is a non-profit organization backed by local medical men. But it has done work for various doctors and hospitals from Pennsylvania to California.

It was Dr. Giordano who urged the local society to give a season of its programs to catching up on cancer diagnosis and cure. A session was conducted by a medical man from the University of Illinois who showed motion pictures of cancer treatment. One picture, I remember, demonstrated the effect of radium treatment on the malignant growth. Said the doctor, as the cancer dissolved: "That is the most impressive demonstration of death by disintegration I have ever seen." He said it so profoundly that I thought for a moment the patient had died. But no, it was the live cancer cells going to their doom that he was referring to.

My series of articles on these meetings attracted a good bit of attention from the readers, and one of the medical society members told me sixty per cent more people offered themselves at local hospitals and physicians' offices for cancer diagnosis after the stories were printed than before.

When Dr. R. L. Sensenich, local man, was president of the Indiana Medical Society, the state convention was held in South Bend and I covered it. One of the meetings I was most interested in was a lecture by a New

York physician on the reduction of pneumonia fatalities through the use of serum. I had written scores of obituaries on pneumonia victims and I thought an extensive report on the new treatment might do some good. I don't know what it did for my readers, but it was one of the biggest breaks I ever had. A month later my own father was sent to the hospital with the disease. He was in Fort Wayne at the time and I told the physician attending him that I wanted the pneumonia typed and serum given. The doctor looked at me in amazement and said, "How do you know about serum? There aren't too many doctors know about it, let alone lay people." So I told him. In twenty-four hours Dad's case had been typed and the serum given and in another day he was on the road to recovery.

But medicine was not the only science whose doings transpired in Hell's Half-Acre. It was there that I met paleontology head-on, too. I was thrilled because long ago, when I was seven years old, I had almost become a paleontologist myself. It happened this way:

Although I was born in a small town I am essentially a city gal. My home was located within spitting distance of the center of the business district and if I wanted to commune with nature I had my choice of looking for four-leaf clovers in a small grass patch in front of the house, or sitting on the curbstone in the shade of a solitary maple tree that grew up through the sidewalk. I accepted my lot gladly until I was old enough to read, and then I found out that the boys and girls in story books were always going off to "the country" when school was out. I had not yet reached the age of discretion which permits me to say, "Thank God, I am not as other men are," and I was troubled by this exodus of young fiction characters. If it was the thing to do, I wanted to do it.

So I took my father into my confidence. "Dad," I said, "I want to go to the country."

He thought about it for a minute. Finally he said, "All right." He called a taxicab and we went to the country. He stopped the driver at a green pasture near a patch of woods and told him to come back for us later. We climbed over a fence and he looked around, selected a tree and lay down in its shade. "Go ahead and play," he said, "this is the country."

So while he took a nap, I ran around in the sun, and then lay down and rolled on the grass, and then got up and plunged into the woods. And there I discovered a treasure. Actually it was a calf's skull. But to me it was an historical find. I had learned about cave-men and dinosaurs at school, and I felt certain these were genuine Stone Age bones. I picked up the dreadful-looking thing, brushed the dirt off and decided to lay it on my Dad's stomach so I wouldn't forget it when we were ready to go. It was there grinning at him, without teeth and without eyes, when he woke up, and it very nearly frightened him into a collapse. He let me keep it, however, and take it home. But Mother said no when I wanted to exhibit it in the parlor from atop the piano.

Throwing it away was unthinkable, so I took it to the County Historical Society Museum and gave it to the curator. She thanked me for it and said she would put it beside Daniel Boone's gun. This gun, which had belonged to Miles Morgan, my great-grandfather and Daniel's gunsmith, had been a gift of my family.

So when I met Dr. Marcus W. Lyon, Jr., a South Bend doctor and president of the American Mammalogists' Society, I shared a fellow feeling as he told me about the Kankakee swamps where red-winged blackbirds flew among the cattails, and the bones of mammoths and mammals were buried. I even got a scoop on some bones that were dug up there, and we had a good feature story with pictures and a statement from the doctor that Indiana ought to keep the bones in the state for historical reasons. But the state had no provision for buying them, and the Buffalo, N. Y., Museum had, so the farmer on whose land they were found sold them for good money.

One summer three of the boys on the *News-Times* and one on the *Tribune* decided they would make a little extra money. Smitten with this idea were Dick Jackson, Jim Doran and Winchell Royce, of the *News-Times*, and Popsy Johnson of the opposition. They organized, promoted and staged "The Midwest Aviation Show." Winchell had previously had some connection with aviation publicity and had the contacts necessary to get the proper performers.

Ted Fordan and Art Davis, ace performers, were among those taking the air, as well as the Bat Boy from Lansing, Mich., who later fell to his death in France. The show was on for two days and was a thrill-packed affair with smoke screens, aerial dog fights, tail spins, parachute leaps. Planes were landed at sixty miles an hour. Pilots showed their skill by picking up handkerchiefs with wing tips. A short race with four planes participating was the climax. It was probably the finest air show ever put on, excepting the annual Cleveland air races.

In fact, the advance publicity indicated it was going to be good enough to be a success, and thereupon the publishers of the papers began to worry for fear the boys would make some money out of it. So they cracked down on the publicity and the coverage was only a fraction of that given the golf tournament. As a result, the boys were out $400 each when the accounts were settled. To Dick and Jim and Winchell and Popsy, a quart of rye apiece. To the publishers for their small potato act, the back of my hand.

One afternoon I was all set to go to Lake Michigan, spend the night with some friends, and come back the next morning. As always, Frank Ahearn caught me with a smile on my face, figured I was up to having some private life, and at three-thirty, just fifteen minutes before I would be on my way, he said, "Miss Smallzried, take a photographer and go interview Mrs. John Ringling."

Now this was more than just an assignment. If I didn't do a good job I would get my goddam neck wrung and nobody knew it better than I. For next to the sea, Frank loved circuses better than anything there is. The day Dexter Fellows, of blessed memory, came into the office with advance publicity on "the greatest show on earth" his eyes lit up, and he lit up, too, all nerves and fury, the way he was when we were getting out an extra. One time Frank sent Hope Halpin up to

Kalamazoo to spend a day with the circus from the time it was set up until it was taken down and shipped on to South Bend. Hope did a bang-up story on it, too. But much good that did me and my Lake Michigan plans.

I discovered from Mr. Fellows, who was in the office, that Mrs. Ringling would be found in her private car at the end of the line on the siding. He smiled and gave me two tickets to the evening performance. Both the smile and the tickets were good medicine and went a long way toward curing my sulks.

Freddy Carlisle, one of our photographers, accompanied me. We trudged over what seemed like miles of railroad track to find the right car. Once there I knocked on a screen door and a voice inside said, "Well, what do you want?" It was such a sharp voice that I was taken off guard and felt myself turning a little red. "I—ah, I wanted to interview Mrs. Ringling for the *News-Times*," I said. There was a moment's pause and the voice said, "Well, what are you waiting for?" Laughter followed this remark, and a woman said, "I guess Charlie has settled it."

I walked in feeling very confused. Lots of people hated me for unwanted publicity I had given them, and some people petted me for good space they had had. But seldom did anyone treat me with contempt. I wasn't used to it, and I didn't like it.

Expecting a shrew, I was agreeably surprised to find an attractive, elderly woman, Mrs. John Ringling. I got a little history of her, which I have forgotten, but it included where she was born, how she met Mr. Ringling, what she did while she traveled with the circus. I recall that she liked to read Willa Cather's books.

I had recovered my composure by this time and was enjoying my visit when a voice behind me went "Awwrrrrk," and I nearly jumped into Mrs. Ringling's lap. I turned around and saw a bright-eyed parrot regarding me with extraordinary curiosity.

"That's Charlie," said Mrs. Ringling.

"Charlie!" I was dumbfounded. "You mean he's the one that let me in?"

"Yes," she said. "He has an unusual sense of the right thing to say, and sometimes the wrong thing. For instance, my daughter-in-law was sitting in the window of the car the other day when one of the workmen walked by. Charlie heard him and said, 'Well, why don't you come in?' The poor man looked up surprised and the girl was too embarrassed to know what to do."

From that point on I didn't worry about my story for Mr. Ahearn. When a parrot grants an interview, it's a natural.

One time I was sent to Notre Dame to cover a lecture and demonstration of the electric eye. The little tube with its supersensitive filament can do any number of useful services, but the one that interested me most was its ability to translate what it saw into sound. I remember that it played a musical disk by peering through the perforations thereon. I shudder to think what this may eventually mean. We may turn on our radios some day and hear a voice saying: "Good evening, Mr. and Mrs. America, this is your friend the electric eye. What

I saw today has been censored by the public morals committee. Good night."

Notre Dame was a frequent source of news. When His Eminence, Eugenio, Cardinal Pacelli, now His Holiness, Pope Pius XII, was touring the United States, he stopped at the university to receive an honorary degree. I was sent to cover the ceremony and took my friend, Dorothy Roberts, with me. It's a good thing I did, too. His Eminence spoke very rapidly with a difficult accent and since she can take shorthand, I asked her to make a record for me. After the ceremony I ran into Tom Barry, Notre Dame publicity man, and he was clawing the air, because the Cardinal hadn't given a copy of his speech to the press representatives, and nobody had understood what he said. Here was one of the most important functions the university had ever staged practically stillborn. So Dorothy and I smirked and said the *News-Times* wouldn't need a copy, anyway. Tom lured us into his office and kept us there until Dorothy had transcribed her notes on his typewriter. Later, he distributed her carbons among the other reporters, and the day was saved. Why didn't we get a scoop, you want to know? Because the event didn't have enough important news value to make an issue of it.

Ross Nelson, my city editor at this time, told me His Eminence had been sent to this country because he was to be the next Pope. It was sort of an open secret around South Bend and I was surprised when the late Pope Pius XI died to find in press notices preceding his election that His Eminence was given very little chance of being successor. If I had only been on a paper then, what a scoop I would have had!

If you are ever in a newspaper office and hear some of the staff members talking about "canned editorials," or "canned features," you may know they are referring to material supplied by newspaper syndicates. For instance, every paper can't afford a full-time cooking editor, Washington correspondent, Paris fashion editor —or lovelorn editor. Hence they subscribe to Prudence Penny, Dorothy Dix and company. The local readers don't realize this. I know, because when I first went to the paper our agony editor was Annie Laurie and her work was sent us by N.E.A., I think. But every now and then we would have a phone call asking for Annie, and then one of the boys, in great glee, would call any of the girls who happened to be handy to the phone. My turn came one morning after I had been particularly hard at it and had decided to take a little extra time for lunch and blow myself to some ravioli. I had my gloves on and was considering my hat when the ax fell. Bob O'Hara (brother to the president of Notre Dame and our desk man, a pal if there ever was one, who had taught me to play Russian Bank) was the rat who called me to the phone.

"It's for Annie Laurie," he whispered.

"Yes?" I said sweetly, as I made a face at Bob.

"Would you help me plan my wedding?" a voice asked.

"I'd be glad to." I wanted to add that I was better at planning funerals, but let it go.

"I want to know what the bridesmaids should wear."

I had no more idea what the bridesmaids should wear than Shirley Temple, so I called for time out to think about it, and countered with, "What are you wearing?"

"Why, a white dress with a wedding veil," the voice answered surprised.

"Why don't you have the girls wear white?" I asked. "That would be different."

"Oh, I couldn't do that," my friend remarked. "That would detract from me."

We were stymied for a moment. Finally she said, "Do you think lace mitts or white kid gloves would be better?"

Glad that the dresses were disposed of I said, "Kid gloves."

"Why?" she wanted to know. This was too much. She not only wanted my help, she wanted theory, too. I was hungry and thinking about my lunch.

"Well, kid gloves or ravioli," I said.

"Or what!"

"They can wear kid gloves any time, and the lace mitts only on certain occasions."

"What about their hats?" she asked next.

How should I know what about their hats! I gave it a thought and replied, "Well, they better get straw picture hats of a neutral color. Then they can wear them often and not just with the dresses."

"Say," she said, "how did you know these girls had to make the clothes do for something else besides my wedding?"

Huh! How did I know? And me making only $13.60 a week!

I'd Tell You if I Could

The last thing I ever expected to do was to come back from getting a story and find a virgin-white satin ribbon tied around my typewriter. But I did. I thought I saw the fine Italian hand of my colleagues in it somewhere. For months they had been looking for a chance to toast me about the part I was taking in the W.C.T.U. and apparently that chance had come. My only misstep was that I'd got friendly with the officers of the temperance union as I listened sympathetically to their telephoned publicity. I knew the names of the members, the order of the programs, and in fact, the whole thing backwards and forwards.

My eyes lit up with something supposed to pass for delight and I said, "What's this?"

Jo Crabill answered, "While you were out the president of the W.C.T.U. called, and I tried to take the item, and I had some trouble. Finally she said, 'Oh, I wish Kay Smallzried was there. I can talk to her just like she was one of us.'"

Everyone in the office whooped at this and I did too, and Jo continued, "If she could see you just once, just one of the times I've seen you putting it away like so much water—"

I tell that little joke on myself conscious of the fact that some people will say, "Just another drunken reporter." The profession, if it is known for nothing else, is known for its inebriety. "Why do reporters drink so much?" people ask, as though drinking were a class

266

mark appropriate only to newsmongers—like stigmata for saints.

I'd tell you if I could, but it's one of those things. You won't believe it when I say all newspaper people don't drink. If I had worked on the *Tribune*, for instance, I would be writing a vastly different story. The publisher of the *Trib* was not only a dry, but he didn't even approve of cigarettes, and his reporters and editors were good boys and girls. There are newspapers throughout the land whose city editors do not swear and never, never take a drink. Of those institutions I know nothing and care to know still less.

So we'll leave it that I worked on a newspaper where a drink was acceptable to the staff members the same as it is to you guys. All right. But some reporters take too much, and then the things they do are pure, unpredictable poetry, however bitter the smack. They have a natural scorn of people, generated by their experience, which comes out when their self-control is taking a well-earned rest.

Whatever story I tell here will be as it was told to me, for newspaper boys are funny and would much rather go around and drink in company with each other than to have girl reporters tagging along. Of course there were times when we drank together, but it was when they were having stag sessions that the more colorful and legendary stories were realities.

One Sunday morning early, just after the paper had gone to press, the boys went out to have a few drinks before going to bed. Herman, our tall, rangy police reporter, fell silent. Such a life, thought he, such a police force! All they do is play dirty hearts. Nothing but dirty hearts! A man needs action—needs to know that the ripple in his shirt sleeve is not an overdose of starch doled out by a Chinese laundryman. Herman looked over at Algy. The latter's supreme creative effort for the day had been a piece about new machinery for the boys' vocational school.

"Algy," said Herman, a tentative note in his voice, "I'd like to take a friendly poke at you. Do you mind?"

Now Algy knew exactly where that proposition stemmed from. He knew that when a boy gets up from making the neighbor's kid holler " 'nough" in his last adolescent fight, a satisfaction goes out of his life that will never be replaced. Let Herman swear never so loudly at the police—it was no comfort. He could lick every man-jack on the force. And the blushing face of the chief poring over one of Herman's stories would never give Herman the thrill that seeing the chief's nose bloody from a good left hook would have provided. Like a knight in flower, Algy stood up. "No," he said slowly. "I don't mind if you hit me."

Herman rose, measured the blow and the time, and let fly straight into Algy's mouth. Algy staggered, but his opponent's arms were around him lowering him gently to his chair. "Thanks, awfully," whispered Herman.

"That's all right," said Algy removing a tooth, "it was loose anyway."

That little story, my friends, is not of two roust-abouts, but of two sensitive young men fully aware that life is not what it had at first seemed to be.

There is a notion current among writers and artists and club women that sensitivity is the exclusive possession of individuals who can point to their hearts and murmur about "something in here." That is pure rot! Being sensitive is a process, and its direction is from outside, in, and not inside, out. A tender heart'll get along. But a tender skin is something else again. And it's a sad fact that a good newspaper man has got to keep a sensitive hide or he'll be no good. Being sensitive is his stock in trade.

And another thing! Newspaper work is a profession entered into during youth. When I went onto the paper I was the youngest member of the staff. I was twenty. Pi Warren, the news editor, was the oldest and he was approaching thirty. McCready Huston, the managing editor, was not yet forty. When Carl Cooper came to the paper he was in his late forties and he was the dean of newspaper men in the town.

Newspaper work, then, is something you grow up with. A personnel manager in an automobile factory may give up his job to become secretary of a Chamber of Commerce, or welfare director in an oil company, or program-maker for the Camp Fire Girls, Inc. But he will not take up reporting or editorial writing.

Since it is a lifetime work, it shapes and seasons, builds up and sometimes tears down its people. Young folk are notably self-centered, serious and sensitive. Your cub reporter is no exception. But with about two oaths from the city editor, he is cured of his conceit. A close-up of clergy and club women purge him of taking life seriously.

But when he finds out that ideals and ideas are as good as the people who are putting them in effect, and not one bit better—his sensitivity asserts itself and he takes up the cudgels against insincerity, intolerance, hypocrisy and false respectability. That is, he would like to take them up. But he can't—his job is to report what he sees, not kill it.

If a reporter calls a business man a bastard, it doesn't mean he himself is a Communist, but simply that his sense of decent behavior has been outraged by the b.m. and quite likely the b.m. *is* a bastard. What has this to do with drinking? Well, the paper runs a story on the b.m.'s having lectured before a club on the sacredness of the American Home, and everybody on the sheet will know that the b.m. has been stepping out on his wife for years. Make no mistake, now. They don't care that he philanders. But let him keep his dirty mouth shut and his picture out of the paper in connection with the sacredness of the American Home. Meantime the boys'll have a drink to get the taste out of their mouths.

People who eat a variety of rich food often have indigestion, and newspaper reporters on a diet of varied experience are subject to the same trouble. It's hard to swallow a lot of the facts. And just as brandy settles the stomach, it also settles indignation.

CHAPTER XVII

Blazes

NOTE: IT WAS SAID of Calvin Coolidge, I believe, that
he wanted put on his tombstone, "Here lies a man who
knew his limitations." In this chapter I have met the
boundaries of my own limitations and I am the first to
recognize it.

I never covered a fire.

Not that I didn't have a few experiences with fires.
One Sunday afternoon when I was sitting in the living
room looking out the window, I saw the press room of
the *Tribune* flare up suddenly and become a solid mass
of flame. I went calmly to the phone and called the fire
department.

Next day I told the gang at the office about it and
they looked at me dumbfounded. "Why in hell," they
asked, "didn't you let the damn thing burn to the
ground?"

They were secretly proud of me, nonetheless, and

Pi Warren had Phil Nicar write a story about how a *News-Times* reporter rescued the opposition from ruin. The *Tribune* staff, although they knew about it, carried never a word of my good deed. Mort Reed asked me if the publisher thanked me or made any acknowledgment and I said, "No." He shook his head, unable to understand such indifference.

Another time I was about to stop at the office with some St. Mary's items I was bringing into town. The fire wagon rushed by me, proceeded to the next block and stopped in front of my own home. The roof was on fire.

I hastened along after them and dashed in to save my copy of Rockwell Kent's *The Lovers* and saw the family was comfortably seated in the living room, watching the sweating firemen through the window. They looked up at me and smiled, and I paused. "The roof's on fire," I said.

"Yes," said Mother, "we know."

I didn't know what to say to keep the conversation alive. I thought Cooky ought to be stirring around trying to get the piano out and Mother might at least be rolling up our imitation Orientals.

"Does Dad know?" I asked.

"Yes," said Ellie. "He's upstairs asleep, and Mother went up and woke him and said, 'The house in on fire,' and he said, 'What do you care, it ain't our house, we only rent it.' "

I remembered suddenly that two of my grandmother's brothers, Mike and Dan, had once deliberately burned down Dan's river house, which he had built himself, simply because they had a bottle and felt like celebrating.

At this point Mercy Prell, who lives across the street, appeared in our midst, having come through the back door. She seemed not to have noticed we were afire— or maybe it was just social tact. Anyway, she was holding a dark-looking glass jar above her head. "Could I interest you in some pickled prunes the grocer sent by mistake?" she inquired.

I don't know what happened next, because that was the moment when I gathered myself together and stole away.

But these were unofficial fires, so to speak. I never got to one in my capacity as reporter (in spite of the fact that I had a fire- and police-line pass) because girls simply were not sent to fires. The reason for this is supposed to be something vaguely chivalrous, as that we might get killed. Actually, however, girls aren't sent because the boys want to go themselves. Fires are the last frontier of hardy manhood. So I've asked George Scheuer to let me put here a revised feature he once wrote for the *News-Times*:

By George A. Scheuer

COVERING FIRES can get to be quite a hobby, sometimes even an obsession. A newspaper with a few fire fans on its staff is certain to have excellent coverage of any "good" blaze no matter where or at what ungodly hour it should "ring in."

The old *News-Times*, of happy memory, had in the

person of Gerald Holland, then officially designated as Sunday editor, a fire-truck follower second to none. When I came onto the *News-Times* Holland's desk was just under the office fire bell, and the chart of box locations was pasted to the wall at his back. He knew most of the common ones without consulting the list and was always on the lookout for a "district ten." That district, at least during the prohibition days, was popular with amateur firemen because it was well dotted with spots where the inner fire might be quenched after the other blaze was under control.

Holland saw some really good fires with me. We were often alone in the office after the "pre-date" or morning mail edition rolled so when the bell tapped out one that sounded interesting we hopped into my Chevvy and investigated. If I couldn't get away Holland sometimes took a taxi and called me in case the fire turned out to be a good one. The night the engineering building burned at Notre Dame he couldn't get through on a regular telephone line so he found a cab stand and had the dispatcher relay the word to me.

That turned out to be quite a night for the fire laddies, for after we had seen the Notre Dame blaze under control and were back at the office pounding out some notes on it for the day staff, a good "tenth district" rang in. We were just in the mood for that and lost no time getting out there. It was a junk yard and not very spectacular so we soon deserted it, only to find next day that the damage reached something like ten times what the fire chief had thought when we walked it off. Burning rubber never did smell good to us.

Despite his name, Holland was what I would call a "rabid" Irishman. He was born in Canada and came to Hoosierland via the sunny state of California, but before all else he was Irish. The night foreman of the composing room sometimes accompanied us on these runs, especially if one came in about his quitting time of 2 A.M. He loved to twit Holland about his Irish pride, and was along the night the wild Irishman got the shock of his life.

It was "district ten" again and turned out to be a Negro pool room. Jerry, always painstaking, picked his way through the tangle of hose to check the name and address of the place on its front window. There in big block letters was the name, "O'Brien's Pool Hall." Earl Rutherford, that was our printer pal, never forgot that. Nor did he let Jerry forget it.

We ran into some pathetic ones, such as tar-paper-covered shacks in which children were trapped and fatally burned. In one blaze in a district near the city limits there was some delay about the fire department's answer to the call, as the first telephoned alarm went to the adjoining city of Mishawaka. By the time the firemen figured out which station should answer the call a grandmother and several children were suffocated. Meanwhile two frantic girls, one of them a proofreader at our paper, and their escorts were pounding on the side of the house and making repeated attempts to fight their way through the smoke to rouse the occupants. My job on that was to call on various neighbors, some of them relatives, and run down school group pictures, snapshots, or any other available photographs of the children.

The proofreader, Elizabeth Anderson, dictated a swell story that would put any sob sister to shame with its reality and heartfelt pathos. She later became an obit writer and eventually was society editor of the sheet.

Jerry and I also "attended" one fire—I still can not get myself to say we covered it, because we didn't. That's just the trouble. It was a Saturday night with a Sunday morning paper coming up, but somehow I happened to be off duty and Jerry, who had quit the *News-Times* a few weeks before, was back in town for the week end. We were celebrating his new job over a pair of brandies at a night club. We were both "sippers" and hated to be rushed with our serious drinking, but a good fire was something else. We heard the sirens and phoned the office to ask "Where?"

It was "district ten" and to keep up old tradition we couldn't let it pass. The bar-keep set the freshly poured brandies back for us and we were off.

A bungalow in the foreign neighborhood was the scene. Apparently a cigarette had ignited the upholstering of a davenport or chair. There was lots of smoke but the damage seemed confined to one room at the front of the house. It was pretty much of a mess when we went up onto the porch to talk to the firemen. They had given the place a good soaking and had ripped the furniture apart with their usual effectiveness so there were heaps of upholstering scattered about. The lights were out, too, and all we could see was what the firemen's lights happened to catch.

The side window of an adjoining room was out and one of the firemen said a man had jumped through it. We hunted up the man, whom we found clad in his pants and undershirt. He said, "Sure, I jumped out of the window. I was taking a nap and when I smelled smoke I just jumped up and started running. When I came to the window I just went right through."

His wife had been the only other occupant of the house although there seemed to have been a party there earlier in the evening. He had been told his wife was at a neighbor's but hadn't seen her yet. We couldn't find anyone at a couple of the neighboring houses we tried, so we decided she was in the crowd.

The firemen were still soaking down the upholstery when we checked out. After stopping at a filling station to phone the office what we had on the smudge we went back to the brandy we had parked on the backbar. Halfway down the glass I was called to the phone.

The city editor wanted to know why we hadn't told him a woman died in the fire. We didn't believe it, but he said we were nuts because the coroner had been called to the scene. This time we didn't park the drink. There was only one finger to go so we killed it and went back to the fire.

There we found the police ambulance crew carrying a woman's body out of that front room at the door of which we had chatted with the fire laddies. When the smoke died down they had found her curled up in a corner where they had thrown some upholstery. The coroner told us his verdict probably would be "death by suffocation."

The filling station we had phoned from before was closed up then so one of our police pals got a garage near by to open up for us to phone.

And after that short delay we went back for another brandy in which to drown the ignominy of having overlooked the body.

There were fires and fires, but Holland had to miss the biggest wild-goose chase of them all. That was the Edwardsburg, Michigan, mill fire.

It broke late one afternoon when a telephone operator tipped us off. Edwardsburg is a small town within the trading area of South Bend, and the only mill we could think of was the Central Michigan Grain Corporation's elevator. We used their grain quotations every day on the market page. Their plant was right next to an oil company's bulk station. With visions of the oil tanks blowing up most of Edwardsburg we decided this fire would have to be covered.

Since "pictures tell more than words," there must be good photographs of the fire, too. Ralph (Dutch) Hennings, sometimes called Hemmingdorfer, was the chief photog and had a fast car so I hopped in with him and we were off.

We watched the sky line for smoke as we neared Edwardsburg but failed to sight even a smudge. Soon we could even see the towering elevator itself and as we pulled up business seemed to be going on as usual.

The fire, we soon learned, had been on the other side of the railroad in a little old feed and flour mill. When we finally arrived on the scene there was nothing left but the foundation and some smoldering embers.

Across the street we located the man who had owned and operated the mill in a barnlike structure that had been more than fifty years old. He was sitting in a battered and slightly charred rocking chair he had saved from the fire. Dutch made a shot of him there while I asked about the mill and the fire.

It hadn't been a very profitable business, he said, with most farmers either selling their grain or taking it to places with more modern equipment. He had managed to get along, however, by keeping down expenses. The mill had been his home, too, with a bunk and a stove in one corner he had boarded off. A kitchen cabinet, a trunk and some tools were about all he'd saved besides the chair. He was quite proud of having saved the chair. "Darn comfortable old chair. I made it myself," he mused. "Don't know what I'd have done without it."

He didn't seem as much concerned about the loss of the mill as he did about getting me to promise that I'd send him a couple of copies of the previous day's paper. When I asked why he wanted that issue instead of the one which would carry the story of the fire, he explained that his daughter had just died and yesterday's paper carried the account of her funeral. "I want to save it," he said. There he sat, with all he had left of a lifetime's work the little rubble around him. His family, his home, his business were gone. And what he most wanted was a newspaper clipping.

He was going to stay with one of the neighbors and said to have the papers sent there. (Sure, I sent them, together with what we used on his fire.)

Dutch, meanwhile, took a shot of the foundation but

was quite disappointed at not getting there soon enough to get some smoke and flame.

The old man said he thought one of the firemen took a picture. With that clue we were off to find the volunteer fireman who took time to photograph a fire.

The fire truck, a red Ford with a chemical tank and a couple of ladders, was kept in a garage so we went there to see if the garage man, who drove the truck, knew which fireman had the camera. He didn't know but he thought the barber next door, who rated as "chief" of the department, might know.

The barber was shaving a customer but didn't mind talking to us while business went on. He paused now and then to gesture with his razor while telling us his story of the fire and giving directions to the house of the fireman who might have taken the picture. The customer, too, rose up now and then to put in his "two bits' worth."

Our next stop was at the home of the fireman the barber and his customer thought might have taken the picture. He hadn't, however, and was more interested in telling us about a new fishing rod he was setting up when we found him in the garage. He thought a boy from Mishawaka who had been visiting a farm home a mile and a quarter west of town had been there with a camera and might have a picture.

We found the farmhouse and when the farmer's wife finally got the idea that we wanted a picture, and not some "spring fries" a roadside sign advertised, she said it was taken by a boy friend of her niece. She told us where the niece lived in Mishawaka and added that the boy worked at a gasoline filling station on the north side of Mishawaka, the one on the south side of the street at the cemetery.

A stop at the filling station brought us to the boy who had taken the picture. It was his girl's camera, however, and she had gone to a movie, he thought. We stopped at her house just to make sure and found no one at home. After another stop at the filling station to ask the boy to get the film and bring it to us the first thing in the morning, we went back to the office.

Dutch got to worrying about the chance that the Mishawaka contingent might forget all about bringing in the picture, so later that evening he drove over to the girl's house and on the promise of making prints of all the pictures on the roll got the film we had rambled over a couple of counties seeking.

With forebodings of a foggy negative or some other photographic disaster Dutch went into the darkroom and I started to get caught up with the work I had dropped. When Dutch pulled the negative out of the soup for a look before drying it he yelled for me. It was a perfect shot of the fire. The building was still intact but smoke was pouring out in one great cloud that blotted out the sky.

We ran the picture on the first page of the "state" edition, along with a piece detailing our search for it. The city editor was a fire fan, too, and grabbed the whole works for the city edition, so Dutch didn't have a bit of trouble collecting mileage for the tour.

CHAPTER XVIII

Sex Appeal from a Convent

IN THE SPRING OF 1932 there was very little news with any lightheartedness in it, the depression being what it was. So the city editors were put to it to drum up ideas for features that would take a reader's mind off his troubles.

Ahearn, pouting about this situation at the city desk one day, looks over at me and says, "Smallzried, find out from Notre Dame and St. Mary's students what their ideal girl and ideal man are like."

I knew a boy at Notre Dame and I called him, told him to round up a few friends, and made a date to talk with them at Sorin Hall, a college dormity. I called Sister Marie Pieta, C.S.C., publicity director and journalism teacher at St. Mary's, and told her I'd like to interview some girls. Now she demurred at this and asked if it wouldn't be the same to have one of her journalism students write up the story I wanted and bring it in. I queried Ahearn and he said, "Decidedly no! You talk to them." I had one acquaintance among the students at the school, so I called her and told her to bring some girls and meet me in town.

Because of the repercussions which this story had I'm going to quote parts of it. Frank gave me seven-column headlines as follows:

IDEAL HUSBAND WILL BE TALKATIVE ST. MARY'S GIRLS SAY; NOTRE DAME BOYS SHUDDER AT "HOT CHA" TYPE OF HELP-MATE.

The boys' story comes first:

Equal privileges to the double standard, the right to smoke, the right to drink and other contested matters of ethics were granted to girls by a room full of Notre Dame seniors but—

The ideal girl of 1932 will have a sense of humor, femininity, mental and physical attractiveness, frankness, sobriety, some college education, and loyalty. . . .

Picture a room in a college dormitory. There is a desk with assorted textbooks, *English Poetry, Logic, Metaphysics,* a picture of Knute Rockne, one of Norma Shearer, a drawing or two and perhaps a cartoon. There will be a trunk, suitcase, several chairs and a cot.

Seven seniors are gathered about a reporter who has just asked: "What has the ideal girl of 1932?"

"Money," said the Cynic. (The Cynic liked to talk but begged to keep his name a secret.)

"Femininity," said the one who accentuated maturity with a cigar.

"A sense of humor," added a third.

And the remaining four simply look wise and say ummmmmmm—

"I want a girl from the Junior League, one who's been places and has a sense of values. One without illusions," declaimed the Cynic. . . .

"And I want one who knows where money comes from," said a Chicago chap. "I have just a certain amount of money to spend. If I like a girl and we enjoy going out we can go much oftener if the girl will go Dutch. If a girl is dependent at home it's different, of course."

It's quite all right for a girl to smoke, but let her buy her own cigarettes.

How about drinking? "If a girl can take a drink or two to be sociable and not get tight it is perfectly o.k.," came from a heretofore quiet member.

The ideal girl is to possess good looks accentuated by smart and neat clothes. She must be mentally attractive, be adept at small talk, but avoid sham and pseudo-sophisticated opinions.

The manly man asked for sobriety in the girl, meaning a certain reserve but not formal distance. She is to like necking in normal proportions.

"I don't expect a girl to kiss me the first time we go out, but I expect it the second or third time, and I expect frankness in the enjoyment of it," one stated.

"But," someone asked, "couldn't you go with a girl for six or eight weeks simply because you have common interests and a good time together?"

"A platonic friendship! Certainly not. Why, I've

never known the girl who could keep an interest of that kind going for six or eight weeks without necking, too." This from the Cynic. "There may be girls like that, two in a thousand perhaps."

The boys no longer believed in double standards of morality.

"Could you marry with any feeling of confidence?" he of the philosophy of life asked. "I could have optimism and trust but no confidence."

The rest admitted they would not be confident of the success of marriage. . . .

Girls are quite marriageable up to the age of thirty. It is better if she doesn't work after marriage and she must be adaptable to the home life her husband can provide her. The economic situation is to govern the size of the family. As a final touch she will not say: "hot cha," "ducky," "fetching," or "cute," and she will "understand moods."

––––––––

So much for the boys. I thought that, for a group in their later adolescence without much practical experience, they had done pretty well in thinking things out for themselves. They had actually mentioned "birth control" in speaking of governing the size of the family, but out of respect for the priests at the university I only hinted at it.

The university officials, however, were enraged at the story. The prefect of religion who edited a little religious bulletin printed an item in the sheet something like this:

"Spain has opened an institution for broken-down

scribes. We think of one writer of a certain feature story in a local paper recently as the first who ought to be nominated for admittance."

With nearly 3,000 students it was impossible for the officials to find the "culprits" who had given such uncensored confessions to the press. At St. Mary's, however, the situation was different. I quote from the girls' story:

If by any chance you (meaning a man) dress well, are an able conversationalist, have a job, dance well, have good manners, sincerity, frankness and a sense of humor, you are the ideal man for 1932. And the belles of St. Mary's will be ringing out for you! At least an interview with a group of St. Mary's girls indicates as much.

Over the remains of a pleasant tea, a reporter put the blunt question, "What about the ideal man of 1932?"

"Ability to cook," says the girl whose technique at giving the breakfast bacon a permanent wave may be a little weak—but can she wear clothes!

"Now, I'm engaged," says another with a practical, albeit romantic, air. "I think he should be an able conversationalist. Able to talk about small things."

"And of course he will dress well," this from all four.

"During the depression he should have a job," continues one, and another adds, "He shouldn't ask a girl to marry him unless his prospects are fairly good, and secure."

The girls, like the boys, felt that good dancing was taken for granted. . . .

The pleasures of courtship, if you don't mind or if you do, are to be continued after marriage.

"There is no sense," said the engaged girl, "in a fellow's thinking that simply because he's married he can let down, and not take you places, or keep as attractive, or open auto doors for you."

All the girls agreed, and furthermore stated that good manners were a decided requisite—but good manners without effeminacy. For he must be popular with the boys. And a mutual respect for each other's friends will be part of the bargain. He must hold his liquor well, smoke cigarettes or pipes.

There will be no going Dutch. The girls don't want a lot of money spent on them. And you shouldn't think that every girl is "gold digging" for every cent you have. After all, you know whether you can afford to take out the girl you want.

"He will treat a girl with intelligence, too," said the practical-minded one. "I mean with a respect for her intelligence and ideas. He won't act as though she might be a half-wit for having an idea of her own which disagrees with his."

"They will, of course, have things in common," a rather idealistic student was speaking, "an appreciation of art, music and literature."

"And he will be frank and sincere," a voice added, "and even-tempered and enthusiastic. He will also be a social equal."

You are wondering now if they spoke of love, the first kiss and such. The answer is—

"Kissing is o.k." But a spokesman continues, "I don't

believe in love at first sight, and petting is taboo. I don't believe in a fellow being so crude he tries to see how far a girl will go the first time he meets her. I don't like the—the—"

"Trial and error method?" it was suggested.

"Yes."

He is to appreciate a home and family as much as the girl. And the economic situation is to govern the size of the family. A college education is to be planned for the children from their birth, and preparations for it made from that time on.

Among the don'ts for boys are: don't be crude; don't croon off key; don't tell about your experiences with other girls; and finally, she of the twinkling eyes admonished, "Don't do a h——l of a lot of swearing."

———————

I thought that wasn't so bad, and there were a lot of newspaper people who thought it was pretty good, because the wire services carried a briefer rewrite on it. But what the nuns thought of it would terrify even so expert a sharpshooter as Westbrook Pegler.

In the first place, the president of the college called Mr. Ahearn and ordered him to come to her office. I sat at my desk waiting for him to return, wondering what in the etc. He appeared simply wreathed with smiles.

"I had to promise," he said, "never to send you to St. Mary's again on any assignment whatsoever."

(My, how he loved it when people hated me!)

The promise was o.k. with me. I could take 'em or leave 'em. But reports began to trickle into town about what had happened to the girls, and I felt sorry. I had told them never to confess they gave me the interview, and the school would never find out from me who had done it.

But the sisters called a convocation and announced that the student body would stay convened until the girls who had given that interview got up and apologized to the school and their classmates for their misstep.

The girls were young and they were embarrassed and frightened. They admitted their crime. In addition to the humiliation of public confession, they received heavy campus sentences all the way around. It wasn't long until one of them became afflicted with screaming nightmares, and another became hysterical. If these girls had wanted to, they could have said I misquoted them. The sisters would have taken their word against mine. I've seen lots of cheap publicity chiselers come up with the "misquoted" gag when they talk out of turn. But not so with my friends. I realize my admiration for them is put on record pretty late in the day and that it will not help them for what they suffered. Nevertheless I'm glad to say I think they were as good sports as I've ever met.

Alas for Mr. Ahearn's promise! When he gave it there were still three girls left on the *News-Times* staff. But the day came when there was only the society editor and me.

Each August 15th, Assumption Day, the Mother General and Council of the Order of Holy Cross Sisters announce the obediences for the coming year. In case you aren't up on your conventual terms an "obedience" is simply the job to which a nun is assigned. For instance, the president of the college may suddenly be changed to be principal of one of the high schools operated by the order. The sisters have many friends and relatives in South Bend and their assignments have a general news interest.

I was sent to get the list from one of the nuns acting for Sister Marie Pieta who was away on vacation.

Everything went fine until she asked me my name. I thought for a minute. I didn't want to get Ahearn in trouble and yet I wasn't so ashamed of anything I'd done that I wanted to give a false name. I said, "Sister, I'm Kay Smallzried."

She smiled. "You're the girl who wrote the story."

I nodded.

"That was a pretty good story," she said. "And besides you had to write it. It was your assignment."

She went on and told me the college was to have a new president, Sister M. Madeleva, poet and scholar, widely known in Catholic literary circles and also in the field of Chaucerian scholarship. The suggestion was made that I interview her and make my peace with the college.

If ever one thing led to another that first interview with Sister Madeleva was it. I observed her closely as she talked. She is small, has violet eyes, a radiant clear skin. The habit could not become her more if it had been designed by Schiaparelli. It is black with a deep white collar and a pleated halo topping the veil.

She explained to me that the classes at St. Mary's would be open to day students from South Bend. This was a new feature. Heretofore if a local girl wished to

attend the college, she had to live there and pay room
and board. Another innovation was the teaching of a
creative writing class by Sister Madeleva herself.
"Could a person enroll in that one class?" I asked.
And she said yes. I told her I would. After I got
away and was back at the office I wondered why I'd
said it. I no more wanted to study creative writing than
I wanted to take up steamfitting. I looked around the
office littered with waste paper and cigarette butts—I
saw the boys, their sleeves rolled up, mopping their
foreheads and cursing the weather. I thought of Sister
Madeleva, cool and serene, the spotless office with the
mingled odor of fresh-cut flowers and furniture polish.
The top of her desk looked like a fountain-pen advertisement clipped from *Vogue*. The top of mine could
easily pass for an illustrated fire hazard.

The comparison didn't end there, I knew. For her
mind was like her desk. She wrote down her thoughts
as they ought to be written. And I struggled with my
brain processes as Laocoön did with the snakes. What in
the world had I let myself in for, I wondered unhap-
pily? A hot September afternoon found me parted from
eighteen bucks, and for this good money I got a ring-
side seat with a group of creative writers listening to
Sister Madeleva.

Never mind about what I learned. This book ain't it.
As I sat in those classes, though, I did get a kick out of
being on forbidden territory. It all seemed so unlikely. I
confessed this feeling to Sister Marie Pieta, who was
also in the class. She smiled and was inclined to let bygones be bygones. Suddenly, without knowing why I

was doing it, I began telling Petey (as Sister Marie Pieta was known behind her back) that St. Mary's ought to hire me to be publicity director. If I worked for them, I pointed out, I couldn't write any more naughty stories.

When I was at the college it always seemed like being in another world. The buildings are beautiful cream-colored Gothic, massive and imposing. The interior is seductively rich, with marble floors and pillars in the halls, walnut walls, thick, thick rugs in the reception room, and furniture whose color and design might have been dreamed up by the tempted St. Anthony himself. Working there, I decided, I would have more time for what I referred to as "my writing." (I had started a novel and got to seventy pages. I knew I had to make it two hundred and seventy, because McCready Huston once told me it took at least that many pages to make a novel.)

The hand of God moves mysteriously, indeed. For in February or March He struck down both the dean and her assistant with appendicitis. Sister Marie Pieta was named dean of women, which meant she would have little time to do publicity for the college. She conferred with Sister Madeleva and Sister Frederick, dean of studies, and they hired me.

Just how much good I did that first spring I was there I don't know. I sent stories and pictures to newspapers in all parts of the United States and although I didn't have a clipping service, the girls told me that letters from their parents indicated my efforts were printed. I had a little talk with Sister Marie Pieta and told her if the girls could wear shorts instead of bloomers I could get lots more pictures printed. "You've got to have sex appeal," I said. To the horror of the conservative nuns the shorts were voted in.

Sex appeal from a convent! There it is. Not what you thought it was going to be, I'll bet. But you might as well know now that any slanderous propaganda about the behavior of nuns and priests is a downright lie. The wishful thinking of intolerant, bulbous-headed bigots like Klan members has always got my tag and I want to go on record as saying the conduct of all the nuns and priests I ever knew is of the finest.

I went back to the *News-Times* for the summer and promoted the Soap Box Derby, and then when school opened I returned again to St. Mary's. I had some misgivings about going back. I knew I was a bone of contention.

There was a situation there, and as I see it, it is one that is bound to develop in any convent. Most women enter convents very young, at sixteen or seventeen. Since they are in part withdrawn from the world they lose a sense of progress and change in method which the incoming younger sisters take for granted. The older sisters didn't see any sense in spending money for a publicity director, while the younger sisters, aware of the competition in the scholastic world, knew the investment was more than warranted.

I persuaded Sister Marie Pieta to subscribe to a clipping service so the college could have a check on my work. St. Mary's got more publicity that year than it ever had before. Sister Madeleva opened a smoking and recreation room for the students, and newspapers from coast to coast carried her remark that she didn't want St. Mary's girls to do "back alley" smoking.

She withdrew from the American Association of University Women because they went on record favoring birth control, and again the clippings poured in from all parts of the country.

Audiences were enchanted with her lectures and it was easy for me to pick out catchy quotations. Example:

"A question that comes into the discussion of poetry is 'Why should we write it?' And the first answer is as a means of self-expression, although, fingernail polish being what it is today, some easily find other means of self-expression."

Another time she was lamenting the complaint of some people that Middle English Chaucer is hard to read. Said she:

"Anyone who can read the sports pages can read Chaucer."

The students supplied copy in a routine fashion, for the most part. That is, I sent out pictures of those holding offices, winning scholastic and athletic honors. One day in convocation, however, they voted to support the United States in the event of any war, and I think I received more than fifty clippings from newspapers throughout the country on that story.

The big name in Notre Dame football then was Bill Shakespeare, and it was news when he came over to sing Christmas carols to the girls. You can imagine the "merry old England" story I made out of that. It appealed to editors, too, I guess, for it ended up by being a wire story. Once when Shakespeare came over to ice-skate on our lake I got a picture of him and one of the girls, and it was carried far and wide.

The result of this publicity, so one of the sisters told me, was a greater springtime inquiry for catalogues than the college had had since before the depression. This sister said she gave the publicity credit because the college had not altered its advertising program one bit. (As a matter of fact, the enrollment jumped to capacity the following year and the income stepped up nearly $100,000.)

That was my job. But nevertheless I was on the spot as a person. I sat up late playing bridge with the lay faculty members. I made a lot of noise with my heels when I walked down the hall. I was working on a novel with Dorothy Roberts, a member of the faculty. (I had shown her the seventy pages and she said, "There's lots of work to be done. Get busy!") I enrolled in Dorothy's Chaucer class and enjoyed it no end. My action was approved by some nuns, frowned upon by others. We missed the last bus out one night and asked a police officer friend of mine to take us out in the patrol wagon. And wasn't it true that I sat in on a Communistic circle in South Bend whose leader was a "fallen" Catholic? This last question made my flesh crawl with rage. This "leader" was indeed a friend of mine. But our circle had spent more time listening to Beethoven and discussing El Greco than it had given to the cause of Communism or any other "ism".

As spring rolled around again, I began to feel wrong

on my insides. I told Dorothy about it and she said, "Indiana Gothic doesn't agree with either one of us." She was right. I was all caught up with poverty, chastity and obedience.

Impressions were crystallizing in my mind. I thought about the gold satin, down-filled quilt which had been given to one of the sisters. Once when I stayed all night at the college another sister had put it on my bed as a little joke. I thought about the fine books, the elaborately carved statuary, the Holy Ghost chapel with its rich simplicity and purple stained windows, and I thought about the expensive gifts that are showered on the sisters at Christmas and Easter time as mail trucks drive up and unload. For that matter, I thought about the simple minimum which membership in the order guarantees—clothes, shelter, food, education, medical and dental care. And finally I thought about the years abroad at Oxford and the Sorbonne which the more brilliant sisters seem to rate.*

Shortly before Commencement it was my job to go among the lay faculty and collect money for a gift we were giving as a group. I stopped at Marta's room— Marta was a widow with one child. She laid me out a dollar. "I'm sorry it's so little, Kay, but this month—" She didn't have to tell me. I knew: insurance, a bill from

---

* Poverty in the vows of nuns means they are not permitted to amass personal fortunes. Some orders are not allowed to keep personal gifts. In the Order of Holy Cross at St. Mary's this is permitted. I hope it is clear that in describing the environment and possessions of the sisters, I do not begrudge them a single thing. But when I think of the hundreds of families I saw on relief during the depression and compare their environment with that of the nuns I must question their definition of the word "poverty," if not its use.

the dentist for a brace for the little girl's teeth, summer clothes for both of them, and a few pennies put by for the long stretch until the first fall pay day. It was all done on a salary the income tax collector wasn't interested in. Next I talked to Edna. She'd just made the last payment on her winter coat (this was in June, mind you!) and was trying to figure out a way to trim her next year's budget to include tuition at a nursery school for her young nieces. It was that way all down the line. All those girls were trying their darndest to get organized for the coming year's fight for survival.

When I called on Cora I found her sitting on the bed looking at the floor. "What's the matter?" I wanted to know. "Oh," she said, "I've got twenty dollars coming for tutoring from a student who's owed the sum for a couple of months. I've just been over to ask a sister if the college wouldn't please bill the parents, and sister says, 'What! Bill them for only twenty dollars?'"

You know the rest. I walked down to the front office and resigned. Only twenty dollars! Clearly I was out of my depth hobnobbing around with people who could refer to twenty solid dollars as "only."

I remembered the story of a woman saint who prayed to have her troubles increased. Her father, thereupon, got a sore on his forehead and she thanked God for the evidence of His love in sending HER this new tribulation!

My need was to get back to work with people who walked up to facts head-on, who could look real poverty in the eye, and who didn't spend too much time thinking over moral luxuries.

Mysticism, I had discovered, was, like other ways of life, more attractive when couched in satisfying comfort. It lacked the hard challenging smack of reality. I wanted to get back to a place where I could let out my breath and say, "Well, I'll be goddammed," or even, "Oh, dear me!" Meantime "my writing" could take care of itself.

CHAPTER XIX

As Sure as God Made Little Apples

TAKE A COMPASS, adjust it to a fifty-mile scale, put the point on South Bend, draw a circle and you will have the circulation territory of the *News-Times*. You will also have in the southwestern Michigan section, the fruit center of the world.

If I haven't said so elsewhere I want to say here that South Bend is only six miles from the Michigan state line. So, you see, what concerned southwestern Michigan also concerned us. And every spring, as sure as God made little apples, what concerned this fruit-growing valley most was its annual blossom festival.

Washington has its cherry blossoms that don't have any fruit; Atlantic City has its beauty contest and the fishy smelling ocean; Pasadena has its parade of roses that you can't eat—but Michigan has the blossoms, beauty queen, parade, *and* a good cash crop to follow the springtime spree.

It's functional, and that's what I like about it. The blossom festival is not an idea dragged in from outside and superimposed on a lot of phony props for the purpose of advertising St. Joseph and Benton Harbor, Michigan. It's simply a party that celebrates the way the fruit farmers make their living.

You can drive for miles and miles in the country in springtime without ever losing sight of a blooming tree, and always the air is full of the special polleny sweetness of fruit flowers. There are crooked apple trees all pink and white—thick, clotted peach blooms—rigid candelabra patterns which turn out to be pear trees, plum blossoms like white buttons on the black branches, and sour cherries, puffs of white foam ready to float away if you cut the strings that hold them down. Oh, I know these Michigan cherries make the best pie in the world, but in the spring I can really love the flowers better.

And while the vineyards and berry patches don't put out spectacular flowers, they're good to look at, too. There's something streamlined about a well-laid-out vineyard. It's as orderly as a plaza full of trained gymnasts doing their one-two-three-fours.

This fruit belt runs along Lake Michigan. Driving north on the highway there you see the boastful, blooming, fertile earth on one side and on the other the sand dunes left by the Glacial Period. Beyond these lies the lake. I don't dare try to describe the dunes for you, because when I want to get away from it all that's where I go. And you know how extravagant people are in describing places like that.

Small towns and villages spot the region and, come spring and the bucolic plague, that urge to be one with nature, the citizens begin preparations for the blossom festival. The first step is to select the village queen, Miss Niles, Miss Baroda, Miss Buchanan, Miss St. Joseph, Miss Kalamazoo, Miss Benton Harbor—some forty or fifty maidens unspoiled by anything except lipstick, rouge, powder, eye-shadow, color rinses, the latest fashions, and whatever else Fifth Avenue can offer.

As each queen is chosen her picture is printed in the South Bend papers with a little story about her. In fact, reporters from the *News-Times* and *Tribune* were often asked to take their lives in their hands and be judges and select the queen at the local contests. I served once in choosing Miss Niles and was somewhat alarmed to see the row of seats in which the judges were to sit was roped off. But the entrants, parents and friends interested in these contests have a much better sense of sportsmanship than the parents of Soap Box Derby drivers, so I was not only safe, but I enjoyed it.

Community winners go to St. Joseph or Benton Harbor for the event which chooses the Blossom Queen. These towns are a mile apart and are the shipping centers for the fruit growers, so it is natural to hold the main festivities in one place one year, the other the next.

The selection of the Queen starts a week's elaborate program. Her Majesty is surrounded by all the other winners as a court of honor. They visit the various towns, attend receptions, plays, concerts in their honor. All the time the enthusiasm is working up for the big day which falls on a Saturday in the middle of May.

That's when the parade will be held and the ball which winds up the festival.

When I was at St. Mary's, Pi Warren was news editor, having returned to the sheet, and he never could take my work at the college seriously. Whenever he wanted me to cover anything he called me up and told me so, just like old times. So the day for the Blossom parade came along and Pi gave me a ring and told me to take a run over and cover it. I asked Dorothy to go along with me because the day was too nice to drive by myself.

Once we were on the Dixie highway we were part of an endless chain of automobiles all headed for St. Joe. I began to notice those little excitement feelings that always started up inside me when I went on an assignment I liked or one that was new. No matter what illusions exploded in my face I never got so hard-boiled that I lost them. I could hardly wait to get there. Although I realized that the blossoms, which had originally inspired the fiesta, were now running second place to the Queen, I did not care. I zipped along at sixty to seventy miles an hour singing "The Stars and Stripes Forever."

"If I had known it was going to be like this," Dorothy said, "I would have written to Mother before I left."

So I slowed down to fifty-eight and felt certain the parade would start before we arrived. It was a distance of about thirty miles. We left at ten o'clock and the parade was to begin at one, so you see there wasn't much time.

We dropped into the Hotel Whitcomb for lunch. It was just a gesture so far as I was concerned. I was much too excited to eat. Thousands of mamas, papas, children and sweethearts were already milling about the streets. The restaurant was crowded and people stood over you while you ate, so they could leap into your chair as soon as you got up. The woman waiting for me not only got my chair but also my lunch, for just as the waitress was serving it someone yelled, "The parade's started."

Dorothy said, "You run along."

At least I guess that's what she said, for I was out the door and down the street. On top of a truck were Dutch Hennings and Leon Russell, our Benton Harbor correspondent. I yelled at them to help me up. I can't imagine that I looked very cute shinnying up the side of a truck, and I thought I would fall apart before I made it. Dutch and Leon took hold of my arms and some bystander pushed obligingly from the rear. I don't suppose the whole procedure took more than a few seconds but I could hear a band playing and I was certain the parade would be half-over before I'd ever make it. I was relieved when at last I stood on top to find the first drum major strutting down the street, the color bearer holding high the American flag, the rum-a-dum of the drum corps following. The parade was on and I was there.

There were two long miles of it, scores of floats, some commercial, showing refrigerators or ice cream or automobiles, some beauty floats, like the House of David prize winner (it was a garden and fountain, very

elaborate), and of course the Queen's float, the poor
girl sweltering under a blazing sun, bowing right and
left, her court of beauties arranged on a series of steps
around her, fifty bands playing their hearts out and
100,000 people lining the streets cheering for all they
were worth.

Dutch says, "Look up here, Queenie," and she does
and smiles, and he gets a picture of her. It's fun to see a
girl as happy as this one is on her big day. Of course
she is surrounded by a group who didn't quite make
the grade. But for this or that judge, each may say to
herself, I'd be on that throne. All the same when they're
sitting there on the float, dressed in smart pastel afternoon gowns setting off all their endearing young
charms, with thousands of people yelling and clapping
for two hours, they wouldn't trade places with a sweep-
stake winner.

Leon invites us to come up to the Whitcomb bar
afterwards for a drink, but Dutch can't. He has to go
back to develop his pictures and get them to the en-
graver so a page can be made up for Sunday's paper.
But I don't have to be in to write my story until after
dinner so I say, "O.K." I join Dorothy who has been
watching the parade from beside the truck and we go
together.

"A girl fainted," she says.

"She did!"

"Yes. She was standing with her mother and father,
and she kept saying, 'I'm going to faint,' and ma says,
'Oh, you're just excited.' And in a minute over she
went. Her people were provoked with her. They took

her into the bank on the corner, laid her on the marble floor, and left a solitary clerk to revive her while they went back to watch the parade."

"I know it," I say. "This parade takes people like that. What's a daughter more or less, compared with a float full of beauties?"

The bar at the Whitcomb was crowded to the gunwales. We found ourselves in the midst of a big party of people whose names I no longer remember, except Miss Cecilia Eisenhart, one of the former Blossom Queens. Miss Eisenhart told us the ex-Queens have a sorority and hold meetings and do charity work and have lots of fun talking over old times. The parade has a float for them each year, which I think is very decent.

The reporter from the *Chicago Tribune* was also there enjoying things and trying not to be bewildered by it all. There was a boy in costume for a play who just drifted over to the table and sat down, and another tall, tall boy in an open-throat shirt looking enough like Abe Lincoln to be his twin brother. The talk was all about the parade and the likely prize winners, and about the Queen and her boy friend and the dance that night.

I was drinking Bacardi cocktails, at whose expense I don't know. I do know Dorothy said to the waiter, "Is your name George?" And he said, "Yes, how did you know?" But she wouldn't tell him, just acted mysterious about it. I had one drink on George. He said to me, "May I ask you a question?" And I said, "Yes." He said, "What are you doing with all those Bacardis?" I looked up into his eyes. "I'm a reporter," I said softly. "Oh," he replied, "in that case the next one's on me."

Isn't it lovely to work on a paper? When I got back to the office, after having stopped at a small hotel in Berrien Springs to eat fried chicken, I wrote a great, long story about it and Phil Nicar, city editor at the time, said it was good and gave me a by-line.

I went home happy and content and slept the sleep of the innocent. But next morning, wouldn't you know it, the phone rang and Mother called me. It was the director of one of the high school bands and he wanted to know why I mentioned every band but his.

"We're proud of our band, too," he said in a very hurt voice.

It would seem that for me blossoms, like roses, have their thorns!

CHAPTER XX

What's the Use of a Big Heart?

THE LONGER I WORKED ON a newspaper the more certain I became that there were two things a reporter
could count on to turn up in the course of a week's
work: something screwy and something sad.

I had learned from my experience the one thing people insist on doing is making fools of themselves. And
the sad cases will be with us so long as the poor are.

It wasn't often, however, that I had really classic ex-
amples come side by side to prove my point. But once,
not long before I left the paper for good, I did. If they
had been specially ordered they couldn't have been
more complete.

The first assignment in this discordant duet was to
interview a New York City judge who was the guest of
the pastor of a fashionable church. As I remember it,
the judge had done some commendable piece of work
in New York by establishing a court of family relations

to solve domestic difficulties without actually having the parties brought into court. This procedure has saved innumerable families the expense of lawyers, and relieved the courts of the congestion of little cases.

In the judge's discussion of family difficulties, the subject of birth control came up. And here the Methodist minister contributed a phenomenal sociological pronouncement.

"I think birth control should be enforced," said he, as though it were a law, "so that we would have more Republicans than Democrats."

It was things like that made me feel victimized, as though I was coming off much the worse in a tussle with an octopus.

"I don't get it," I said.

"Well," said the Methodist, "there's no doubt but what our wealthier people who have few children are Republicans, and the Democrats are the masses who have six and eight in a family. If they could be encouraged to use birth control, things would even up and the Republicans get back in office."

I give you my word this man was as serious as a senator up for re-election. I sat there wondering what to do with this piece of "news" when he said, "Don't quote me."

I was relieved. The bad thing about printing an asinine idea is that you never know what asses will take it up. Remembering the lengths to which the Methodists and other drys went in enforcing prohibition, I shuddered to think where a drive to "enforce" birth control might lead.

Shortly before I turned the judge's story in to the desk, I had a phone call tipping me off on the birth of a twenty-three-ounce baby, and the address of the child's grandmother. I took my copy to Ross Nelson and said, "I've got an exclusive on a pint-size infant, but it may take me a while to dig up the story."

We were usually kept within phone distance of the office until after the paper was out because of possible emergencies, and if I went on this story, he would be unable to get hold of me if he needed me. He said, "How do you stand?"

"I'm all up," I said, meaning all the stories I had had on my desk were in the hands of Ross, himself. "And if anything else comes in Marge can take care of it." I referred to a grand friend, Marge Fotheringill. I was training her to take over part of my work.

He said, "O.K."

I found the grandmother's house, and she told me my information was absolutely correct, and offered to go with me to the home where the youngster was born.

At the edge of town we left the paved highway to drive along a dirt road. At the top of a hill we came on half a dozen tar-paper shacks. "The last one on the right is my daughter's," said Grandma.

I remember that the old lady was talking to me constantly, but I have no idea what she said. I stared at the shack with unbelieving eyes. The worst I can say about it will flatter it. It was a one-room, one-story affair, and the sheets of tar paper overlapped each other, sagging at some places, bulging at others. The flat roof protruded over the sides of the house, the uneven edges accentuating the flimsiness of the structure. Compared with this drab green "home," a house of cards is firm as a vault.

In the center of the front wall of the wretched hovel was a door with a wooden step from around which the dirt had washed away. I walked inside. Opposite me was a round coal stove, to my left the mother and child in a dirty, sagging bed, to my right a cook stove and kitchen table and cupboard. Several children squatted on the floor around the stove. A thin girl in her late teens sat in one of the chairs, and in the other, leaning back against the wall, was a pale-faced youth with peering, nearsighted eyes. These two, Grandma explained, were "sister-in-law, who is separated from her husband, and her new boy-friend." As nearly as I could make out the three adults now present, the father of the new baby, and the baby itself, all slept in the bed together. At any rate, there was no other sleeping accommodation in the room. The children, I suppose, crawled under the tables and chairs.

Grandma began going over the details again and by this time I had adjusted myself to the situation enough to listen to what she was saying.

"Violet was standing over by the stove yesterday getting dinner," she said, "and I happened to be here, and she complained about having a pain and not feeling well, and I looked at her, and I said, 'Vi, I believe you're going to have a baby.' And she said, 'Oh, I don't think so.' But I went into town and got a doctor and the baby was born."

"You—ah, you mean she didn't know she was pregnant?" I asked.

"Noooo! Never suspected it for a minute!"

Grandma unwrapped the little bundle and handed me the infant. It was dressed in doll clothes from the ten-cent store. I picked it up, felt its little heart beating. I could hold it safely in one hand, and my hand measures six and one-half inches from the base of my palm to the tip of my middle finger. Its head and bottom rested easily in my hand while its tiny legs and feet kicked in the air.

I laid it carefully back on its blanket and wrapped it up again. In my mind I began outlining a little campaign to save its life, which obviously was going to come to a quick end in present surroundings.

The infant's brother had a bad cold, the kind that had made a sore on his upper lip from too much nose-running and too little blowing. I looked at him while he was in the act of urinating into the stove. Relieved, he picked up a hot-pad to close the door, but "boy friend" said, "Wait a minute, Buddy," and spat into the stove. "O.K.," he said.

I went back to the office and told Pi and Ross about it. "Blow it up," they said, "we'll make a big feature for tomorrow."

For once in my life I wanted something more than a big feature with my name at the top of it. It was the business of reporters, I had learned, to tell what they saw and heard. But couldn't I, as Kay Smallzried, try to save a life if I wanted to? Did I, through my very last day, have to be nobody receiving the shafts of multiplied impressions and giving them out again in some sort of organized form? This once I was going to break the pattern of non-identity for the sake of a twenty-three-ounce baby.

The first thing I did was to call my sister, Ellie, and tell her about it. Ellie belongs to the Service Guild, a club interested in charitable work. The girls had around a hundred dollars in their treasury and hadn't decided as yet what worthy enterprise they would undertake. I suggested the baby, saying how it needed hospitalization and the care of a competent physician. Ellie called the president of the group, Ann Regan, and Ann said, "Sure, we'll do it."

Then I called Miss Evelyn McGuinness, superintendent of nurses at Epworth Hospital, and her assistant, Miss Dorothy Mason, head of the children's ward. I also got in touch with Sister Amanda, a honey of a person, who asked her grade school pupils to bring old clothes for the whole family. One of her pupils told his father, a Bendix official, about it, and he said he would give the baby's father a job.

Encouraged by my success I wrote my story, a human interest yarn about the tiny life that was bringing manifold blessings to the whole family. Dutch Hennings and I went out late in the afternoon to take pictures. To give an idea of the infant's size, we held it beside a quart milk bottle. The two were equal. Then we snapped one of the mother holding it, and still another of the baby lying on the bed. This was to be enlarged to life-size. It was almost dark when I made my third trip of the day to the tar-paper shack. Miss Mason was with me and tried to explain to the family about the hospital. For the food, the clothes and the job, they thanked me. But to the hospitalization and medical care they said, "No!"

An infant's place, it seems, is with its mother, its snotty-nosed brothers and sisters, sister-in-law and her boy friend. In vain we pleaded for the baby's life. In vain Miss Mason pointed out the dangers of leaving it around for promiscuous petting and handling. They still said, "No!"

The father of the baby kept saying after each argument, "My brother was taken to a hospital when he was a baby and fed with a bottle and he had stomach trouble all his life."

I was mad enough at them to be a capitalist. Here was an arch-example of the unappreciative poor. Here, God knows, were the ill housed, ill clothed and ill fed. And they were living up to the major criticism the rich thrust at them—resistance to the opportunity to better themselves. In my heart I knew why. These people, and their neighbors, living in their tar-paper shacks with dirt floors, were ignorant—not only of what medical science *could* do to help them, but of what anyone *would* do. They were unused to good intentions being exercised on their behalf. Why should they lift themselves above the routine of their destitute existence for a moment's comfort, and then be thrust back into it when I went on to another story, and the hospital on to another case? They felt themselves not the type of family likely to interest that mythical creature, Dame Fortune. They were suspicious, resentful—and rightly so. The society that threw them into their wretched squalor on a deserted hilltop hardly deserved their grateful thanks for a moment's pity and some castoff clothing. Nevertheless, I meant to carry my good deed through if I could.

I had another idea and signaled Miss Mason to retreat. I took her back to town, returned to the office and called Mrs. J. R. Dumont, girls' probation officer. I had known her a long time and I could trust her to act without involving me in the proceedings. I told her the story.

Late the next day, after Mrs. Dumont had been out to the shack, she called me and told me she had informed the family the baby's life was unsafe in its surroundings, and she would give them twenty-four hours to do something about it before the authorities stepped in and took over. We both thought they would yield to hospitalization at this. I went to see if I could help them make arrangements and found the family gone.

I tried the grandmother's. They were all there. They had decided the baby could be sufficiently isolated at Grandma's to save it. Grandpa was home, and he had read the story I had written, and was highly indignant about my having mentioned the brother's cold and the sore on his lip, and the general poverty-stricken condition of the family. He was drunk and yelled at me, calling me a liar and walking toward me waving his fist in the air. Grandma intervened as I backed to the door to make an escape.

But I knew when I was licked. I ran down the steps while they followed and shouted loud opinions about me and the efforts I had made. I went home wondering what in hell was the use of a big heart.

Sunday's paper carried the follow-up stories and pictures on the infant. Monday's papers carried its obituary!

I hope that when Methodist pastors find out there are other uses for birth control than making more Republicans, I will be there to get the story. That will be news!

CHAPTER XXI

Is That Girl Married?

(NOTE: Because the people involved in the story of this chapter have had enough trouble already, names marked with an * are fictitious.)

Having finished with writing my Soap Box Derby copy for the next day, I sat down at the city editor's desk, pulled out a drawer, put my feet on it, and settled back to read the afternoon paper. It was around nine o'clock and I was waiting for Helen Minczewski to get back from Buchanan, Michigan, where she had gone with Dutch Hennings—on a murder story.

The paper I was reading carried an account of it. Joseph Edward Torrence*, thirty-four, the preceding evening had found his wife, Gretchen*, being intimately embraced by Robert Pellman*, a next-door neighbor. The surprised lover had ducked out the back door and started on a dead run over the broad garden lots of the village, and after him rushed Torrence, gun in hand. In less time than it takes to tell it the enraged husband had squared his account with honor. Pellman was dead.

It was a hot, sticky July night, so hot the palms of my hands were moist, and I began to be restless. I was on the point of writing Helen a note and telling her to meet me for a glass of beer at Zimmers' when I heard her come in the downstairs door, laughing as though she had heard for the first time the story of the artist's model and the cane-bottomed chair.

"Oh God," Dutch bawled as they came up the stairs. "It's a lulu! It's the funniest story we've had in a long time."

I lit a cigarette and sat back to listen. I could tell by the resonance in his nasal voice that Dutch was in rare form. A funny yarn became an untouchable classic when he told it.

All Helen could say was, "Oh, Kay, you should have been there."

"I'll say you should," twanged Dutch. "We've got to go to bat now and save Torry from the chair."

"Torry?" I asked.

"Yeah. He's Buchanan's favorite son. They all call him Torry, and when I say all, I mean all. Jeez, he's got more friends than Santy Claus."

"Every place we were today," Helen went on, "little groups of people were standing or sitting around talking, and you would have thought from the expression on their faces that war'd been declared."

I looked at my companions. Their eyes were bright, and they were grinning at the remembered pleasure of their day. I hastily thought over the murders which had come up since I'd been on the paper and I couldn't recall one that provided a laugh. I realize that to most people a man who has committed murder has removed himself from the commonplace. To a reporter who sees a number of such cases each year, however, the murderer has merely removed himself from one commonplace to another. I was looking for the yardstick by which to measure Torry and his crime.

"What's he look like?" I asked.

"Boyish and perplexed," said Helen, "like Jimmy Stewart in the movies."

Dutch sat on the desk and rerolled his shirt sleeves. Helen, George Scheuer, Tom Philipson, King Detzler, and Bobby Hoenig gathered round to hear about it, too. "Well, in the first place," Dutch began, "Torry's a good boy."

"He's worked hard all his life," Helen put in.

Dutch nodded. "He was an orphan raised by his grandparents. And he saved his money and got himself half ownership in a filling station and auto agency."

"And he married well," Helen said.

"Yeah, he married the daughter of a wealthy farmer. And he went on working hard and gave her everything she wanted and they had a couple of little boys."

"Oh, now, look," I said. "Are you telling me about a murder, or an American success story?"

"It's got everything in it, Kay," said Helen. "That's what makes it so perfect."

"Torry worked awful late," Dutch went on, "and his

wife complained about it. When he got home he was so tired that—" Dutch spread his hands.

We all laughed. The implication was flawless.

"And if he did have any time off, he went fishing or hunting with the boys."

"What'd she do?" Tom asked. "Join the Lonely Hearts Club?"

"Maybe she could have left some of those strongman ads around as a hint," Detzler said.

We all had ideas on how the situation could have been more happily resolved. The story of the remiss husband was old in Chaucer's time and is still a joke the race doesn't outgrow.

"Next door," said Dutch, "was a young man, a Virginian—"

"No!" I said. (I remembered suddenly: when a Vuhginian makes love to you . . .)

"Yes," said Dutch, "and moreover he had red hair."

"I told you this story had everything!" Helen crowed.

"Fate," said Scheuer.

"Fate writing movie scenarios," I said. "That redheaded Southerner business is the Hollywood touch."

"Well, Torry got next to the fact that his wife was carrying on with this guy, and last night he lays a trap for 'em and catches 'em. After the killing he tells the police he was only rushing to the protection of his wife. That's a hot one. Torry goes out, and Pellman comes over, and Gretchen says to him," Dutch jumped off the desk and began gesturing with his hands, "she says, 'Come on into the bedroom. I can defend myself better in here.'"

"The front and back doors were locked," Helen said.

"That's right," Dutch agreed. "They kept Torry running from one door to the other yelling his head off, and finally when he bangs at the front, Pellman runs out the back and starts off across the fields with Torry after him. There was Pellman, holding his pants up with one hand and jumping fences with the other. Jeez, I'll bet when those bullets were whizzing around his head he was thinking, 'Was it worth it!' " Dutch threw down his cigarette and stepped on it while we laughed. He looked up. "A guy can't run fast with his pants down, y'know. He never had a chance."

"If he's confessed," I said, "how're we going to save him?"

"Oh, don't be naïve, Kay," Helen said.

"Save him! Jesus!" Dutch said. "He better be saved or Buchanan'll secede from the Union. Why, the prosecutor is ready to cry right now. He's up for re-election next November and the trial is scheduled to come off in October. If he convicts Torry he'll lose every vote in Buchanan, and if he doesn't, what kind of a prosecutor is he?"

Dutch opened his bag and showed us some pictures. Two he had swiped from the Torrence house. There was one of Gretchen and her lover which they had posed for at a dime-store gallery. The other showed the children. He went into his darkroom and returned in a while with wet prints of Torry, and of the little bungalow where the murderer and his wife had lived happily until the soft-spoken Southerner appeared.

Years before in my bloodthirsty childhood I had

read the crime stories in the papers and had decided capital punishment should be made mandatory for all self-confessed murderers. I looked at the pictures and tried to tell myself Torry was guilty and he should be punished. But I couldn't. I wanted him to go free. We all did. Pellman's character explained, if not vindicated, Torry's action. He had the reputation of being a seducer of women. And it was possible the world would not be poorer for having one red-haired Virginian less. And another thing! When Torry shot his enemy and, turning over his lifeless body, said, "He's dead, I guess," he had given all of us a vicarious satisfaction. How many times a person longs to take a gun to somebody who ought never to have been born anyway! So, hurray for Torry! I wanted to do something about it. I wanted to help him. The thought of going on with the Soap Box Derby made me feel as though I'd been sentenced to eat cardboard and sand while others had chicken. As far as excitement, thrills, and the vital stuff of life were concerned, I might better be covering the knitting classes of new brides.

The story was front page stuff for several days, and I envied Helen her assignment with a pure agony. The trial was set for October. I knew Helen was going to be married that month, and for days I went around in a sweat that assumed crisis proportions: would she set the date for a day before or after the trial? If before, then I might be assigned to it since I'd be through with the Soap Box Derby by then. At last she told me she was going to be married the Saturday before. "Oh, Helen, how lovely," I said. I really was glad about her happiness and all. But I'd never covered a murder, and I'd been burning to for years and years. And this was a natural, with the tremolo full organ. I kissed her, in sheer delight. I know she'll understand my feelings.

Her last big story for the paper was a resume of the case, which was printed the Sunday before the trial opened. She did a marvelous job. In the course of it she dubbed Torry "the honor slayer," and plainly asked the citizens of South Bend and Buchanan if he was to spend the rest of his days behind bars for protecting his wife and home?

No! Of course he wasn't. I knew that, and so did the citizens. But a trial had to be held anyway. A jury of his peers who had never heard of the case and had no opinion on it would decide Torry's fate. Uh-huh! To get a jury like that in southern Michigan the prosecution would have had to dig up the remains of Cro-Magnon man.

The defense attorneys, James and Charles Stuart*, of Niles, Michigan, were after an acquittal. They were prepared to plead "temporary insanity," the first time such a plea had been used in the history of the state. But they also wanted to advance a secondary element of self-defense.

The trial was held in the courthouse at St. Joseph, county seat of Berrien County, in which Buchanan is situated. When I got to the office and found that Leon Russell, our Michigan correspondent, was to cover it, I was in such a fury that I almost resigned then and there. I was so enraged that I swore I wouldn't read a line of Leon's copy, and it was only that same demon com-

pulsion that makes you read streetcar ads and mem-
orize the Alka-Seltzer rhymes that drove me to the
afternoon paper.

Leon had caught Mrs. Torrence's testimony. She was
called as a state witness, to establish the causes and inci-
dents leading up to the crime. Defense attorney Charles
Stuart cross-examined her:

"Did there ever come a time when your relations
with Pellman were not proper?"

"Yes, about the middle of January."

"Did they continue to grow—to increase?"

"Yes."

"At home or when riding?"

"Both places."

The account continued with, "There followed a description of many of the times they had spent together."

Here stands the adulteress, I thought, ancient of
wrongdoers, admitting the oasis in her love-parched life
was only a mirage of the devil. Her parents, who had
nursed her through the sicknesses of her childhood, her
friends, who had given her gifts when she married, the
townspeople, who had looked up to her as the wife of a
leading citizen, widen their eyes as they listen, and their
scorn falls on her like whiplashes.

Poor Gretchen Torrence! She takes the stand not to
tell her story, not to plead for understanding and for-
giveness. The case against her is not a legal one, and
can't be pondered by a jury. If she had murdered Torry
for neglecting her, then she could have had a trial. But
as things stand nobody cares whether or not she had a
reason for her actions. She is on the stand to score a

point for the prosecution, for she must say her husband was guilty of murder. Later the defense will drag from her the admission that her conduct was enough to drive any good man to murder. She will give it pitifully enough, humbly aware that her human rights to privacy and comprehension are gone. She went on with her story.

The first or second week in June, she says, Torrence came home and said, "Honey, I'd like to talk to you." She was in bed at the time, and he crept in beside her.

"He told me, 'People are talking about you. What have you been doing? Why do you go out with that man?'

"I was cold and indifferent," she testifies. "He told me how he worked to make money for me—how he wore the same work shoes for three years. How he was too dead tired to go out with me when he wasn't working. He always told me to take the car and go with the neighbors and have a good time. He often came home, and I hadn't been there to get his supper. He often went to bed hungry.

"He turned over on his side and buried his head in the pillow and just cried." Her voice falters, and she stares back to that evening, remembering. "I felt sorry for him, but still I had this other image in my mind, and what Torry said didn't matter, it seemed like." (How many nights had she buried *her* head in the pillow and cried? I'm for Torry, all right, but she did have her side.)

She said when Torry had warned Pellman to stay away from her, the Virginian had grabbed a catsup bot-

tle in a threatening manner. Another time Pellman had
told her he always carried a gun and would just as soon
use it on her as on her husband.

The next day Leon phoned Pi Warren he was going
to be too busy with other news to take care of the trial,
and could somebody be sent to St. Joseph? Pi slammed
down the phone and without looking at me, said, "Kay,
go catch the Torrence trial." I didn't know whether to
dance, faint, or kiss him. But right away he began muttering, "Jesus Christ! No God damn excuse for it.—
Boy Scouts and Camp Fire Girls, and they expect me to
get out a paper!" So I just ran down the stairs and got
going. It was MY MURDER!

The courthouse was filled with people, downstairs
and up, and the excited murmur of their voices echoed
throughout the building. As many of Torry's friends
as could had crowded into the courtroom, and others
lingered in the hall outside. I was to sit at a table near
the judge's rostrum. The court gave me a yellow tablet
so long and heavy I felt like Moses receiving the law.
My heart pounded so hard my hand trembled.

The first witnesses to take the stand were Torry's old
grandmother, who cried and said what a good boy he
was, his wife's parents, who testified on his behalf that
he was a good, stalwart young man they were proud to
have as a son-in-law, and some of his friends. I wrote
down every single question and every answer, objections sustained and overruled.

When the defense questioned the friends, they said
Torry was not normal on the night the crime was committed. The temporary insanity plea was being built up.

The prosecutor scored a point (reluctantly?) when he asked each witness, "You're here to help Torry, aren't you?" Sadly they nodded, "Yes."

Torry took the stand! I stared at him, fascinated before that most enthralling of human beings, a man on trial for his life. The mark of Cain, however subtle, must somewhere show on him. But he wore an ordinary blue suit, his manners were mild and unexceptional, his voice was the flat, unresonant drawl of all my friends and neighbors. I tried my heroic best to find some unique pathos, some peculiar dignity in his testimony. But it simply wasn't there. Joseph Edward Torrence repeated dully the platitudes of his little life. Yes, he had always lived with his grandparents. Yes, he had walked three miles to school. Yes, he had worked on the farm and then in a factory. No, he had never sown any wild oats. Had he, the defense inquired tenderly, idealized the young girl who was to become his wife? Torry muttered that he supposed so.

After too much of this sort of questioning, designed to establish the prisoner's homespun virtue, the lawyer got down to the business we had come for. Ah-hem! Kaff-kaff! Now, Mr. Torrence, regarding the events which lead up to the night of July 28th—

Now surely, *surely* something must happen! These are the things that drove him once to curse and kill. Lived over again here, with his wife looking on, his neighbors straining in their seats, the jury, the judge, the prosecutor, and the press attending every word as though it were revelation, he must transcend himself, become a symbol of what is primitive, passionate, fatal.

326

"What did you do," the defense attorney hummed, "when your wife admitted her meetings with Pellman?"

"I told her I was going to tell her mamma and daddy on her."

At this humdrum pace the lawyer trundles him through the account of Gretchen's exhaustless deceit and the wreck of his happiness. A little color begins to sting his pale cheeks and he stirs uneasily, wipes his mouth, shuffles his feet. "I said to her, 'I have reason to believe you are stepping out on me.' I cried. My heart was broken. I said, 'I have tried to give you everything, a home, a new car. I built two extra rooms. We have our little boys. If you have no respect for me, you should have for our boys.' I said, 'You shouldn't go out with Pellman. He is no good. He is just a drunkard. He was driven out of the South because of an unwed mother. He has no love for you. He is only using you as a toy.'" His voice broke and tears came to his eyes.

I scratched down in the margin of my yellow tablet, "weeps." I am remembering another wronged man, for whom the worst bitterness was that looseness and depravity were preferred above worth. You know the place where Hamlet comes in to his mother and shows her pictures of her murdered husband and of the man who killed him:

"Look here upon this picture and on this;
  The counterfeit presentment of two brothers.
  See what a grace was seated on this brow; . . .
  This was your husband: look you now what follows.
  . . . Have you eyes? . . .

Could you on this fair mountain leave to feed
And batten on this moor?
                    . . . and what judgment
Would step from this to this?"

The trial went on. The prosecution objected that the
defendant was having a pleasant afternoon visit with
the jury, but the objection was overruled. The defendant had the right to tell his story in his own words.
Finally: now, Mr. Torrence, will you tell us what happened when you heard Pellman run out the back door?
Torry settles back and says in a relieved voice, "I dunno.
My mind went blank." So the plea of temporary insanity is built up!

He is given for cross-examination to the prosecutor
who clears his throat timidly. "Recall that part of your
testimony beginning, 'Any man with red blood in his
veins—' "

"I can do that," said Torry. "I was going to say,
'Any man with American red blood in his veins, any
man on the jury or in this courtroom would have done
the same thing I did. He would have rushed to the protection of his wife.' "

"American red blood in his veins—" I might have
known, I thought, that when I was finally sent to cover
a murder trial it would turn out to be some kind of
farce. For years I had entertained visions of myself in
the role of reporter-detective solving a series of crimes
that would make the *Murders of the Rue Morgue* look
like the recreation of an anemic missionary. And what
did I get! A lecture by the murderer on the American

Way of doing things. I expected he would continue by saying "What helps business helps you." I felt let down. I still wanted him to go free. He was dumb, but he was good (that is, he had never done anything bad but commit this one little murder), and virtue should be its own reward since it isn't a reward to anyone else. But all at once I knew I wasn't covering a trial at all. There was no element of chance in this. It wasn't sporting.

"Why," asked the prosecutor, "when you were running to the protection of your wife, did you proceed to run away from her in the direction of the victim?"

"Because I couldn't get into the house," said Torry. The jurors nodded approvingly. That was the sort of logic the thing was founded on.

At this point the prosecutor called an alienist to the stand with some idea of establishing the prisoner's sanity the night of the crime. What a piece of impertinence on the part of the prosecutor! The last thing anyone wanted in this purely local (one might almost say family) matter was the opinion of an outsider.

Everybody hated the alienist on sight. It made no difference to them that this quiet little old man had spent a lifetime gathering facts and learning to offer impersonal judgments. The damned squeak wanted to put the heat on Torry, their Torry, who was a good, etc. I watched him take his place on the witness stand and wondered if he knew he was the villain of the piece.

The prosecutor, with the zeal of cold cigar ashes, asked the question: "Excitement on the part of the murderer, following his crime, doesn't indicate insanity, does it?" (That was safe enough.)

Alienist in thoughtful voice: "No."

The prosecutor questioned him on paleness, trembling, and excessive saliva as indications of insanity, and the alienist said that none of these things indicated an insane condition. He was then excused. As a scientific interlude the alienist's testimony was an innocuous little flop.

Although I knew Torry would be acquitted, the opinion of the doctor carried some weight with me, and I wrote a story saying how the prosecutor had spiked the insanity plea of the defense. I made it look pretty bad for Torry, and everyone was anxious to hear the defense's cross-examination the next day.

I think Attorney James Stuart sat up all night getting his cross-examination ready. As he rose to begin it everybody stared, surprised, at a thick manuscript he was holding in his hand. He inspected the nails of his free hand daintily, explaining in a dulcet voice that he wanted to ask the doctor a question—just one question. He had a copy of it here—tapping the manuscript. Might he read it? The doctor nodded gravely. Attorney Stuart took a stance before the jury and began. Ten minutes went by, and he was still reading—a half an hour—an hour—he was slogging along like Kipling's boots. And there hadn't been a period yet in this gargantuan question of his, because it was made up of about a hundred parts beginning, "Assuming that—" and going on to describe some major point in Torry's story as the defense was presenting it. So the lawyer managed, before his official summation, and under the pretext of cross-examining the alienist, to rub into the jury every single scrap of his case all over again!

I looked at the lawyer, so dapper, so clever. When he got to his fourth paragraph, "assuming further that in his young manhood he met a young lady—" I suppressed a feeble smile. The fact that every man-jack in the courtroom knew by heart the story being rehashed didn't dampen anybody's spirits. They sat forward in their chairs gulping down all those "assumings" as if a brand-new murder was being described. That's the way people are. Their own emotions are inexhaustibly fresh and thrilling to them. It's the same way with funerals, as any seasoned obit writer will tell you. You know how the notices run: "There will be a prayer service at the house, funeral at the church, and burial rites at the cemetery"—three chances for the bereaved to live their grief over more or less officially, and sob, as it were, for publication. And why not? For them it is just as good the third time as the first.

So with these Buchanan folk, who had read all about Torry's crime when it happened, heard the testimony of every witness, and were now simply flapping their ears in order not to miss a word of Stuart's "question." As for the attorney himself, he was full of sunny happiness. Aware that acquittal was a foregone conclusion, he was lowering the case into its grave of oblivion amid the appreciative weeping of his audience. Like a singer who has won an operatic contest and relaxes to sing for pleasure, he was letting himself go in a grand finale of love-death music.

When he said, "Assuming that he thereupon flashed his flashlight through the window, whereupon he saw the deceased and his wife standing in a close and endearing embrace, and that the wife's dress appeared to be pulled up in the vicinity of her waist—" the color sprang up into the faces of Torry and his friends like a sunrise in the sky. Gretchen's head was bowed into her handkerchief, her thin body shaking as she tried to hold back her sobs.

I had been so absorbed by the lawyer's act and its effects on the spectators that I forgot this was the cross-examination of the alienist, and was startled to hear Mr. Stuart drop his sweetly pleading voice and say harshly, "Now, Doctor . . . will you state whether in your opinion the conduct of the accused from the time he looked in the window of the porch until he was at the city hall following the shooting, as appears from the evidence in this case that you have heard, was consistent with sanity?"

The crowded courtroom draws its breath and I make ready to write down the doctor's answer. And the judge calls a recess! Of all times! I felt like I'd had a double chocolate sundae with whipped cream and nuts slapped out of my hands. But I suppose if the judge had to go—

In the court library I am introduced to Torry. How did I feel, shaking the hand that held the gun that murdered Robert Pellman? I felt old. Before the trial I should have been all goose flesh, but now I knew things are not what they seem. This legal festival hadn't really been an attempt to find out whether a murder had been done and who was guilty; it was a little country parliament sitting on the question: "Should our neighbor, Torry, who's been a good boy all his life, git hung for what he done?" We smiled at each other, and I said, "I hope you go free."

"Thanks," he said, "so do I."

When court resumed, the prosecutor entered a flock of objections to the wording of the question, all of which were overruled. And the defense, by way of adding an extra flourish, got the alienist to take back practically everything he'd said for the prosecution. The patient doctor admitted that "insanity is not a medical term, but a sociological term"; that another mental specialist called into the case had refused to testify for the prosecution when he got the facts, and so on.

The testimony was over. The prosecutor, after a brief speech about the difference between sentiment and duty, sheepishly asked the jury for a verdict of "guilty." Mr. Stuart, who had been much petted during the recess for his "question," jumped in and told the story all over again, pulling out his vox humana stop and wiping his eyes at the touching places. The judge, a little old man with a voice hardly audible beyond the end of his gavel, charged the jury—I don't know how, and neither, probably, did they, but that didn't matter. The verdict came in after the first ballot: "Not guilty because acting while temporarily insane."

Magna est veritas, et praevalet!

The next day Pi sent me to Buchanan to see Torry and find out if he was going to divorce his wife. I took Devon with me to get some pictures. When we arrived we found that Torry was at the home of his business partner, and I went there and explained what I wanted.

The partner puffed himself out with righteous rage. "After the shameless publicity you have given the poor boy, you have the nerve, the gall—" he slammed the door in my face.

Shameless publicity, indeed! Who did the old buzzard think had built up his poor boy's defense, even before the crime was two days old! But that's the way people are about papers. Devon drove me to a drugstore where I could get a coke and figure on my next move. Providence was looking after me that day, for who should come in but a man who used to work in the *News-Times* composing room and was a native of Buchanan. He knew Torry and the indignant partner well, because everybody in Buchanan knew everybody else well. With his help I reached Torry and made my peace with the partner.

Devon and I bundled the two of them into the car and took them to their filling station where Devon made pictures of Torry working a gasoline pump. But we didn't have him to ourselves long. People crowded around him to slap him on the back and shake hands. In a minute the plaza in front of the station was jammed.

"Haven't his friends seen him yet?" I asked the partner.

"Sure—lots of them. I took him to my house last night as soon as he was out of jail. But a big crowd—more'n five hundred, I guess, collected here, and so I brought him down, and they sure did cheer him, I'm telling you. And pretty soon there was an extra on the street about him, and I saw one old woman grab a bunch of papers

334

from a kid and start shouting, 'Torry free! Torry free!' Jeez! And then they came and got him and carried him on their shoulders through the streets."

"Has he seen his kids?" I asked.

The partner shook his head. "No, they're out in the country with their grandparents."

Boy, what a break for me! I shoved my way through the mob, plucked Torry's sleeve and said, "Now, Mr. Torrence, we want to take you to see your children."

As we were crossing the street he was stopped by a woman who had brought her two little sons, tow-haired youngsters about two and three years old, to shake hands with him. As he climbed into Devon's car another woman with tears in her eyes clasped his hand and cried, "God bless you, Torry. God does answer prayer. I have prayed for you every night."

While we were driving him along, I asked him if he was going to divorce his wife. He admitted, with composure, that he had thought of it, but he didn't know yet. (It's my hunch he would have taken Gretchen back on the spot if the townspeople hadn't been so dead set against her.) He said he'd been in jail for eleven weeks and he hadn't made any plans because he hadn't known whether or not he'd have to go to prison. (He was the only one who didn't know.)

I asked him if he was going back to work soon, and he said, "No, I think I'll do some hunting. Did you ever hunt?"

I admitted this was a pleasure outside my experience, and he looked me over appraisingly. "You'd take about a sixteen-gauge shotgun, I'd say."

This talk of guns had me not knowing which way to look. It seemed so unlikely that a man just freed for murder would be planning to go shooting. But who am I, etc.?

We stopped at a schoolhouse where we thought we might find the children. The teacher told me with tears in her eyes that the dear little boys were at home that day. She said they were model students.

So we went on to the grandparents. The boys were in the yard, and when Torry climbed out they looked at him for a moment, rigid with joy, and then went yelling up to the house, "Grandma, Pop's here! Pop's here!" In a minute they swarmed back down the lawn and into his arms. "We're going crow-hunting," they announced proudly.

Lord! Such a family for hunting!

On the way back to the office I felt pretty smug, because I not only had a hot exclusive in the reunion of father and children as well as the honor of having brought it about, but I had taken Torry away from any possibility of the other paper's seeing him in time to get an interview for their afternoon edition.

I noticed Devon was smiling to himself as we drove along and I asked him why. He said, "You remember when you got out of the car to go into the school and ask about his kids?"

"Yes," I said.

"Well," chortled Devon, "Torry leaned over to me and he said, 'Say, is that girl married?' "

336

CHAPTER XXII

"Thanks for the Memory"

AFTER LEAVING the *News-Times* I kept in touch with staff members, and always went to see the gang when I was home. Toward the last not many of those I told you about in "Meet Me Friends" were left.

But I felt a bit sentimental about the place and never went up the steps without a hundred memories fighting for precedence in my mind. You know most of them now.

My last trip was Christmas Eve of 1938. And Liz Anderson told me the paper was going to fold. Tom Philipson, Dutch Hennings, Dan Mahoney and Pi were all being funny about it—what else was there to do?

A week later Mother sent me a copy of the last edition and on the front page was this editorial:

"30"

In the newspaper profession "30" means the end.
The *News-Times* will suspend publication with
its last issue today.

It is with genuine regret that we make this an-
nouncement, but conditions have made it inevi-
table.

Since 1931 the *News-Times* has been published
at a loss. It will interest our friends and readers to
know, for instance, that the 1938 volume of business was less than half that of ten years ago. It is of
course obvious to everyone that such a shrinkage in
volume is bound to result in heavy losses.

The decision to retire from the field is based
upon the conviction, justified by years of experience, that two newspapers cannot be published here
with a fair profit for both under present conditions.

Nor is this situation peculiar to South Bend. During the past two or three years mergers and sus-
pensions have converted almost every city of this
size and below in the nation into "one-paper
towns."

In Worcester, Massachusetts; Toledo, Ohio;
New Haven and Hartford in Connecticut; Providence, Rhode Island; Portland, Maine; Albany and
Rochester in New York; Louisville, Kentucky;
Des Moines, St. Paul, Memphis, Youngstown,
Akron—the list where similar action has been taken
is almost inexhaustible. It is simply a trend of the
times. It cannot be blamed upon local conditions or
lack of local interest in existing publications.

As stated before we regret the circumstances

which make this action necessary. During our years of close association with the people of Michiana we have made many friends and these friendships we regard as ample repayment for any effort we have made in behalf of the general welfare.

To the fine people of South Bend and all of Michiana we wish the best of everything. They have been loyal, friendly, helpful.

We suspend with the same feeling of friendliness for the *Tribune* and its people. We write "30" in fact without the slightest tinge of malice or bitterness toward anyone.

Joseph M. Stephenson,
Editor and Publisher.

I read that editorial and reread it and I went out to have a glass of beer and think it over. It seemed to me there is a danger in one-newspaper towns. Suppose I owned a dozen newspapers in such towns in a single state. I could team up with the politicians and pretty well control not only the twelve towns but the state, too. How are the people in a one-newspaper town going to know that the publisher hasn't sold out to the city hall? The press has been crying a good bit about threats to its freedom, but the only threat to the press I can see is self-strangulation through all these fold-ups.

Well, I was a reporter long enough to learn that what I think isn't news and maybe that applies to writing books as well as reporting.

Incidentally the paper suspended publication while I was writing this book. For instance in "Meet Me

Friends" I spoke as if Jim Costin were still on the *News-Times*, which he was when I was writing that chapter. He is now on the *Chicago Tribune*. Others of "me friends" have made changes, too. But I can't go back now and change it all around and say where everybody is and who has married whom since I started to write. I suppose I could, but I'm not going to and I hope nobody minds.

It might interest you to know how all of us who were on the paper, all of us who worked such long hours for so little, who laughed so much, and drank so much, and cussed so much, are keeping in touch with each other.

George Scheuer (thank God for people like George) writes a bulletin several times a year and mails it to us. We write to him and tell him what we're doing and thinking and he makes up half a dozen sheets newspaper style, and sends them out. It is called the *Ex-News-Times Bulletin*. The alumnae of the paper have a name too, The Associated Beer Schooners of the Extinct *News-Times*. The first letters of the capitalized words spell *ABSENT*.

The gang is thinking of writing a book about the paper, and it will be a good one if they do. For, much as I have written about it, it is still only part of the story.

Having been out of the newspaper world for three years, I find I was wrong in going into business. It's being a reporter that I like better than anything else. Indeed as I think back over this book I believe it is probably the longest and most complete application for a job I ever wrote.

—30—

DATE DUE